# SCATTERED UNDER THE RISING SUN

# SCATTERED UNDER THE RISING SUN

*The Gordon Highlanders in the Far East*
*1941–1945*

## Stewart Mitchell

Pen & Sword
**MILITARY**

First published in Great Britain in 2012 by
PEN & SWORD MILITARY
an imprint of
Pen & Sword Books Ltd
47 Church Street
Barnsley, South Yorkshire
S70 2AS

Copyright © Stewart Mitchell 2012

ISBN 978 1 78159 025 6

Typeset in Ehrhardt by
CHIC GRAPHICS

Printed and bound in England
by CPI Group (UK) Ltd, Croydon, CR0 4YY

Pen & Sword Books Ltd incorporates the imprints of
Pen & Sword Aviation, Pen & Sword Family History, Pen & Sword Maritime,
Pen & Sword Military, Pen & Sword Discovery, Wharncliffe Local History,
Wharncliffe True Crime, Wharncliffe Transport, Pen & Sword Select,
Pen & Sword Military Classics, Leo Cooper, Remember When,
The Praetorian Press, Seaforth Publishing and Frontline Publishing

For a complete list of Pen & Sword titles please contact
PEN & SWORD BOOKS LIMITED
47 Church Street, Barnsley, South Yorkshire, S70 2AS England
E-mail: enquiries@pen-and-sword.co.uk
Website: www.pen-and-sword.co.uk

# Contents

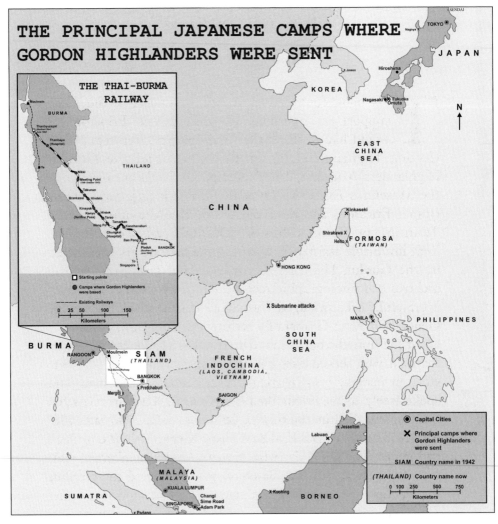

Map of south east Asia including inset of Thai-Burma railway.
(*Courtesy of Gordon Highlanders' Museum*)

# Acknowledgements

This book could not have been produced without the support and assistance of many people. Principally I would like to thank the Chairman and Trustees of the Gordon Highlanders' Regimental Trust and the Gordon Highlanders' Museum, Aberdeen. Special thanks are also due to the Museum's Executive Director (Claire Petty), the Curator (Jesper Ericsson) and the members of the Museum Research Team (Major Malcolm Ross, Charles Reid and Bert Innes) for their invaluable assistance. Much of the material used is owned by the Gordon Highlanders Museum and free access to the archives and photographic records and permission to use these is gratefully acknowledged. I would also like to thank Lieutenant General Sir Peter Graham for writing the Foreword.

At the time the book was written it was a sad fact that few of the men who served with the Battalion were alive to tell their story in person. I am particularly grateful to those men who spoke freely to me about their experiences. They were Angus Cassie (who died in 2009), Jack Jamieson, James Mowatt (who both died in 2011), Bill Kellas, William Niven, Alistair Urquhart and James Scott and I also wish to thank family members of men who had served with the Battalion who contacted the Gordon Highlanders' Museum with information about their loved one. This was invaluable and gave an opportunity to expand my knowledge about them, obtain photographs and documents outlining accounts and details of their personal and the Battalion's actions during the period which is described and illustrated in this book.

Prior to this project being undertaken, a number of Gordon Highlanders who had been Prisoners of War had produced their memoirs. These included Bill Young (*A Gordon Highlander if Ever I Saw One*, written by John Duff), John Murray Melville (*Tomorrow - The New Day*, an unpublished biography edited and introduced by his son, David Melville), George McNab (*George S. McNab – Gordon Highlander & Far East Prisoner of War*, compiled and edited by his grandson Brian Coutts) and Archibald Black (*Threads*, an unpublished autobiography). It was extremely generous of John Duff, David Melville and Brian Coutts to agree that I could use some of their material. I am also indebted to Lieutenant Colonel Alaistair Cumming who contacted Mrs A. Black and obtained her permission to use material from her husband's autobiography. In addition Paul Gibbs Pancheri, a Straits Settlements Volunteer, had also written his memoirs, entitled *Volunteer*, with many references to Gordon Highlanders detailing his contact and friendship with many of them in Singapore and Thailand. It was very generous of his son, Michael Pancheri, to allow me use of relevant material from his father's book. Ampleforth Abbey Trust kindly supplied photographs of Lieutenant V. I. D. Stewart and, whilst retaining the copyright on these, kindly allowed their use.

In addition it is important to acknowledge the valuable source of original research material at the National Archives, Kew, London (Files WO344 361/1 to 410/1). Aberdeen City Library allowed me to consult and copy their archive material, particularly in local newspapers of the period. Aberdeen Journals, through Mr David Knight, kindly agreed that the stories and photographs of men included in some of their newspapers could be used freely.

Additional information has also been obtained from the Commonwealth War Graves Commission, both abstracted from their website and in direct communication. For those men who were held prisoner in Formosa (now Taiwan) a collaborative project was mounted with Michael Hurst MBE, Director of the Taiwan PoW Camps Memorial Society. His assistance was invaluable in this regard. I was also assisted by Agnes Dougan and Campbell Thompson of the Lanarkshire Yeomanry Memorial Group, Jim Grant, Webmaster of the Kinnethmont website (www.kinnethmont.co.uk) and the families who provided photographs to his website. Jonathan Moffat, Rod Beattie, Linda Dahl, Jim Erickson, Wes Injerd and the late Roger Mansell also assisted greatly in helping me understand movements to Japan and the transport of men on the 'Hellships'. In all these respects I wish to acknowledge my gratitude for their invaluable support. I also wish to thank Dr Rathin Khaund who gave me a better understanding of some of the tropical diseases, etc. that affected the PoWs. I would also like to thank my wife, Hilda, and my family, Hilary, Nicola and Judith, for their support and encouragement.

Every effort has been made to ensure that facts presented in this book are wholly accurate and faithfully reproduce information passed to me. However, if any discrepancy or inaccuracy has occurred I apologise in advance and, if possible, will seek to make appropriate corrections in future.

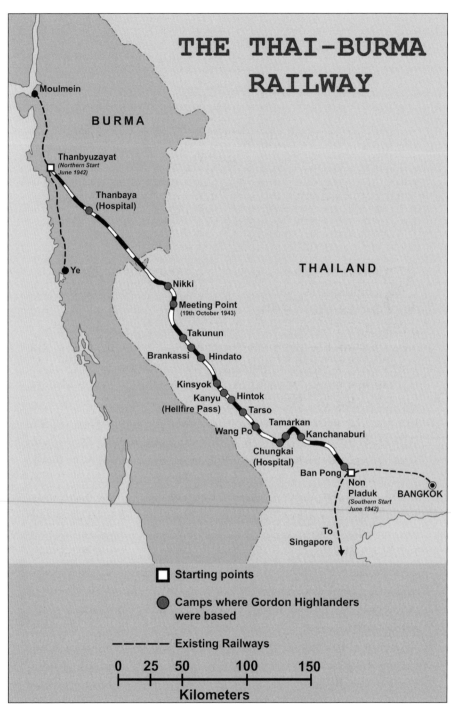

Thai-Burma railway showing PoW camps where Gordon Highlanders were mainly held (*Courtesy of Gordon Highlanders' Museum*)

# Foreword

by
## Lieutenant General Sir Peter Graham
## KCB CBE
## Last Colonel of the Gordon Highlanders

Stewart Mitchell is a dedicated Volunteer at the Gordon Highlanders' Museum. Though not a Gordon he has stuck by the story of the 2nd Battalion Gordon Highlanders during their tour of duty in the Far East which culminated in a large part of the Battalion becoming prisoners of war of the Japanese 1942–45. The old Regiment owes him a great debt for writing this unique account of the horror of captivity under the Japanese that the Battalion faced with courage, resilience and humour. Indeed, as far as I know, while many individuals have written about their experiences as prisoners of war, no one has written before about a Battalion as prisoners of war of the Japanese

The 2nd Battalion was proud to trace its ancestry back to the original 92nd Gordon Highlanders, raised in 1794. In the 1930s and at the outbreak of war they were regarded as a very professional, first-class, infantry battalion with a wonderful history. The vast majority of them came from the small towns and villages of the North East of Scotland and made excellent soldiers. This book tells how, in captivity, they maintained that reputation.

In my early years as a Gordon Highlander, Colonel Willie Graham was Colonel of the Regiment – indeed he interviewed me for the Regiment and spoke about his time as a Far East

Prisoner of War (FEPOW). I served alongside Major George Elsmie, who was later to command the 1st Battalion, Major Francis Moir-Byers, who was a wonderful and amusing raconteur, Major Charlie Michie and his brother Captain George Michie, both ex-RSMs with the Regiment and wonderful soldiers, and ORQMS Dick Pallant, a remarkable Chief Clerk. Among my brother officers were Lieutenant Colonel W. D. H. ('Dukie') Duke who had commanded the 1st Battalion in Malaya and was admired by all who knew him; Major Alan Close, another great character, and Lieutenant Colonel Billy Innes who was one of the last survivors.

But perhaps the most telling thing was to be invited to attend a 2nd Battalion Old Comrades/FEPOW Reunion. These were usually organised by Norman Catto, the 2nd Battalion's Carrier Platoon Sergeant, who had served alongside Reggie Lees on the 'Railway' and after the war did so much to look after his fellow FEPOWs and their widows in the North East of Scotland. There you would meet strong characters such as George McNab, Bill Kellas and Johnny Laing, who as a piper in the 2nd Battalion kept his pipes all the way through his captivity; they are now played by his grandson Michael Laing. These reunions were very special. You quickly appreciated these men had suffered as others had not and were strong in character and belonged to a really close knit family. It was a privilege to be with them and the atmosphere was fantastic.

So I am particularly delighted that Stewart Mitchell has written this book. He has put in a vast amount of time and energy researching the facts and the story of their captivity and the characters of the officers and men of that wonderful Battalion. He has done a real service to the old Regiment and I am most grateful to him as all Gordon Highlanders will be.

Peter Graham
December 2011.

# CHAPTER 1

# Introduction

The inspiration for this book came mainly from two items in the collection of the Gordon Highlanders' Museum, Aberdeen. The origins of these were very different but together they 'kick-started' a journey back in time to search out the individual and collective stories of a gallant group of men. These were the men of the 2nd Battalion Gordon Highlanders. They served their country courageously in battle and then showed tremendous dignity and fortitude in captivity. They toiled under a harsh regime of arduous work, with inadequate food and filthy conditions imposed by a fanatical enemy who showed them no mercy, excusing their lack of any basic humanity on an ancient warrior code of *Bushido* (The Way of the Warrior). Ironically three of the seven pillars of this code were respect, benevolence and honesty, which were absent in full measure in the Japanese Army's treatment of their helpless captives.

The first item from the Museum collection was the Nominal Roll of the 2nd Battalion Gordon Highlanders, listing who was present in Singapore before the start of the war in the Pacific on 8 December 1941. This is a contemporary record created within the Battalion administration in Selarang Barracks, Singapore around 1940. It is a handwritten alphabetical list of every officer and enlisted man in the Battalion, together with information on their rank, next of kin, transfers, etc. Whilst all of this basic information on the men involved was the starting point for putting together this story, its most fascinating aspect is the notes added during the battle for Malaya and Singapore, detailing casualties (both wounded and killed in action). Thereafter, while the men of the Battalion were prisoners of war (PoWs) this practice continued, giving details of those who died of disease, etc. and movements to other areas, such as Japan.

The man responsible for compiling and maintaining this was Sergeant Archibald (known as 'Dick') Pallant (2867720), illustrated leafing through the book after the war. It is not clear today, after almost seventy years, how Dick Pallant managed to maintain this record. This was, of course, originally an official document being held within the Battalion for administrative purposes but once the capitulation had taken place its status would have changed dramatically. The Japanese were completely against the maintenance of records of any kind, including personal diaries, by their prisoners and the Battalion Nominal Roll would have had to be kept secret. Dick Pallant assumed responsibility for this and hid the document in his bedding and it was a fantastic achievement that he managed to preserve this through his time as a PoW, in both Singapore and Thailand, so that we have this unique document today. Dick Pallant was assisted by Company Sergeant Major Angus Collie (2874524) who also kept records while working on the infamous Thai–Burma Railway and later passed the information on to Dick Pallant, who updated his master record. One possible additional clue to the means whereby the book survived detection by the Japanese came out during a discussion between the author and Angus Cassie (2878447). He indicated that, after the Japanese surrender, in 1945, he was taken by Lieutenant Colonel Stitt to the large War Cemetery at Kanchanaburi where many of the British soldiers were buried. He was instructed to dig at the head or foot of some of the graves. Angus Cassie stated, 'Colonel Stitt had a diagram and he knew exactly where he wanted to dig and we recovered jars and tins that contained the Battalion's papers from before the war. These had been buried with the casualties to hide them from the Japanese'. This suggests that a combination of mechanisms were employed to deceive the Japanese and keep track of the men on the Regiment. Dick Pallant's exceptional conduct during his time as a Far East Prisoner of War was formally recognised when he was mentioned in recognition of 'gallant and distinguished services' after the war and the Notice to this effect was published in the *London Gazette* on 12 September 1946.

The second strand in the conception of this book was, unlike Sergeant Pallant's Nominal Roll, a completely unofficial personal initiative. This was a scrapbook produced by the labours of Mrs Irene Lees, the wife of Major R. G. Lees who was second-in-command of the 2nd Battalion Gordon Highlanders in Singapore.

Irene Lees was, even before her marriage, steeped in the Regimental traditions. Her father, Sir Harry V. Brooke KBE of Fairley House, Countesswells, Aberdeen, had been a captain in the Gordons during the Boer War and three of her brothers served with the Regiment during The Great War. Two of them were killed and the eldest, Lieutenant J. A. Otho Brooke, was awarded the Victoria Cross (VC) for an action in Belgium in October 1914 while serving with the 2nd Battalion Gordon Highlanders. (He was also posthumously promoted to the rank of captain).

Mrs Lees lived in Singapore with her husband and was only evacuated by ship on 12 February 1942, together with the other wives and families of the men. This was only two days before the capitulation of the colony to the Japanese. Once back in Aberdeen she started a support group for the families who had men in Singapore. She created a scrapbook in which she pasted photographs of some of the men, acquired from their relatives, adding newspaper cuttings and comments, etc. From 1943 onwards some PoW postcards were received by the relatives from the men and her Battalion family network facilitated the sharing of information as none was available from official sources. She also recorded the PoW camps the men reported they were being held in, together with the name of each soldier's next of kin with whom she was in touch, and the man's eventual fate, e.g. liberated, died or missing at sea. After the war, this scrapbook was presented to the officers and men of the Battalion, who had been Far East prisoners of war and now forms part of the Collection at the Gordon Highlanders' Museum.

Once the starting point had been established it was then necessary to trawl through the Museum's collection for further photographs and items donated giving details of the Battalion's actions and their experiences during captivity. In addition visits were made to the National Archives at Kew, London, to glean information from the Prisoner of War Release Questionnaires. In Aberdeen, the City Library newspaper archive was consulted for material and, in addition, contact was made with the few Gordon Highlanders still alive at the time of writing. Information also came from the families of men who contacted the Gordon Highlanders' Museum who were curious to know more about their relatives' time while serving with the Regiment in the Far East.

In March 2010 I travelled to Thailand to see the Thai–Burma Railway for myself and visited Kanyu Cutting, known as Hellfire Pass to the PoWs and the bridge on the River Kwai at Kanchanaburi. Here I also visited the war cemetery where there are 108 Gordon Highlanders buried, re-interred by the Commonwealth War Graves Commission after retrieval from all along the railway up to the border with Burma. (Graves from north of this are located at Thanbyuzayat, Burma, now Myanmar). One of the aims of my project was to obtain a photo of every man who served in the Battalion and became a casualty of the battle for Malaya and Singapore or a PoW. It was a bonus, therefore, to find, lying on the ground next to the grave of

4

Robert Willox (2883815), two laminated sheets, one a photograph of him and the other a short life history. These must have been left by a family member of his only a few weeks before. As I did not have this photograph it was a great find and perhaps ironic that I had travelled several thousands of miles to Thailand to obtain a photograph of a man from Boddam, Peterhead which is only thirty miles from my own home in Aberdeen. In addition, by an amazing coincidence, the home address for Rob Willox was the same farm as that for Jack Rennie, who was not related to him, but also served in the 2nd Battalion Gordon Highlanders but who had left Singapore for service back in Europe in 1939, just as Rob was joining the Gordons in Aberdeen.

With the passage of time and the greater insight afforded by the greater knowledge of the ordeal the men went through, individually and collectively, it became all the more imperative that their remarkable story was told. This follows in the subsequent chapters.

# CHAPTER 2

# Prelude
# The Road to Singapore
# 1934–1937

In the first half of the twentieth century, most Regiments in the British Regular Army operated a three Battalion system and the Gordon Highlanders were no different. This comprised a Regimental HQ or 'Depot' (Aberdeen in the case of the Gordon Highlanders) and a 1st and 2nd Battalion each of a nominal strength of thirty officers and 930 other ranks, together with some twenty attached specialist trades from other Corps. In addition to these there were the Territorial Army Battalions (TA) for part time soldiers and the Gordon Highlanders had the 4th (Aberdeen City) Battalion, the 5th (Buchan & Formartine) Battalion, the 6th (Banff & Donside) Battalion & the 7th (Deeside) Battalion. At any particular time only one Regular Battalion (1st or 2nd) would serve at 'home' (i.e. somewhere in the UK) while the other was overseas (i.e. somewhere in the British Empire).

In 1934 the 2nd Battalion Gordon Highlanders had been stationed in Aldershot for three years while the 1st Battalion were at Peshawar in India. For the 2nd Battalion 1934 was a busy year in ceremonial terms. In February they recovered their drums, which had been left in Ostend in October 1914, just after the Battalion landed and moved to the front at the start of the First

World War. Willie Graham, who would go on to command the 2nd Battalion in Singapore was only a young second lieutenant in 1914 and found the transport wagons grossly overloaded, so it was decided to leave the seven drums in the safe keeping of the local police in Ostend. Immediately after the Armistice, in 1918, Willie Graham went back to Ostend to recover the drums but found that the Germans had found them and, on their evacuation of Ostend, had taken them back to Germany as a 'war trophy', where they were deposited in the Armoury Museum, Berlin. The Colonel of the Regiment (General Sir Ian Hamilton) made a personal approach to President Hindenburg of Germany, then Head of State in name only as Adolf Hitler had come to power, and requested the return of the drums, to Sir Ian's great delight President Hindenburg agreed, as a gesture of friendship and reconciliation. Sir Ian travelled to Berlin where they were taken to the 'Reichswehr Ministerium' (Defence Ministry) and later recalled how they were shown into a large room where they were met with the sight of the drums decorated with bay leaves and flanked on either side by sentries 'as motionless as statues' and with their eyes apparently fixed and switched on half-right and half-left. They were dressed in service kit, steel helmets and rifles with fixed bayonets. Here, General Von Bloomberg (the German War Minister) presented the drums in the presence of some thirty other high ranking officers and dignitaries. In his address he recognised the Gordon Highlanders as one of the most famous regiments of the British Army and recalled how their Colours once flew side by side with those of the Prussian Army at the Battle of Waterloo. He went on to say how pleased he was to fulfil the request for the drums to be returned to their rightful home. After the ceremony, Sir Ian was received in private by the 'Reichspresident', Field Marshal von Hindenburg, allowing time for a cordial conversation between these two men, both veterans of the previous bloody conflict between their two nations.

On return to Aldershot, these drums were received with great ceremony and at Farnborough were taken back to Barracks with an escort of two officers, fifty men, the Drummers, Pipers and the Regimental Band. Once back in the Barracks the whole Battalion was drawn up on the Square and, after speeches, the entire Battalion marched past in fours.

These drums were echoes of the First World War, in which the Regiment had been involved from the very beginning incurring 30,000 casualties, of which 440 officers and 8,500 other ranks were killed. One such casualty was the father of James Gordon (2876032), who was now serving with the Gordon Highlanders himself. The Regiment had fought in all the major actions of the Great War and their gallantry was recognised by the award of four Victoria Crosses; fifty-one Distinguished Service Orders; 175 Military Crosses; 193 Distinguished Conduct Medals, and many other decorations. One of those on parade that day was Private Alfred Dick (2875875) and he could have had no thought that a mere five years later (in 1939), would see Britain plunged into another war with Germany and in ten short years (in 1944) he would be fighting for his life in the South China Sea, after suffering more than two years of hell as a slave labourer of the Japanese Empire. Many others with him on parade that day would not live to see the end of 1944 but for most of them Adolf Hitler was not to be their problem.

Later that year, in April, they paraded again for their Majesties, King George V and Queen Mary (who was later to give her name to the great liner which would take a large number of the men home at the end of the next war). However, at this time, in 1934, just sixteen years after the end of the 'war to end all wars', another war was still an unthinkable prospect.

The 1st Battalion serving in India were due to come home and consequently the 2nd Battalion were fully aware that they were due an overseas posting. This was to be to Gibraltar and, in the period prior to their departure, the 2nd Battalion was being brought up to full strength by a recruitment campaign. The North East of Scotland is a fertile area and boasts some of the best farmland in Scotland. Consequently, large numbers of men were employed in agriculture. The agricultural tradition at this time was that men were engaged on a particular farm for six months only and at the end of this 'term' they would assemble at the local 'Feein' Market' where the farmers would also come to engage, or re-engage, men for the following six months, offering a fixed fee for their labours. These were also great social occasions where friends and relations, who had often been working on farms all over the county, came together to catch up, have a drink and it was, in a sense, a great holiday occasion. Naturally the seasonal nature of farming meant that the work available varied throughout the year, so making this an uncertain means of earning a living. Recruiting sergeants would tour the traditional recruitment area of the Regiment in North East Scotland (Aberdeen City and the Counties of Aberdeenshire, Banff & Kincardine and the Orkney and Shetland Isles), visiting the Feein' Markets to persuade young men to sign up. This was not particularly difficult at this time as there was a worldwide depression and there was little work. Many of the recruits who were working on farms enjoyed poor wages and conditions with no job security so the army offered a secure haven, where they could sign up for a minimum period of seven years' guaranteed employment. In addition, for those with a spirit of adventure, the army offered foreign travel, which could be offered as a specific 'carrot' at this time as it was known that a foreign posting was a clear possibility. In addition, The Territorial Army (TA) was a popular pastime, where men would meet and socialise in the local Drill Halls, earn a small bounty, and have a regular holiday at the Summer Camp which was a welcome bonus in these hard times. These men of the TA also provided a fertile recruitment ground for the recruiting sergeants. Irrespective of whether they had any Territorial Army (TA) experience or not, these recruits were sent to the Depot at Castlehill Barracks, Aberdeen, to start their five months' basic training. Once this was completed the men were ready to be posted to their Battalion and many were sent to Aldershot to join the 2nd Battalion to bring it up to full strength.

When the date of their final departure dawned, the 2nd Battalion made an impressive sight as they marched, kilted, to Farnborough Railway Station, to the accompaniment of the Pipes and Drums of the Cameron Highlanders and the Band of the Royal West Kent Regiment. After the short train journey to Southampton, the men and their equipment boarded HMT (Hired Military Transport) *Somersetshire*.

The Battalion's married families had already boarded the day before the main body of men arrived. The four-day voyage to Gibraltar was in exceptionally calm conditions, considering the late time of year but, despite this, there was the inevitable problem of many passengers being seasick. However, one highlight for many was the sighting of a school of porpoises riding the ship's bow wave. On Sunday 21 October they were all relieved to disembark in glorious sunshine, in stark contrast to the cold they had left behind, and the general view was that Gibraltar was an improvement on Aldershot. After unloading, the Battalion marched to their new home on 'The Rock'. The Colony's Governor, and distinguished soldier, Sir Charles Harrington GCB GBE DSO took the salute and the parade was cheered on by a large crowd lining the route. In a sense, the Regiment was coming home as it was here, at Windmill Hill, Gibraltar, in December 1794, that the Regiment received its first Colours, after being raised earlier that year, back in Aberdeenshire, by the Fifth Duke of Gordon.

As time went on the Battalion began to settle in to their new surroundings. Their Barracks were splendidly situated with commanding views over the Bay of Gibraltar looking over to Spain and North Africa. However their first duty was none too pleasant as they were required to carry out a rigorous cleaning programme and debugging of their barracks, which were infested with numerous insects, including bed bugs. Their new location also called for changes to their normal operational procedures. New skills had to be learned, such as the use of donkey carts for transport. In one amusing incident, a donkey showed it was quite as smart as the average private soldier. When carting a load of bedding down the hill to the guardhouse at Buena Vista Barracks, it stubbornly refused to proceed when it reached the steep decline so Private Milne, who was the driver, unhitched the cart and laid the shafts on the ground. When the cart began to roll downhill of its own accord, he left the donkey and ran after it and the donkey followed closely behind, showing it knew how to get down the steep hill without the loaded cart!

On 5 January 1935, the two Regular Battalions (1st and 2nd) met up for only the second time in their histories, the first occasion being the Boer War at the turn of the nineteenth/twentieth century. The 1st Battalion, which was en route back to Scotland from Palestine, from service in India, had been given special permission to call in to Gibraltar. The occasion was marked by the visit to Gibraltar by the Regiment's Colonel-in-Chief, Sir Ian Hamilton, and the meeting resulted in a highly memorable spectacle. Both Battalions paraded together and were inspected by His Excellency, Sir Charles Harrington. A display by the combined Pipes and Drums of both Battalions also took place and, on the social side, there was also an opportunity for many of the men to catch up with former comrades. More elaborate and lengthy celebrations that had been planned had to be abandoned as the ship carrying the 1st was only allowed to dock for a few hours since there had already been some delay in their trip home.

The 2nd Battalion then began to settle into the routine duties of a garrison force, with weapon training, guard duty and ceremonial events, such as trooping the colour and participating in the King's Silver Jubilee celebrations, on 6 May 1935. This latter event also meant that the Silver Jubilee Medal was awarded to five members of the Battalion. The band and pipe band were in demand to play at various official and social functions both civic, such as at a garden fête in Jerez (the famous home of sherry), and recreational, e.g. the various concerts, and other entertainments, for the many ships' companies in port. Also in May, an invitation was extended for the Band together with the Drums and Pipes to play in the Stadium Metropolitan, (the predecessor of the Bernabeu Stadium), Madrid. The sight of a famous Scottish Regiment, resplendent in their full formal highland dress uniforms of dark green and gold Gordon tartan, playing in their capital was extremely novel, greatly impressing the large Spanish crowds who attended both performances. In later life, in the TV age of Champions' League football, this concert allowed Piper Johnny Laing (2876421) to boast, mischievously, to his young grandson that he had played in Real Madrid FC's stadium. However, he would neglect to mention that he was not playing football!

With Gibraltar being a large naval base, there was the usual inter-service rivalry which was at its most competitive in the field of sport. Boxing, rowing, polo, athletics, tennis and fencing were all popular. Sports such as polo, horse racing and hunting were beyond the means of most in the UK but in Gibraltar the opportunity was opened to those with much more modest means. In their spare time some men chose to learn Spanish, while many others, particularly those with families, enjoyed the relatively relaxed situation with easy access to the warm waters on the beach at the North Front, a stretch of sand lying just below the sheer face of the rock which gave the colony its distinctive appearance. Life on The Rock was novel and interesting and when off duty individual Gordons could explore the caves or climb The Rock to feed the Barbary Apes. These were also a great hit with the young children who were living in the married quarters. The North Front was also the venue for sporting events including the annual Highland Games, which drew large crowds of interested spectators. There were separate games both for individual Companies and the Battalion as a whole. In addition to the serious sporting events, the games were all day family fun affairs with transport and meals laid on for the wives and children. There were races for the children, wives and even for 'old' soldiers. In May 1936 the young 'Boy Soldier', Jim Murch (2876243) proved himself to be a very promising athlete by becoming Headquarters Wing Overall Champion, just two weeks before his eighteenth birthday. He also became the battalion Junior Champion. There were many excellent athletes in the Battalion. Robert (Bob) Morgan (2875457) was running the mile in four minutes ten seconds when the world record was just four seconds less and he and his brother, Arthur (2876361), excelled at the three-mile distance also. The sporting prowess of the Gordons was not limited to athletics and included a number of disciplines, with the Battalion winning the Gibraltar Garrison Inter-Regimental Challenge Cup for boxing in 1936.

The social calendar was also full with friendly visits to and from the messes of the many other military units stationed on, or visiting The Rock, particularly naval, with whom a strong bond of friendship was developed. During the two-and-a-half years the Battalion was in Gibraltar there were many informal opportunities for the men to go to sea on naval vessels. This included exercises and manoeuvres but, in addition, parties of Gordons went as guests of ships' companies to give them an insight into the role of the Navy. However, on 12 June 1936, the Battalion went to go to sea on a serious operational role. After some initial confusion, they were given only twelve hours' notice that they were being rushed to Egypt, as a reserve force to contain unrest in the British Mandated Territory of Palestine. The first leg of the journey through the Mediterranean to Malta was aboard the battle-cruiser HMS *Repulse*.

Here the Battalion was divided and transferred to the two, slightly smaller, heavy cruisers HMS *Exeter* and HMS *Shropshire* for the final leg of their journey to Alexandria, arriving there on 17 June 1936. During the voyage from Malta to Egypt the Gordons gave a display of sword-dancing on deck and a number of the crew clambered into the cutter to get a better view but one man slipped and fell overboard. Lifeboats were immediately lowered from the *Shropshire* while *Exeter* stood by and the man, Ordinary Seaman Milne who, by an amazing coincidence, was from Aberdeen, the home of the Gordons, was rescued none the worse for his ordeal. As HMS *Exeter* pulled into the port the Gordons' Pipe Band was playing on deck and the Admiral Commanding Alexandria Harbour signalled to Captain C. E. Douglas-Pennant of HMS *Exeter* to congratulate him on 'providing the most impressive spectacle seen in the harbour for months and months'.

The Battalion disembarked and moved to the outskirts of Alexandria and were based at three separate locations, Sidi Bishr, Dekheila Camp and Aboukir. Here they made ready to move into Palestine, to counter the Arab revolt against the British rule and the mass immigration of Jewish settlers. However, while there, things were sufficiently quiet for the Pipers to perform at the gymkhana of the Grenadier Guards. The emergency situation in Palestine subsided fairly quickly with the result that only thirty-four days after their arrival the Battalion were back aboard HMS *Repulse*, bound for Gibraltar. Sailing at the fast pace of 24 knots they arrived back in the early morning of Sunday 25 July 1936.

About this time, the Spanish Civil War had begun and from their vantage point on the Rock of Gibraltar the Battalion had a 'ringside seat' watching the factions opposing each other at the nearby Spanish fort at Ceunta and the Batteries of Algeciras. In addition, there were air attacks on Spanish ships in the bay. The war meant that it was necessary to impose restrictions on movement so it was no longer possible for the Colony to have normal relations with parties in Spain. This also meant the loss of the polo ground, which lay on the Spanish side of the border. The Battalion was employed in patrolling the border, manning roadblocks and generally assisting local police, particularly because there was an influx of refugees. The Governor commented that there were very friendly relations between the Battalion and the civilian population which gave rise to a harmonious atmosphere and at least one man married a local woman.

In the summer of 1936 it became known that the Battalion were to be posted to Singapore the following year and, with this new location being so far from Britain, there was an opportunity for some men to get leave to travel home but this was not universally available and not all had the means to fund such leave. In addition, with the impending move, men who were due to finish their service with the Colours left to complete their service back home, making room for the draft of new men, both new and old hands from the 1st Battalion. At the start of the year, Arthur Morgan (2876361) wrote to his brother Rob wishing him a Happy New Year and obviously pleased to hear that he had been posted to join him in Gibraltar and was due to arrive as part of a body of thirty-seven men, replacing those men posted back to the UK. The 2nd Battalion left for Malaya on 3 March 1937 aboard HMT *Dorsetshire*, the sister ship of HMT *Somersetshire* which had taken them to Gibraltar three years earlier. After handing over their barracks to the Norfolks they marched to join their ship to the music of the 1st Battalion, King's Own Yorkshire Light Infantry. The warm relationship which had formed with the Royal Navy resulted in magnificent displays of admiration and friendship from the combined Home and Mediterranean Fleets, both of which were in port at that time. HMS *Repulse*, which had taken the Battalion to Egypt the previous year, broke out an enormous replica of the Regimental flag at her masthead. Not to be outdone HMS *Royal Oak* (later to become the first British battleship to be sunk in the Second World War, as she lay at anchor in Scapa Flow) had two pipers on deck, playing 'Cock of the North' (the Regimental anthem).

The voyage to Singapore was fairly uneventful, travelling through the Suez Canal and calling at Port Said, Aden and Colombo. The posting to Singapore was anticipated eagerly as the prospect of this eastern tropical paradise had a certain fascination, being a new experience for almost all of them. The first impressions of their new base at Selarang Barracks, Changi, about twelve miles from Singapore City, were very favourable. These brand new modern barracks, built in a light airy style, provided many comforts not available at Gibraltar and the men had sprung beds with integral mosquito nets and large lockers.

Following a long period of planning, dating back to 1926, when the need to protect the vital strategic location of Singapore was realised, the previous four years had seen the entire Changi area of Singapore Island transformed. This mosquito-infested wilderness area of mangrove swamp and virgin jungle was converted into a modern military complex comprising of Kitchener Barracks (Royal Engineers), Roberts Barracks (Royal Artillery), India Barracks (Indian Army) and Selarang Barracks (Gordon Highlanders), together with living quarters for service personnel's families. Recreational and sporting facilities, including a swimming pool, were still under construction when the Gordons arrived but were completed by the end of 1937. In addition there were the necessary school and hospital facilities. A large naval base and dockyard was developed for the Royal Navy in the Straits of Johore and an airfield was constructed at Seletar. Together, these combined to form the new Singapore Fortress, with Headquarters at Fort Canning, in the south-east of Singapore Island.

The 2nd Battalion soon settled into their new surroundings and marvelled at the exotic plants, animals and insects. A piper playing alone on the edge of some lush vegetation was surprised to find that, like some Indian snake charmer, the sound of his pipes attracted two large snakes which slithered out of the undergrowth. The cosmopolitan nature of the colony was also a novelty as the population comprised not only the native Malays but large numbers of Chinese, Indians, Tamils and Japanese together with European and Eurasian (mixed-race) settlers. Singapore embodied everything that was the 'mystical East', with the exotic fragrances, unusual sounds, colourful customs and cultures, which all combined to make this tropical paradise an exciting place to live. The families were also well catered for by the Army. There were separate quarters for the married officers and men in a small village of brand new bungalows near their base.

The pleasant climate and access to the beach and pool, together with well-appointed sports and social facilities, allowed them to have a standard of living far beyond their means back home in Britain. The single men also enjoyed the delights available in nearby Singapore, far better than in the UK and more exotic and 'sensuous' than those available in Gibraltar, which they had so recently left behind.

The Battalion continued to be involved in ceremonial duties. Following an impressive parade on 12 May 1937 for the coronation of King George VI, involving detachments from all services stationed on the island, the Battalion, headed by the Pipes and Drums, marched through Singapore, much to the delight and awe of the large crowds. Afterwards, the Pipes played at the garden party at Government House and were complimented on their programme by His Excellency, Sir Shenton Thomas, Governor of Singapore.

Routine training continued with mock attacks and defence in the countryside to ensure familiarity with the terrain and acclimatisation of the men. At one such exercise on the Malay Peninsula at Mersing, Johore Bahru, local troops of the Johore

Military Force held a local village and were engaged after the Gordon Highlanders had rapidly trekked through twelve miles of thick jungle, referred to as 'ulu' by the men. This was followed up by another mock attack at Kota Tinggi. This trip north was not all work and there were opportunities to relax and swim at the beach and engage in soccer and cricket matches against local opposition of Malays and Chinese. This was also a rubber, and pineapple, growing area and local commercial companies entertained the Battalion who reciprocated by conducting ceremonial marches, musical performances and highland dancing exhibitions, much to the delight of the local inhabitants who had rarely seen European troops before, never mind a strange and exotic Scottish Highland regiment with a pipe band at its head.

Back in Singapore, combined exercises continued to test the readiness of the garrison force and more training was instigated. An exercise designed to simulate an attack which resulted in heavy casualties was undertaken in May 1938. The howls and screams of some of the 'casualties' were so realistic that traumatized civilian bystanders had to be hurried from the scene, casting anxious glances over their shoulders at some apparently distressed Gordon Highlander enthusiastically acting his part and struggling with harassed stretcher-bearers at the roadside. The roads were congested with 'walking wounded' and converted rickshaws carrying additional stretcher cases to a Regimental Aid Post (RAP), located in a rubber plantation. One stretcher case arrived at the Military Hospital at Tanglin with the cryptic label 'GSW [gunshot wound] left thigh and fracture'. This luckless soldier had a rifle securely attached to one leg, in lieu of a splint, bunches of lallang grass for padding and several miles of field dressing and his feet bound together with putties!

In another unplanned incident at Regimental HQ, the Battalion Gas NCO had just started up a tear-gas generator for testing in the vicinity of the Orderly Room when a sudden change of wind resulted in the ingress of gas to the building which resulted in its sudden and rapid evacuation. This incident created much amusement for bystanders, especially when an officer, in his hurry to escape but with his eyesight impaired by the effects of the gas, collided with an innocent passing cyclist! All this gave added interest to the anti-gas courses which were also taking place at this time.

In February 1938 the Commanding Officer, Lieutenant Colonel George Burney, was invited to join a party going to Shanghai aboard HMS *Duncan* and he took along Piper John A. Findlater (2876231), the 'Orderly Piper'. En route the ship called at Saigon, the capital of French Indochina, and after HMS *Duncan* had docked safely, he was allowed free time to go ashore and explore. Tiring of his sightseeing he decided that he would like a drink. The locals, he presumed, were unlikely to speak English and, not being able to speak French, he looked around for a suitable European candidate who might speak English, to ask for directions. On seeing a well-dressed European he approached the man and enquired if he spoke English. John Findlater was astonished to receive the reply 'no verra weel but I think I can speak Scots as weel as you'. This turned out to be a man from Banff, Scotland (some forty-five miles from the Gordons' home base in Aberdeen). On investigation it was discovered that he was the chief engineer of the MV *Loch Lomond*, a British merchant ship lying at anchor in the harbour. Continuing their journey, calling at Manila and Hong Kong en-route, they reached Shanghai and John saw a 'window into the future', which the rest of his comrades would become all too familiar with. Following Japanese attacks, much of the great city of Shanghai lay in ruins and numerous Chinese refugees were fleeing the area.

Taking account of the climate in Singapore, it was normal for the Battalion's routine duties to be completed in the mornings, often with an 04:00 hours start and a parade every day at 06:00

hours. After this there was a compulsory afternoon siesta for all those off duty and not engaged in some sport. For the off-duty soldier there were endless opportunities to take part in many sports, including soccer, cricket, hockey, boxing, athletics, rowing and sailing. These were played for fun and in intra-Battalion and inter-unit competitions, often with silverware at stake and many photos from the time show teams of proud Gordons posing with their end of season silverware collections of cups and shields. Ominously, many of the photographers working in Singapore at this time were Japanese spies who were naively given easy access to all the military establishments to take these photographs. One example is a photograph of a group of Gordon Highlanders in Selarang which is now held by Rod Smart, the son of Private Alexander (Sandy) Smart (2877319). 'Nakajima & Co.' is the name of the photographer which is proudly printed on it. This simple device presented these photographers ample opportunity to record the details of the military capabilities in the colony, which were then reported back to Tokyo.

In addition there were the social activities of drama and concert groups and on the camp there was the NAAFI. For those with money in their pockets, the attractions of Singapore City, some twelve miles away, were enticing. The men could get into the city in a taxi and would go out dressed in their 'whites' (smart tropical suits). A popular venue was the Union Jack Club but the heady cocktail of alcohol and inter-unit rivalry would often lead to a disturbance requiring the intervention of the Red Caps [Military Police].

On the social side, the Ladies' Club offered entertainment and companionship for the Battalion ladies, where they organised whist drives, concerts and parties which included older children and occasionally the married men. They also participated in sports and rifle shooting and took full advantage of the tropical climate for hiking, cycling, picnics and trips to the beach and swimming pool. Peggy Coutts and Winnie Bent went on a family holiday with their children and Winnie's husband, Percy. They travelled by train to Kuala Lumpur and, describing her trip up Fraser's Hill, Peggy said she was thrilled to be above the clouds but nearly fainted as the air was so rare! Another holiday had been taken at Port Dickson, on the western side of Malaya. Peggy's husband, Willie, had been there previously on manoeuvres with the Battalion. While on holiday they stayed in a bungalow and had access to a private beach where Peggy learned to swim.

In the spring of 1939, after two years in Singapore, the Battalion expected another posting and barrack-room speculation of where they were destined was at fever pitch. The rumours given the most credibility for their next destination were Jamaica, as the authorities wanted a pipe band available to play at the World's Fair in the USA, or Shanghai, as Madame Chiang Kai Shek (the wife of the Chinese ruler and a very influential woman in her own right) had specifically requested the Gordons. This rumour was presumably sparked by the earlier visit of the Commanding Officer, Lieutenant Colonel Burney, and Piper John Findlater to Shanghai the previous year.

Therefore, when the news finally came that they were to be posted to Mhow, Central India, it came somewhat as a shock to many. A few old hands, who had served in India with the 1st Battalion earlier in the decade, claimed that 'no Indian Station could be a good one' but this was in contrast to news the Commanding Officer received in a letter from the Commanding Officer of the Suffolk Regiment, who the Gordons were to relieve. Mhow was described as having a good climate and, being at an elevation of 1,900 feet (580 metres) above sea level, the summers were not too hot and with fine cold winter months, quite a contrast to the tropical steamy heat of Singapore.

However, with rising tensions in Europe and the eventual outbreak of the war in September 1939, all plans to relocate the unit were shelved and the Gordons were held on in Singapore. Army life continued and the Gordon Highlanders, being professional soldiers, continued to be called on to assist other units. One amusing example was when Sergeant Milton, who hailed from Banffshire, was detailed to act as an instructor to a company of Chinese Straits Settlements Volunteers based in Penang, on the Malay Peninsula. After his tour was complete their Commanding Officer reported that these Chinese volunteers were all speaking with a Scots accent. Another example was the close ties with 1st Battalion Straits Settlements Volunteer Force (SSVF) in Singapore where the Gordons' Pipe Major (Jimmy Dickie) always led the 1st Battalion (Scottish Company) SSVF to church on Sundays. In addition, Company Sergeant Major Angus Collie (2874524) and Regimental Quartermaster Sergeant Robert Spence (2871799) gave a lot of instruction on how to organise and maintain their equipment and stores.

The Battalion also underwent a major reorganisation in February 1939 to put it on a war footing and make full use of all its personnel in a combat role. In addition, the Battalion was strengthened by the posting of additional men from the 1st Battalion for a specific Transport and Carrier Platoon. There were quite a lot of organisational changes such as deployment of the Pipers to become 'Tock Monkeys' (trench mortars) and the Drummers to become ack-ack (anti-aircraft) gunners. The Pipers, keen to show off their skills, after their annual weapons' training, decided to challenge the Battalion's Ladies' Club to a shooting match at the miniature range but were embarrassed by their defeat!

Back home in the UK, conscription began in April 1939, following the introduction of the Military Training Act 1939. This required all single men, aged twenty to twenty-two, to serve in the armed services for six months' military training before being transferred to the Reserves. However, events overtook this plan. Even before the first batch had completed their six months' training, war was declared on Germany on 3 September 1939, and they were, therefore, immediately incorporated in Britain's armed forces for the duration of the war. The conscription rules changed at the outbreak of war with the passing of the National Service (Armed Forces) Act 1939 which introduced conscription of all men eighteen to forty-one years old. Some men were rejected for medical reasons, and exemptions were available for those engaged in industries or occupations of vital national importance and/or the war effort, e.g. coal miners, munitions workers, police officers and the clergy. These were referred to as Reserved Occupations.

Inevitably some of the men conscripted into the Gordon Highlanders were posted to the 2nd Battalion in Singapore. One such conscript, called up in June 1939, was Jimmy Mowatt (2883082), who travelled with a number of others including (John) Murray Melville (2888645). The group was in the charge of Lieutenant Robert Chaytor, assisted by Second Lieutenant George Roberts with both relying heavily on the vastly more experienced Sergeant (Tibby) Burnett (2874727). When mobilised they went by train to Liverpool and sailed on the MV *Batory* at the beginning of August 1940. They were part of a large convoy and the ship had some 200 children on board who were being evacuated to Australia from the large industrial cities in Britain which were the target of Nazi bombers. The Gordons were asked to keep the children amused and played games, such as hide and seek, with them. The ship's route was via Sierra Leone and Cape Town, South Africa. Here the men were given shore leave where they found the welcome and hospitality given by the local population overwhelming, with many families taking soldiers home for a meal. Although delighted to be taken for a home-cooked meal, it was the first time that most had ever seen rice being offered as a savoury part of the meal and not the familiar rice pudding they had at home. Little did they realise that in quite a short time they would have to survive on little else. On leaving Cape Town, the convoy split up with the larger part going on to the Middle East. The MV *Batory*'s voyage continued eastwards, calling at Bombay and Colombo en-route and arriving into Singapore on 15 November 1941, just three weeks before the war in the Pacific began. It was a fairly slow journey of three and a half months, partly as they were often zig-zagging to avoid submarine attack. On arrival at Singapore good-byes were said to the children with many tears being shed on both sides.

Among the men who sailed on this ship were Jimmy Scott (2880277), Robert Anderson (2882177) and Peter Taylor (2882550), all of whom had already seen quite a bit of the war. Four months earlier, at the end of May 1940, these men were evacuated back to England when both the 4th and 6th Battalions were taken off at Dunkirk. Their comrades in the 1st and 5th Battalions were not so fortunate and as part of the 51st (Highland) Division were captured by the Germans at St Valéry en Caux and became prisoners of war for five long years. Among those captured was Brigadier (formerly Lieutenant Colonel) George T. Burney, who commanded 153 Brigade and had been the Commanding Officer of the 2nd Battalion Gordon Highlanders in Singapore until December 1938. He died in captivity on 7 November 1940, while in a hospital in Munich, Germany. The men of the 2nd Battalion in Singapore were much affected by the losses of their comrades in France, now languishing in PoW camps in Eastern Europe. Deciding that they would like to assist them in some way, a series of concert parties was organised and performed to various audiences around Singapore to raise funds. These shows proved a great success and $600 was raised and sent to the Red Cross to buy parcels for the 'boys in the Stalags'. This was not just a comradely gesture to show solidarity. Many of those captured were close family members of the men in Singapore. The Gordon Highlanders, being the local regiment drawing recruits from Aberdeen and its hinterland had many close family members serving together within the 2nd Battalion and across the Regiment, both Regulars and Territorial Army. For example, 2877049 Jim Barclay's two brothers (Bill and Jake) were both captured at St Valéry and he was not alone in worrying about his family members; many more men had family members who had suffered the same fate. As a consequence of this anxiety, when the new draft arrived with men who had served in France the opportunity was taken to question them about their experiences in action and whether they had any news about their friends or relatives.

However, these men were by far not the first of the conscripts to arrive. Others, such as Alistair Urquhart, who was called up on 23 September 1939, almost immediately after the introduction of National Service (Armed Forces) Act 1939, was sent to Singapore immediately after completing his basic training, arriving there with twenty-seven others in December 1939. Their journey, on board the MV *Andes* had only taken three weeks as the Mediterranean and Suez Canal were still fairly safe for the passage of troopships since France was still undefeated and Italy had not entered the war. George McNab (2885735), another conscript, arrived on 15 May 1941 after leaving his six-day-old child back in Aberdeen. He was initially refused permission to go and see his wife and new baby daughter before he left but after he declared that he would go AWOL (absent without official leave), so that he could see them. Fortunately, common sense and compassion prevailed and the authorities relented and he was allowed to visit his new family before leaving Aberdeen, with nineteen other men, on 16 March 1941. They travelled by train to Liverpool where an air raid was in progress, but they were not affected by this and eventually were able to board their ship which was to take them overseas. At this point they did not know where they were bound and presumed it was to the Middle East, where Britain was engaged in fierce fighting in the North African desert.

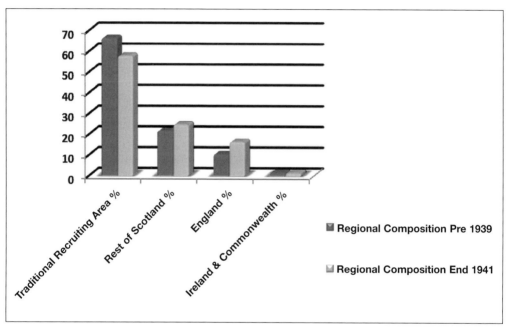

**Changes in Regional Composition of Men in 2nd Battalion
1939 to 1941**

The influx of thousands of conscripts in 1939, as part of the rapid expansion of the British Army to counteract the threat from Germany, such as invasion, and the loss of so many men (killed or captured) in France in 1940 meant that during the early part of the war, the British Army urgently needed numerous additional Instructors. The best candidates were experienced Regular Soldiers such as the men of the 2nd Battalion. As a result a number of men were sent back to Britain from Singapore, among whom was Corporal Jack Rennie who had been with the Battalion from the time they left Aldershot back in 1934. In 1939 he volunteered to be a training instructor and returned to Britain on the cruiser HMS *Cairo*, the ship stopping at several places en route to collect other Regular Army men serving oversees. As the ship passed through the Mediterranean they were running low on fresh food so a depth charge was dropped and the dead fish collected for supper. Jack spent the next five years in the south of England as an instructor, earning a commission in August 1942, and by 1944 had been promoted to the rank of captain. Just after D-Day' (6 June 1944), he volunteered to resume his active front-line service. By an amazing coincidence, he was posted to the newly-reformed 2nd Battalion Gordon Highlanders (the phoenix of his former unit in Singapore), serving with the 15th (Scottish) Division in Normandy and seeing fierce fighting there and in Holland. He rose to the rank of major and took command of a company that fought its way across the Rhine, finishing his war, on VE Day, in Tripoli.

The arrival of this new blood was not therefore a coincidence; these were the men to take up the reins following departure of many old and experienced hands. From the middle of 1939 to late 1941, just before the war in the Pacific began, the turnover of men amounted to just less than 25 per cent. This large influx of new men inevitably changed the nature of the Battalion which had until then been comprised only of professional ('Regular) soldiers, many with long service. The change of personnel not only increased the numbers of young and inexperienced men, their motivation was different. The Regulars had all volunteered for a career in the Army and in most cases had specifically chosen to enlist in the Gordon Highlanders, their local regiment. For most of the conscripts, life in the army had not been part of their future plans, so life in a Regular Army Highland infantry regiment, such as the Gordons, with a strong emphasis on strict discipline, spit and polish, precision drills, and ceremonial duties was quite a shock to their systems. These new recruits, 34 per cent from England and 33 per cent Lowland Scotland, quickly realised there was an additional problem. The Gordon Highlanders had to them an alien culture, especially among the enlisted men, with the language spoken being 'Doric', a strong distinctive dialect of Scots spoken widely but almost exclusively in the North East of Scotland.

In addition, the 2nd Battalion Gordon Highlanders were a close-knit unit and even after the addition of the conscripts, at the end of 1941, just fewer than 58 per cent of them were from Aberdeen and surrounding area, and 54 per cent of them had served for six or more years together. In addition many of the men were from very small communities, with very small populations and so would have known the families of other soldiers from that area. These not only include small towns like Buckie, Keith, Huntly and Turriff but also smaller villages such as Portsoy, Methlick, Fetterangus, New Deer, Crathes, Rhynie. Although far from the North East of Scotland, the Shetland Isles were linked culturally and, in a sense, physically, by the ferry from Aberdeen. There was only a small population there but there were eight Shetland Islanders in the Battalion of whom only one, Sergeant Christopher Robertson (2876680), was to survive the war. Of these eight men, two, both from Lerwick, joined together in 1935 with their service numbers being consecutive, Robert Wiseman (2876580) and William Goodlad (2876581). When called up at age twenty, Andrew McIntosh (2888556), from Drumnadrochit, a small village on the shores of Loch Ness, asked to join the RAF with his two pals but found he was enlisted into the Gordons. He was instructed to report to Bridge of Don Barracks, Aberdeen. He was not very pleased at first as his two friends were both accepted for the RAF but, the Gordons' camaraderie soon won him over. Their officers were, however, from a more privileged class of society. Unlike most of the other ranks (ORs) they were very well educated, including several old Etonians, with others from Harrow, Ampleforth College and other prestigious public schools. They were also very well connected, one officer being a Godson of Queen Victoria while others were from titled Scottish families. The Territorial Army and War Emergency commissioned officers were generally from the professions. Despite this potential gulf between the officers and the other ranks there was a great esprit de corps and the bond between them was strong, developed through long association and on the sports field. The officers often coached and led Battalion teams of boxers, field athletes (including the heavy events such as hammer throwing, caber tossing and tug o'war), swimming (including water polo) and cricket. Some of the officers were themselves outstanding sportsmen. Second Lieutenant George Roberts was a Scottish international rugby player (capped five times) and amateur golfer, playing for Scotland in 1938, while Captain Gordon Ludovic Farquhar held a 'black belt' in judo.

However, the saying goes that 'blood is thicker than water' and there were many blood relatives serving together in the Battalion in Singapore. The Bremner family was deeply woven into the fabric of the Battalion with four men being inter-related. John S. Bremner (2876172) and William Bremner (2869632) were brothers. William Bremner's son, William John Bremner (2890085), had enlisted, in Singapore, as a band boy at the age of fourteen, while his daughter (Isobel Ruth Bremner) had married Percy (known as John) Brown (2876136). In all there were twenty-eight sets of brothers, all pairs with the exception of the McGregors (Arthur, John and Alexander), from Keith, Banffshire and the Milnes (Fred, Charles and Colin), from Rhynie, Aberdeenshire, who were trios. Brothers James and Peter Milton, joined together and their service numbers were only two digits apart. Similarly the Christie brothers William M. and Donald, whose numbers are only fourteen digits apart,

30

joined and trained together in the same squad (India Squad, June 1933). They had both been farmworkers and they almost certainly enlisted at the May Feein' Market in the Castlegate, Aberdeen, which was overlooked by Castlehill Barracks, then the 'home' of the Regiment. At this same market, brothers William (2876251) and John Pirie (2876252) both enlisted, their service numbers being consecutive and while William trained in the India Squad with the Christies. John Pirie trained in the Afghanistan Squad at the same time, also at Castlehill Barracks. Fifteen men from the 1933 India Squad and nine from the 1933 Afghanistan Squad were destined to be posted to Singapore. When the colony was attacked by the Japanese in 1941, the twenty-four of them knew each other extremely well, having served together for over eight years, from their first day in the army.

In addition there were four sets of cousins and two men (George Sim and Alexander Watt) who were both brought up together as brothers by George's mother. William Bremner (aged fifteen), Patrick Brind (aged fifteen) and Frederick Brind (aged fourteen) all joined the Gordon Highlanders in Singapore at about the same time, Freddie joining as late as 23 January 1942, when hostilities had already begun. They were already living there, William Bremner in family quarters at Selarang, his father being a serving soldier with the Battalion and the Brind boys lived at Taiping, the sons of a prison warder and former sergeant of the Wiltshire Regiment.

These three young boys remained together in the early days of the conflict, immediately after the Japanese invasion, as they did not join the rest of the Battalion when they took up their battle station at Pengerang, just across the Johore Strait from their barracks at Changi. All three were sent up to Fort Canning (British Army HQ) where William John Bremner was put in the care of Private John 'Ginger' Stewart (2880733) and the Brind brothers were placed in the care of Corporal Alistair Urquhart, who was given the task, by the Education Officer, of educating them for their Army General Certificate of Education.

The family connections with the Regiment took many forms and spanned or traversed the generations. For example, the fathers of Corporals James Gordon (2876032) and George McNab (2885735) both served with the Regiment in the First World War and unfortunately both were killed in action. John Laing, as a 'Boy' soldier, stood and posed for the team photo after winning the Gibraltar Garrison Inter-Unit Athletic Challenge Cup in 1935 but little did he think that the man standing next to him, Cruden Watt (820156), was to become his relation by marriage. Another comrade, Albert Middleton (2869710), married another sister of his and so also became his brother in law. In addition, Lieutenant Forbes Sandison and Captain Gray Grant (from the Grant's Scotch Whisky family) had been school friends from Huntly, and when commissioned in Malaya in 1941, Lieutenant Sandison found his way into the 2nd Battalion Gordon Highlanders. These longstanding school friendships also extended into the wives and Major Walter Duke's wife (Yvonne) had been at the same school in London as Pam Roper-Caldbeck (wife of Captain Reggie Roper-Caldbeck) and, as a consequence, Pam later became Godmother to Bridget, the Dukes' daughter.

The Battalion came under the command of Lieutenant Colonel Graham from December 1938. Willie Graham's association with the 2nd Battalion stretched back to the Great War when he landed with them at Zeebrugge, Belgium, in October 1914 as one of the Old Contemptibles. (This was the nickname the men of the British Expeditionary Force gave themselves, following the remark, by the German Kaiser, that the British had a 'contemptible little army'.) Colonel Graham distinguished himself in France and won the Military Cross but by the time he took command of the Battalion he was almost forty-nine years old.

The Battalion settled into a routine of training to bring the new men up to scratch. For the men stationed in Singapore the war in Europe appeared a million miles away. A complacent attitude prevailed in the colony and the peacetime lifestyle went on unchanged. Opportunities or suggestions to strengthen the defences of the island were frowned upon by the Governor and Army General Staff as it was considered to be poor for the morale of the civilian population. An unshakable belief still held that the Singapore Fortress was impregnable. The men were still able to get late passes and went out at the weekends into Singapore City, frequenting the Union Jack Club or to nightclubs where the girls could be booked for a dance in so called 'Taxi Dances'. Some men had developed close and lasting relationships with local women, including marriage or, in some cases, a form of 'common law' marriage. The scene was however, set for a dramatic and sudden change!

# CHAPTER 3

# The Battle for Singapore

Tensions in the Far East were rising with Japanese imperialism and their growing confidence in their own military power making them increasingly bellicose. This was in stark contrast to the Western Powers, such as Great Britain, who dismissed Japan and the Japanese forces as any credible threat. In July 1937 Japan invaded and continued in their attempts to dominate China and exploit her vast natural resources. Actions by the Japanese Army included atrocities such as the massacre of defenceless civilians, the rape of women and looting. Tensions continued to mount in the Far East throughout 1941 and Britain and the United States of America imposed a trade embargo on Japan for her actions against China. The main consequence for Japan was the loss of imports of raw materials, especially oil. Japan saw the oil rich Dutch East Indies (modern Indonesia) and rubber and tin rich Malaya (Malaysia) as vital for her ambitions toward her future prosperity and regional dominance. In these circumstances, with a belligerent, military-led government in total control in Japan, conflict with the Western Powers of Britain, the United States of America and the Netherlands was inevitable.

In 1941 Britain, with only its Empire and Commonwealth, stood alone against Germany and Italy. The priorities were to protect the home country against invasion and to safeguard the Middle East, preventing Germany reaching the vast oil reserves there and the commencement of a second front against Russia, through the Caucasus, which also had rich oil reserves. The Far East was, therefore, seen as a lower priority and the government of Winston Churchill in London believed that war with Japan was not imminent. Simple precautions, such as improving the defences on the northern shores of Singapore Island, were not encouraged by the High Command. This, it was suggested, would be interpreted locally as a sign of weakness and bad for the morale of the civilian population.

The threat of invasion from the north, down through the Malayan Peninsula was not, contrary to popular belief, totally discounted by military planners in London and Singapore. One of the main issues in countering this threat was the diplomatic sensitivities of respecting the neutrality of Thailand to the north and possibly prematurely triggering a response from Japan. While Thailand had been an ally against Germany in the First World War, their military, under the Prime Minister Plaek Phibulsongkram, was leaning towards Japan in the 1930s. There were parallels in the two countries' ruling systems with iconic royal households and one example of the close relationship which was developing was that Thailand armed herself with Japanese aircraft in 1938. Furthermore, since Japan had annexed Korea and Taiwan in the early part of the century, the military-led government in Thailand was looking for an opportunity to recover territory and prestige it had lost to the French and the British in the late nineteenth century. This opportunity came in 1940 with the defeat of France by Germany. Japan, an Axis ally of Germany, marched into the French colony of Indochina (Vietnam and Cambodia) while Thailand seized the French colony of Laos. The Thai people were, however, more or less impotent in respect of their country's government.

Tensions in the area continued to grow and, on 1 December 1941, the 2nd Battalion Gordon Highlanders prepared to move to their predetermined battle positions to guard the artillery installations at Pengerang, across the Straits of Johore and strategically placed to protect the approaches to the large naval base. This was very familiar territory for the Gordons, having patrolled the area for many years previously, and a full company had moved into position a little earlier. Prior to their mobilisation, the men packed all their personal effects, which were then stored in boxes in the gymnasium at Selarang Barracks. The Battalion silverware (sports trophies and Mess silverware) together with the Battalion Colours were deposited in a vault in the Hong Kong and Shanghai Bank in Singapore City.

Meanwhile, Sergeant Frank Knight (2874564) had been detached from the Battalion to a specialised group of the Federated Malay Straits Volunteer Force Railway Operating and Maintenance Company, whose task was to travel north up the line, cross into Thailand and blow up railway bridges if Malaya was invaded. This team was alerted in advance of the invasion and crossed the border, unlike the planned operation for other British units, and completed the mission successfully. During this operation Frank later reported that he saw Japanese soldiers crossing into Malaya on pedal cycles.

At Pengerang, the Gordons began to work on strengthening their defences and anti-personnel mines were laid, but not without cost. On 20 December 1941 Privates David Johnston (2876713) and William Mackie (2879250) were killed and Lieutenant Duncan Campbell, Lance Sergeant Robert Laing (2876627) and Private Alexander Graham (2889054) were all wounded in an accident while laying these mines. Private Graham died of his wounds in Roberts Barracks Hospital on 24 March 1942.

On 2 December 1941 a Naval battle group, Force Z, arrived in Singapore, sent by Prime Minister Winston Churchill as a deterrent against Japanese attack. This comprised the battleship HMS *Prince of Wales* and the battle-cruiser, HMS *Repulse.*

These capital ships were escorted by four destroyers, HM Ships *Electra*, *Express*, *Encounter* and *Jupiter*. The aircraft carrier HMS *Indomitable* was an essential part of this force as it was to provide the necessary air cover for operations. However, on her maiden voyage, she had run aground on a coral reef in the West Indies, so her departure for the Far East was delayed for repairs to be effected. This delay proved to be fatal for the other capital ships in the group. The commander was Sir Tom Philips, who had been promoted to the rank of admiral only in October.

Japanese forces attacked the USA's Pacific fleet at Pearl Harbor and almost simultaneously invaded southern Thailand and northern Malaya on 7 December 1941. In a speech to the United States Congress, President Franklin D. Roosevelt famously referred to this day as 'A date which will live in infamy'. Singapore City was also bombed by Japanese GM3 Nell bombers. Although these attacks were more or less concurrent, because of the relative geographical positions of Singapore, Pearl Harbor, Hawaii and the International Dateline, the attacks on Singapore and Malaya actually occurred on the 8 December 1941. At Selarang Barracks, Changi, the evening started quietly. Here the young 'Boy' soldiers, who had been prevented from going up to Pengerang because of their age, and those in the Band, who were detailed to man a medical centre, all remained. However they were awakened in the middle of the night by the sound of explosions and the firing of anti-aircraft guns. There was some confusion as to what it all meant and some thought it was just another exercise although others were adamant that they had heard aircraft and that it had been a real air raid. The situation soon became clear when they were ordered to 'stand to' and the men formed up outside the guardroom and were informed that there had indeed been a raid on Singapore City. They were told to be vigilant and patrols were sent out to look for anyone acting suspiciously, such as signalling to the enemy, but these orders were not very clear. Men spoke in whispers as all lights were extinguished and this merely added to the tension. Archie Black thought this was not what was supposed to happen as the script was that the Japanese would obligingly attack from the sea and would conveniently be blown out of the water by the massive shore defences. Peggy Coutts (wife of 2871271 Willie Coutts) was at home in the married quarters at Selarang when she too was awakened at about 4.00am by the sound of the Japanese planes which came over the city in waves of twenty-five. She remembered that at the time all the outside lights were on and she switched hers off; a little later, a messenger from the barracks came round to ensure everyone switched off their lights also.

Meanwhile, in an effort to counteract the Japanese landings in the north, HMS *Repulse* and HMS *Prince of Wales* were despatched, on the evening of 8 December 1941 to disrupt and prevent these as far as possible. The Gordon Highlanders, at their battle stations in Pengerang, saw the *Prince of Wales* and *Repulse* move majestically out of the Johore Straits on their way north. Many of the men remembered their old friend the *Repulse* from the operation in 1936 when they were rushed from Gibraltar to Egypt to deal with an Arab revolt in Palestine. Private Bob Morgan remembered that a photograph of this ship had been used to illustrate the card he sent home to his family to wish them a 'Happy New Year' in 1937. Admiral Philips had expected to receive air cover from the RAF, to replace the planes from *Indomitable*, but, due to a lack of communication between the services, he was not fully aware of the losses inflicted on British air bases in northern Malaya and so in effect he had no air cover. This proved disastrous as the fleet were spotted by Japanese bombers and sunk on the morning of 10 December 1941, with the loss of 840 men, including Admiral Philips who went down with his ship. Ironically, a squadron (453 Squadron,

Royal Australian Air Force) of Brewster Buffalos, which could easily have dealt with the Japanese bomber threat, arrived over the scene too late. Had Phillips adhered to the plan agreed with this squadron's commander, the Buffaloes could have been in position to intercept the bombers. The escorting destroyers picked up as many of the survivors as they could but the loss of these two ships was a major blow to the defence of Singapore and Malaya. Against all expectations, in the space of just two days the Japanese had eliminated virtually all British and American capital ships in the Pacific area. Two American aircraft carriers, The USS *Enterprise* and the USS *Lexington* were, however, at sea when the Japanese dive and torpedo bombers struck Pearl Harbor. They both escaped unscathed and this was later to prove very costly for the Japanese.

Just before Christmas 1941 all the families were advised they would be evacuated as soon as ships were available to take them back to Britain. They could only take a small amount of luggage with most of their belongings packed away in the barracks gymnasium. At the end of January 1942 four ships arrived with reinforcements and the families embarked on the *Duchess of Bedford* and sailed at 6.00pm on Thursday 30 January 1942. As they left the harbour there was an air raid and bombs dropped all around the ship and, although she was not hit, there were other ships nearby which were damaged. The *Duchess of Bedford* was called 'the most bombed ship still afloat', and was a very lucky ship. During the Second World War, she sank a U–boat, damaged another, was shot at and bombed on a number of occasions. The families arrived in Liverpool on 2 April 1942 and made their way to stay with relatives in the UK. However, not all went back to the UK. Jean Low, the wife of Sergeant William Low (2870244), disembarked when the ship called into port in South Africa and spent the duration of the war in Natal, as did the wife and family of Sergeant Jock Webster (2865818), but they settled there permanently after the war. Company Quartermaster Sergeant James King's family had a tragic time at the beginning of 1942. His wife died in childbirth, just before the families were evacuated, so his children (twins) were taken care of by a nanny who ensured their safe evacuation. When their ship called at Colombo they called to see their uncle (his brother), who was stationed in Colombo. However, on their onward journey tragedy struck this family again as the twins died of cholera before they reached Durban, South Africa. Major Walter Duke's wife (Yvonne) and daughter (Bridget) also reached South Africa and stayed in Mtunzini, Zululand (now Kwa Zulu-Natal) where sadly Mrs Duke died in 1943, a fact quite unknown to Major Duke until after the end of the war. Jane Middleton, the wife of Private Albert Middleton (2869710), left Singapore with her two sons on a ship bound for Australia and they spent the war in Victoria, not returning home to Scotland until March 1946. Mrs Jeannie Winton, wife of Company Sergeant Major Andrew Winton (2872532), and her friend, the wife of Lance Sergeant James Ewen (2870233), also made it to Australia and shared a house together. Mrs Winton was pregnant with her second child who was born in Wagga Wagga, New South Wales, in June 1942. She was named Andrea after her father.

Not all the families of the Gordons escaped the clutches of the Japanese. The wife of Corporal Bert Logan (2875425) did not manage to get away and she was interned in Changi Gaol. Sergeant Douglas Hepburn (2876059), in a romantic gesture, married his fiancée, Marie Paglar, at Singapore on 11 February 1942, just before the surrender. She was evacuated from Singapore on 12 February 1942 but was captured by the Japanese and interned in Palembang, Sumatra. Gabrielle Lyon, the wife of Captain Ivan Lyon and their five-month-old son, Clive, had been evacuated to Australia at the beginning of February 1942. In April 1942, they left Australia bound for India to join Ivan but, while passing through the Indian Ocean, their ship was attacked by a German warship. The Germans handed over the ship, including the crew and passengers, to their allies, the Japanese, and they were interned in Japan, Clive Lyon possibly becoming one of the youngest British internees.

Air raids on Singapore continued relentlessly throughout January, causing very heavy civilian casualties and on the 18th the naval base was hit and the oil storage tanks there, holding 100,000 gallons (half a million litres) of fuel oil, were set alight. A thick plume of smoke blackened the skies and for those men who had escaped from Dunkirk twenty months earlier the scene was remarkably similar. The Gordon Highlanders were part of the Singapore Garrison Force and as a consequence were not initially involved in the fighting against the Japanese in northern Malaya. These men were, however; fully aware that their families back in Britain would be worried by the reports coming out of Singapore and being reported in their newspapers and on their wireless sets by the BBC. Some of them took the trouble to send home a telegram to reassure their loved ones that they were still alive and well. One example, sent on 18 January 1941 from Private Jock Campbell (2884170), said everything that needed to be said: 'All well and safe. Please don't worry. Best wishes for Christmas and New Year.'

The situation regarding the defence of Malaya in the north grew progressively worse and the Gordon Highlanders were relieved at Pengerang on 21 January 1942 and committed to the battle. On 26 January 1942 the battalion took up position at Milestone 45, on the Ayer Hitam Road, where they dug in either side of the highway in a rubber plantation. There were several attacks by the Japanese that day; six men were killed and ten wounded but they held their position. In this, their first action, there were some who had a fairly casual attitude to the dangers of their situation. Private Davie Clyne (2876454) saw his friend, Lance

Corporal John Iggo (2876209), getting carried away and standing upright to fire at the Japanese while enemy bullets were thudding into the trunks of the rubber trees all around them. He shouted to John to get down and lie flat on the ground where he would get some cover from the longish grass but, just at that moment, he heard him scream that he had been shot and was seriously wounded in the arm, which subsequently had to be amputated above the elbow.

The next day further attacks occurred and one man was killed and three wounded, including Captain Francis Moir-Byers, who was visiting the GOC 8th Australian Division, and Lieutenant General Henry Gordon Bennett, who was later to become a controversial figure in both Britain and his native Australia. They were having tea together when a low-flying plane bombed the Brigade HQ and Moir-Byers was wounded by shrapnel. Heavier fighting on the 28th and 29th caused the deaths of five men and twenty wounded. This was another sad day for Davie Clyne as among the dead was Private George Clyne (2878924), his cousin. George was a champion runner and heroically thought he could use his speed in a charge to surprise and eliminate a Japanese machine-gun position. Tragically, he was cut down in a hail of bullets and, with multiple gunshot wounds, was rushed back to Alexandra Hospital, Singapore, but was pronounced dead on arrival. Also evacuated back to Alexandra Hospital with George was Bob Morgan, who had been wounded in the jaw by shrapnel. Bob survived this wound but sadly his brother Arthur, who was also wounded in the fighting, died of his wounds in Alexandra Hospital on 4 February. At this point in the battle Corporal Mark Allen (2875307), who was a bandsman and consequently deployed in a support role, and stretcher-bearer acted with great bravery. This was to result in him being awarded the Distinguished Conduct Medal, second only to the Victoria Cross (VC) as a gallantry award available to an enlisted man and widely regarded as a near miss for a VC. He was the only Gordon Highlander to receive one of the ten DCMs awarded in the entire Malaya Campaign. His citation states:

> During the action at 41 Milestone on the Ayer Hitam-Johore Road in January 1942, this Non-Commissioned Officer displayed gallantry under intense machine-gun fire. He organised and led carrying parties for ammunition which he successfully delivered to forward Troops at a very critical juncture. Subsequently he brought back several casualties at a time when machine-gun fire and shelling were continuous in the area. Throughout the fighting in *Johore* and Singapore Corporal Allen set a most inspiring example to his men by his cheerful demeanour, determination and courage.

The Gordons fought courageously and tenaciously throughout their short involvement in the Malaya Campaign. In addition to Mark Allen's bravery, the courage of the Gordons' Medical Officer, Captain Frank Pantridge, was recognised in late January. He won the Military Cross (MC) and his citation stated,

> This officer worked unceasingly under the most adverse conditions of continuous bombing and shelling and was an inspiring example to all with whom he came into contact'.

Major Walter Duke and Captain Ludovic Farquhar were also recognised with the same award. Major Duke's citation read:

> During operations in Johore and Singapore between 25 January and 15 February 1942, this officer displayed great determination and high fighting qualities as a Company commander. He invariably set an outstanding personal example by his gallant bearing and disregard for his own safety. At all times his inspired leadership contributed largely to the successful actions of the Company under his command.

This reflects the comment by one of his men who said 'you never saw Major Duke in a trench – he was always running from one to another checking that all was well with us'. Captain Ludovic Farquhar's citation paints a similar picture:

> As a Company Commander during the period 25 January to 15 February 1942, in fighting in Johore and Singapore this officer by his skilled leadership and personal bravery enabled those under him to inflict severe losses on the enemy on at least five occasions. At all times he inspired those under him with the sole intention of attacking the enemy, and by his determination and gallant conduct set a splendid example to all.

Private Joseph Yeats (2876247) won the Military Medal (MM). General Gordon Bennett complimented the Gordons for their contribution to the defence of Malaya while under his command.

One of the main problems was the Japanese complete control of the air and Private William Niven (2880078) explained that a spotter plane, with a high-pitched engine noise, which he described was 'like a sewing machine', regularly came over their position and was soon followed up by the bombers. On 29 January 1942, while he was dug in adjacent to the road, bombs fell close by and Private Robert Ingram (2876257) lying next to him received serious shrapnel wounds to his back, while the man next to him was killed, yet, on this occasion, Willie Niven escaped unscathed. The continual attention the Gordons received from Japanese aircraft was in complete contrast to the support from the Royal Air Force and Jimmy Scott (2880277) claimed he never saw a single British plane the whole time they were embattled with the Japanese. Many British planes were destroyed on the ground, at the beginning of the conflict when the element of surprise lay with the enemy. The lack of air cover for the troops was not for any lack of courage by the RAF pilots and their Brewster Buffalos but the problem was these were no match the faster and more manoeuvrable Japanese Zeros, which shot them down fairly easily.

The strategic withdrawal of British, Australian and Indian troops continued until, on the morning of 31 January 1942, only the Gordon Highlanders and the Argyll and Sutherland Highlanders remained on mainland Malaya. The Gordons marched across the Causeway back into Singapore to the sound of the pipes of the Argylls piping 'Cock O' the North', the Gordons' marching anthem. The causeway was then blown up but this was not as successful as planned and repairs were achieved by the Japanese within a very short time. At this time observers on the ground in Singapore noticed that the Japanese planes were ever present in the skies above and never seemed to be molested by anything other than the constant thump of Bofors guns. These were fairly ineffective and were no real threat to the Japanese but they scored at least one hit. Corporal Alex McDonald (2871657) managed to get a piece of downed plane as a souvenir and fashioned the aluminium into an identity bracelet for himself. This now rests within the collection of the Gordon Highlanders' Museum in Aberdeen.

The Battalion moved to Birdwood Camp, a hutted camp on Singapore Island, where they were subjected to a number of attacks by Japanese bombers. The worst of these was on 8 February 1942 when a number of the huts were set ablaze. Not everyone had managed to get into the slit trenches when this attack occurred and four men were killed and nine wounded. In addition, as the Quartermaster, Lieutenant William Main, looked on, a direct hit set fire to and completely destroyed his store. This resulted in a serious loss of equipment.

As with the families' belongings, most of the men's possessions and equipment had been stored in the gymnasium at

Selarang. When they returned to Changi they found that the building had been looted and men endeavoured to rescue what they could. The Pipe Major told the members of the Pipe Band that all of the army equipment was to be written off, so if they thought they could use anything they could take. Piper Johnny Laing (2876421) was D Company's piper and was the custodian of a fine set of ivory and silver mounted pipes, so he thought he would do his best to keep them and carried them right to the end of his time in captivity. He didn't flaunt them in any way because of their intrinsic value and in any event felt that, as time went by during his time working on the railway, he just didn't have the strength to play them. However, he brought them home in 1945. Seventy years later, his grandson (Michael Laing), a Pipe Major in the Territorial Army, is still playing them. Piper Sam Robertson (2876427) decided to try and get his bagpipes, which had been a gift to him from his family, 'evacuated' back to Scotland on one of the ships leaving Singapore. He persuaded someone to take care of them for him but, unfortunately, although he survived and eventually got home safely, he discovered that his pipes had ended up at the bottom of the sea after the ship carrying them was sunk by enemy action.

Sergeant Willie Coutts (2871271) went back to his own house to check that things were all right, his wife and daughter (Peggy and Norah) having been evacuated on 31 January 1842. As a precaution against air raids, sandbags had been piled up on the verandahs of the family quarters houses at Selarang. The advice given to the families had been that, in the event of an air raid, they should put a table on the verandah behind the sandbags and a mattress on top and sit under the table. Willie found that for his family this would have been catastrophic as a bomb had gone right through the house, from back to front and under the table where they would have been sheltering.

Like Jock Campbell, Private Bob Morgan also managed to send off a telegram to his parents back in Aberdeenshire to reassure them that he was all right but the situation in Singapore had worsened dramatically since January. As a consequence, Bob's telegram was not delivered until mid-1944. The envelope with telegram message also contained a printed note from the Postmaster General explaining that the chaotic circumstances which prevailed in Singapore in February 1942 meant that many messages had not been sent at that time and had only recently arrived in the UK. His bemused parents would not have known at that time that Robert was now in in poor health in Thailand, nor that their other son, Arthur, had died.

On 11 February 1942 the Battalion moved forward from their position in reserve to Tyersall Park, where incidentally was located the 14th Indian General Hospital. This was clearly identified as a hospital by numerous Red Cross signs including large sheets sewn together to make a huge Red Cross flag strung between two trees. Just after the Battalion passed this position there was an air raid and the hospital was attacked and D Company were sent back to assist in rescuing the injured. The scene was described in detail by Private Archie Black (2879290) who, with Private Robert Burness (2876701), acted as stretcher bearers. These men were bandsmen and had been re-assigned from HQ Company and allocated this task as they had not been trained as front-line fighting men. The hospital was attacked by Japanese aircraft which repeatedly strafed the hospital and grounds. The buildings, being largely wooden huts with atap roofing (palm frond thatch) soon caught fire and many trapped patients were heard screaming as they were burned alive, while others were killed by gunfire or wounded for a second time. It was a scene of absolute carnage and the two Gordons used their medical kits to bandage as many wounded as they could. Their supply of bandages was soon exhausted and they resorted to tearing up bed sheets to make improvised dressings. Archie Black's best efforts were hampered by the wounded men repeatedly grabbing his hand to thank him for his efforts while others chose to try and hide beneath his body to shield themselves from the attacking planes. As the attack came to an end more help arrived and Archie was able to hand over to the hospital's own medical staff. An Indian doctor replenished his supply of field dressings and shook his hand, thanking him for his assistance.

The Battalion pressed on and, as they approached, the front line came under artillery fire, crossing the main road in small groups between shellbursts. On 12 February 1942 the Battalion was in position at Bukit Timah where heavy fighting occurred over the next four days. The Gordons were faced by an enemy advancing with tank support and Private Willie Niven (2880078) described the problem from his own first-hand experience.

On the 12th of February we were in Bukit Timah Road and my Company [C Company] were told to advance, which was strange as the rest of the Battalion were all withdrawing. I heard a noise and then saw a Japanese Gun Carrier. I was with two others, Robert Mearns [2876505] from Oldmeldrum and John (Hank) Stewart [2819471] from Newmill, Keith. We jumped into a large concrete storm drain at the roadside and hid under a bridge. The Jap gun stopped right beside us and at that point our Royal Artillery began to fire at the Japs. We decided this was our best chance to make a run for it and jumped out of the drain and ran across the road for some large houses opposite. We had to climb over a wire netting fence and the bipod legs of Hank's Bren gun got entangled in the fence. I stopped to help him and I was hit by shrapnel in the shoulder and he received a gunshot wound to his wrist. The bullet came out the other side and I told him that that was lucky but he was not so sure. Mearns was also wounded. The Jap gun eventually moved off and we were evacuated to a first aid post. When we got there it was the Fullerton Buildings, adjacent to the General Post Office, which was being used as a Casualty Clearing station. There were a lot of newly arrived troops there, all singing and enjoying themselves and they took no notice of us, even though we were all dirty and dishevelled after our time in combat.

This account clearly illustrates the confusion and hopeless position of the Battalion, who were not equipped to deal with the enemy's armour-supported assault.

The enemy were infiltrating their positions by every means and one afternoon, while Archie Black was sitting on the edge of his slit trench, a British army 15-cwt hundredweight truck drew up in the valley some 200 yards below him. As the soldiers alighted from this vehicle he thought there was something odd about their appearance and demeanour until suddenly it dawned on him these soldiers were Japanese. He quickly adopted a kneeling position and started to fire and the first few men slumped to the ground. A Vickers machine gun, manned by some Australians who had also been watching the truck with some suspicion, opened up and the truck burst into flames. A number of follow-up bursts of fire into the grass at the roadside appeared to deal with the imminent threat.

The British position became more and more precarious and a general withdrawal commenced. On 13 February 1942 the Battalion were at Holland Road. Lieutenant Robert (Bobby) Irvine was briefing a few men whom he was sending out on a patrol when a direct hit by a mortar shell on the slit trench killed him instantly while Privates Bill Kellas (2876651) and Joe Clayton (2876767), alongside him, escaped unhurt. Air and artillery fire continued to trouble the Gordons and, among others, Regimental Sergeant Major Alexander Milne was badly wounded while Private James Thomson (28766360) was killed while trying to identify the position of a mortar which was firing on their position. Thomas Cass (3184402) was also wounded by shrapnel from a mortar round and evacuated to Alexandra Hospital.

One of the worst atrocities perpetrated by the Japanese was during the battle for Singapore. On 14 February 1942 Japanese soldiers approached Alexandra Hospital (later known as Singapore Civil Hospital and now as Singapore General Hospital) and, although no resistance was offered, entered the building and went on a rampage, shooting and bayoneting patients and medical staff. There have been suggestions that they were pursuing a party of Indian soldiers who had retreated through the hospital grounds but there can be no plausible excuse for the murder of non-combatant medical staff and defenceless men who were lying in bed, receiving treatment for their wounds. Those that survived this horror were murdered over the next two days. Initially, they were confined to a small room where the overcrowding and lack of air and water resulted in the deaths of many of those already weak due to loss of blood from their wounds. However, the following day, the Japanese took the survivors out into the grounds in pairs and bayoneted them to death in cold blood. Those awaiting their fate would have heard the bloodcurdling screams of those being murdered and been fully aware that they were condemned to die in a horrific way.

Six Gordon Highlanders were among those who died. They included Captain Henry (Harry) Smith, the Gordon Highlanders' Chaplain, who had been with the men on the front line but accompanied the wounded when they were evacuated to hospital, and Private Andrew Annand (287848), who was receiving treatment for a shrapnel wound he received on 29 January. Chaplain Harry Smith was in the hospital doing pastoral work when the Japanese attacked and was with a soldier when he was bayoneted and killed by a Japanese soldier. However, the man on the stretcher survived as Chaplain Harry Smith's body protected him. Chaplain Smith and Private Annand both have identified graves in Kranji War Cemetery but almost all the victims of the massacre were buried in a mass grave, originally an emergency water tank which had been dug in the hospital grounds. When Kranji War Cemetery was created, in 1946, it was realised that it would be impossible to identify the individuals in the mass grave and it was left undisturbed. Of the ninety-four British soldiers buried there, four were Gordon Highlanders, and the others were patients receiving treatment for wounds at the time of the incident. The Gordons were Private James A. Barclay (2877049); Private Thomas Cass (3184402); Private James Forbes 2876466) and Private Roy Stewart Scott (2879196).

At Gillman Barracks Hospital on Alexandra Road, Singapore, Private Victor J. King (2889874) faced a situation with a chilling similarity to the incident at Alexandra Hospital. He had received multiple gunshot wounds to his legs on 28 January 1942 while in action with the Battalion in Johore and was being treated in Gillman. Just after the capitulation, on 15 February 1942, front-line Japanese soldiers came into the hospital and tormented patients with drawn bayonets. After the war no one was prosecuted or held accountable for either of these actions.

Over the final four days of the battle for Singapore heavy casualties were incurred with seventeen men killed and twenty-one wounded, the Battalion's worst period since entering the battle three weeks earlier. On the night of 13 February 1942 the Battalion Commander, Lieutenant Colonel Jack Stitt, was very concerned by the shortages of water and petrol. As the battle for Singapore was drawing to a close, he was ordered to arrange for the evacuation of one officer and fourteen experienced other ranks (ORs) who could form the nucleus of a new Battalion. He chose Lieutenant William E. Main (the oldest officer and

Quartermaster) and ordered him to leave with his hand-picked team.

In a letter to his daughter (Agnes Anne), written on 6 March 1942, on board a ship bound for Colombo, Ceylon (now Sri Lanka), Lieutenant Main gave details of the events prior to his escape, including the bombing of his house and the Battalion store, where everything was lost. His wife (Annie), together with many other civilians, had been evacuated a little earlier and he expressed the heartbreak of missing her, apparently by only a few minutes when he had gone to see her before her ship left Keppel Harbour. He declared the hope that he would meet up with her in Colombo.

With his orders to evacuate coming at the eleventh hour of Singapore's ordeal, Lieutenant Main and his party arrived at the docks to find a chaotic scene, with some 300 other men trying to get out just as they were. All the ships had already left because of the intense bombing and shelling of Keppel Harbour. The Gordons stayed there all night and were lucky not to have incurred any further casualties, so at dawn Lieutenant Main took his men out of the immediate docks area. Later that day, on Saturday 14 February, they heard that two launches had become available but these had well below the passenger capacity required. A discussion ensued and it was agreed that lots would be drawn for places on board but, as there were too many men for this to be done individually, the units stood as one. The fifteen Gordons were lucky and were allocated a place together with the Straits Settlements Volunteers and 2 MIB (Malaya Infantry Brigade) Signals. Their small motor launch was the *Celia* and they sailed out at six in the evening, leaving behind a blazing Singapore.

At dawn the next day they had crossed the Straits of Malacca to Sumatra and streamed up the River Indragiri for four days, reaching the navigable limit. Here they remained on board for a few days until arrangements could be made for their onward journey. After this short delay they made a hair-raising cross-country journey by bus and train over the mountains to Padang, their port of departure on 23 February 1942. At this point Lieutenant Main was separated from his squad as the ship they had boarded had no room to take him and they left without him and reached Sumatra. On 26 February 1942 they and around 500 fugitives from numerous other units, set sail again. Late on the night, on 1 March 1942, their ship, the SS *Rooseboom* (a Dutch cargo steamer) was sunk by an enemy submarine. Their position, west of Sumatra, was 300 miles from land. The ship sank rapidly and all fourteen Gordons were lost, one of whom was Company Sergeant Major Andrew Winton (2872532) whose pregnant wife had been evacuated to Australia at the the end of January. He would never see his second daughter. Only one lifeboat survived the attack, which soon became overcrowded and, after several weeks at sea, only two people survived. One of these was an Argyll and Sutherland Highlander (Walter Gibson) who wrote about their harrowing ordeal in his book *The Boat*, published in 1952. This brought the Battalion's total casualties, including those who subsequently died of the wounds they received, to sixty-two killed and seventy-nine wounded, of whom eight were successfully evacuated on the hospital ship *Talamaba*. In July of the following year, the *Talamba* was sunk when carrying out a similar mercy operation off the coast of Sicily when she was deliberately targeted by enemy bombers. Lieutenant Main did successful get away on 1 March 1942, firstly making for Java but the Japanese advance meant his party could not make it and ran for Colombo. After arrival in Colombo, on 10 March 1942, he spent two weeks in hospital with an attack of malaria. On discharge he was made Camp Commandant at General Pownall's Headquarters. Despite his ordeal, Lieutenant Main finished off the letter to his daughter in upbeat Gordon Highlander spirit, adding a postscript mentioning to her that he was posting it to her on Good Friday but complaining there were no signs of any hot-cross buns, an unlikely prospect in the circumstances.

Private Hugh McGurk (3054253) had also managed to get himself on a ship leaving Keppel Harbour but his ship was sunk by a Japanese cruiser on 17 February 1942. Instead of being picked up as a survivor he swam ashore and lived in the jungle with native fishermen. After about seven days like this, he met up with and joined four women and three children, survivors of the SS *Van Der Brook*, which had also been sunk by the Japanese cruiser. They were all being cared for by Malay women but the Japanese were closing in and after three days a native informer gave them away and they were captured on 28 February 1942 and taken to Palembang. He was not the only Gordon Highlander to spend the war as a PoW in Sumatra. Alfred Clark (2878440) was captured at Muntok, Sumatra, in February and moved to Palembang in April 1942 and Hugh Gallagher (2876873) also made it to Sumatra and was captured at Banka Straits on 17 February 1942 and spent the war in Sumatra. It is not known how they escaped from Singapore but possibly he accompanied Hugh McGurk and they were separated when their vessel was sunk. They probably were reunited in captivity as they spent time in the same prisoner-of-war camps. These men had used their own initiative to get away as there were strict orders to remain with their units and accept their fate as prisoners of war. Obviously they did not relish this and chose to risk everything to try and fight another day.

Although four other officers of the Gordon Highlanders and two other ranks escaped successfully from Singapore, in the hours just before the capitulation or in the subsequent confusion, Lieutenant Main was the only officer who had been with the Battalion during the hostilities. The other officers who escaped were Lieutenant Geoffrey Hallowes, who had been posted to the Singapore Fortress HQ and was seen by Lieutenant Main in Padang, Captain Neil Gordon, Captain Ivan

Lyon and General Robert A. Wolf Murray DSO MC. Like Lieutenant Main, all escaped via Padang. Private John Bruce (2876328), who had received special training when he attended the School of Demolitions in the summer of 1941, was detached from the Battalion and involved in the destruction of some of the infrastructure and was lucky enough to be evacuated. Lieutenant General Henry Gordon Bennett, who was General Officer in Command of all Australian Forces in Malaya had handed over command of the 8th Division to Brigadier Cecil Callaghan, commandeered a sampan and escaped to Australia, also via Padang, claiming that he had vital information on how to wage war successfully against the Japanese, but this was contrary to the order to surrender by General Percival.

Captain (later Lieutenant Colonel) Ivan Lyon, who had been attached to the Intelligence Corps, had far from finished his war with the Japanese, remaining in Sumatra for some time and assisting many Allied soldiers to escape. His activities were principally centred on the Indragiri River and were a stunning success. Before the capitulation of Singapore he had been involved in setting up the escape route through Padang and stayed in the area for some considerable time assisting stragglers who had managed to get out of Singapore. He was appointed MBE for his work. His peacetime pastime of ocean sailing in the boat he bought and shared with his good friend Captain Francis Moir-Byers had taught him a great deal about local tides and currents. His seamanship was first rate, all of which made him a natural for the role he performed. He left Padang for India in a native prua and eventually went on to Australia from where he would call on the Japanese again, with spectacular results. Geoff Hallowes also escaped to Ceylon from Padang and, like Ivon Lyon, was to harass the enemies of the King in special operations as part of the Special Operations Executive (SOE), a brainchild of Churchill which he said was to 'set Europe ablaze'. He worked in Yugoslavia and in France after D Day, working with the French Resistance with great success and was Mentioned in Despatches and awarded the Croix de Guerre by the French Government.

Geoff Hallowes' escape was somewhat fortunate as all officers and men were forbidden to leave their positions. Hallowes volunteered to act as a courier to take the message of the surrender to one of the two British outposts on the islands of Blakang Mati and Pulau Brani as all communication with these islands had been cut. He was to be accompanied by Major Nick Nicholson of the Royal Engineers. They were told by Lieutenant Colonel Crawford (GSOI Operations, Singapore) that if they were successful in their mission, they could choose to stay with the troops on the island and become prisoners of war or try to escape to freedom. Geoff Hallowes took this latter suggestion as a reward for volunteering for the mission. They took a four-metre dinghy with paddles to cross to the island which took them about two hours. After walking for about four miles they located the British unit and relayed the message regarding the surrender. They now decided to make their escape and set off again in their dinghy but, after only a short distance, one of the paddles broke. This made progress very difficult but eventually they landed on another of the many islands just south of Singapore. Here they came across four stranded British soldiers who had, apparently, deserted from Singapore before the ceasefire but their boat had sunk. These men, two corporals and two privates, had two oars so the officers decided not to ask any awkward questions about their escape, perhaps secretly admiring their initiative in the circumstances. Pooling their resources, the six-man party continued their escape. Working against the wind and tide with only oars for propulsion was difficult. There were planes circling the area and they thought they would be attacked but were left alone, eventually reaching another island where they were able to buy some coconuts and fruit, which they demolished with relish. Geoff Hallowes and the corporals did all the rowing and, as a result, Hallowes' backside became very sore and blistered. The third night was very frightening as they were swept onto a reef by a storm. They were soaked through and became very cold. Going ashore they were able to make use one of Ivan Lyon's food supply dumps which provided them with additional supplies. The following day disaster struck when their boat sank but they got ashore safely. Two days later they had negotiated with the crew of a Chinese junk to take them to Sumatra, arriving there a week after escaping from Singapore. Escape through Padang was still possible at this time but with the advancing Japanese and the lack of ships the opportunities were diminishing fast. They met up with other British refugees and were able to get into a truck which struggled through the jungle with frequent breakdowns and stoppages due to lack of fuel, eventually arriving at Padang on 28 February 1942. They were very lucky as a British destroyer, which had been involved in the Battle of the Java Sea, called in to refuel and they were allowed aboard her. They made for Colombo arriving there on 5 March 1942. Geoff Hallowes went on to Bombay, India.

Another 2nd Battalion Gordon Highlander who was later to strike a blow against the Japanese in Burma was Jimmie Dickie. He left Singapore before hostilities began and was commissioned, in October 1943, into the 2/9th Battalion Gordon Highlanders, which became 100th Anti-Tank Regiment, Royal Artillery. Jimmy saw service in Burma, with the Fourteenth Army, ending the war with the rank of captain.

At the time of the British capitulation Frank Knight was back in Singapore and still with the specialist demolition group, which had been working on bridges on the Malayan line as the withdrawal down the peninsula unfolded. They found an unattended motor yacht at the docks and hoped to make good their escape but were prevented, at pistol point, by an officer with a misguided sense of duty. He then removed the distributor cap from the engine and threw it overboard. Frank made some vain attempts to recover the vital part by diving in the harbour but without success. Shortly thereafter, Frank was reunited with the Gordons at Changi.

Back in Singapore, the end came for the Gordon Highlanders with the British surrender at 8.30pm on 15 February 1942. There was some confusion and uncertainty in the ranks at first but orders came to pile up their weapons. This news was somewhat of a surprise as the men on the front line firmly believed they were holding their own, although they were aware of the shortage of ammunition. At first the order to surrender was received in silence as these dour, hard and naturally reserved men, predominantly from tough agricultural backgrounds in the North East of Scotland, were unwilling to just give in but, being professional soldiers, they obeyed without question. The orders were to remain alert and if attacked they could defend themselves but they were not, on any account, to start shooting. For some there was relief that the fighting was over and the immediate danger to their lives over the previous weeks was at an end. However, they knew that, in any event, there was now the uncertainty of a life of captivity in the hands of their enemy. This was all very ironic for the men who had escaped the clutches of the Germans when evacuated at Dunkirk who were now to become prisoners of a foe with wholly different ideas regarding the treatment of prisoners of war.

It was very galling, therefore, to discover at a later date that General Yamashita's bold demand that the Allied forces surrender was a bluff. His own lines of supply were stretched to breaking point and it is likely if General Percival and his staff had been a bit more assertive, a more positive outcome may have been achieved. Nevertheless, no relief force was coming to the aid of Singapore and surrender was inevitable but time could possibly have been bought to allow more men to get away. The sudden collapse of the Allies also surprised the Japanese who were completely unprepared to deal with the thousands of prisoners. They were, therefore, obliged to rely on the local Singapore Administration to maintain the day-to-day functions of the colony and for the Allied army to manage its own captivity, a somewhat incongruous situation.

# CHAPTER 4

# Captured!
# The Distribution of Gordon
# Highlander PoWs

After the surrender of the British and Allied Empire and Commonwealth forces on 15 February 1942, the Gordon Highlanders were given instructions to march to the Changi area, where they were to be held captive. No transport was provided by the Japanese, so they were forced to march the fourteen long miles. This was very hard as the men were already exhausted, physically and mentally, from the fierce battles of the preceding weeks. Their spirits were low as, with the red-hot sun high overhead, they marched (or more accurately staggered) past the remnants of the battle so recently lost. Bombed-out buildings, streets filled with rubble, burned-out vehicles, some still with the dead bodies of their occupants, and many other gruesome sights met them as they trudged through the city. The Gordons felt degraded and embarrassed as they passed groups of the civilian population who looked on in stunned and bewildered silence as they also tried to come to terms with the rapid change in their own fortunes. Many of the Gordons felt they had let these civilians down. The Chinese members of the population feared the most, knowing the brutal reputation the Japanese Army had already earned, following their operations in China. They were filled with dread as they expected brutal reprisals for it was known that the Chinese community in Singapore had actively supported the efforts to resist the Japanese in mainland China over the preceding years.

Once at Changi they found that their old barracks at Selarang had already been occupied by Australian troops, so they eventually found themselves in a hutted camp at the beach area of Changi at Telok Paku. However, the whole Changi area effectively became a huge prisoner-of-war camp and there was only limited security as the Japanese were overwhelmed by the number of prisoners in their hands. The Japanese were therefore compelled to leave the Allied army to organise itself but some guards were posted, mostly Indian Army and Sikhs, who had defected to the Japanese side.

The Japanese strategy had for some time been to drive a wedge between the British and the Indian soldiers by supporting Indian Independence from Britain and promoting the idea of 'Asia for Asians' in what they referred to as the 'Greater East Asia Co-Prosperity Sphere'. Here the Japanese would take the lead and be mainly in control, although these aspects were generally played down. The Indian National Army of Liberation was raised in Singapore, after the capitulation, and Indian PoWs were given the opportunity to change their allegiance to this new army and so remain 'free' to fight with the Japanese against the British in an effort to conquer India. Many, but not all, took up this offer, rather than becoming prisoners of war.

At this time the men, left to their own devices, had time to relax and come to terms with their new situation. Initially, for many, there was a feeling of relief that the fighting was over but there was the great uncertainty as to what would become of them. Many thought that the Allies would come to their rescue and put great store by the recent entry of the United States into the war, but they did not appreciate how long it would be before the vast resources of America could be mobilised fully after years of isolationism and the efforts of many influential Americans to avoid their country being dragged into another world war. However, not everyone was prepared to sit back and accept the situation. Private Andrew Moir (2876464) escaped from Changi to Singapore where he knew people who could help him. He walked out of the camp on 7 March 1942 and nobody stopped him. He knew the country pretty well, reached Singapore by 8.00 pm and went straight to the house of his Siamese girlfriend (Yoon Saiprasert). Here he remained until 28 June 1942 with the idea of getting away to somewhere still held by the British. During this time he met Sergeant Doran, RAMC, and Private Arnold, East Surreys, and another Siamese girl, the wife of Signalman Hodges. They came into contact with a Chinese youth who was prepared to help contact one of the men who ran junks sailing to the many islands south of Singapore. A meeting was finally arranged and they hired a taxi to go to the harbour, as they had the girls with them and it was too far to walk. As they arrived they were stopped by Japanese soldiers in plain clothes with torches. They took them to their HQ where they were kept for fourteen days. They were interrogated at intervals, beaten and sometimes flogged, on one occasion with horse whips, but they didn't talk. The girls were separated from them and were not seen again. Their fate is not known but it is unlikely to have been pleasant, most probably either forced into being 'comfort girls' for the Japanese or executed.

Unlike PoWs in the European theatre, where there were many thousands of escape attempts, some successful, there was no way for the PoWs in Singapore, or indeed anywhere in the East Indies, (now Malaysia and Indonesia) to blend into the local population. Their white faces made them readily identifiable as PoWs and the Japanese put a price on their heads to encourage the local people to betray them. Despite this risk, in July 1942, Captain George R. Roper-Caldbeck, (Battalion Adjutant) made a report on the escape by a group of four men, two Gordon Highlanders, Piper James (Hamish) Johnston (2876288) and

Private James ('Artie') Turnbull (2879081)) with two NCOs from other regiments. They stole a boat and escaped to Johore, on the mainland of Malaya. Hamish and the two NCOs spoke Malay and hoped to secure assistance from local communist groups who had been active in resisting the Japanese prior to the capitulation. They had prepared well and accumulated food and medical supplies before they made their escape. They left under cover of darkness and landed safely on the island of Pulau Ubin, locally known as 'Granite Island' by the British since a few years earlier it had provided much of the rock which was crushed into aggregate to make the concrete for the construction of most of the military facilities at Changi, including the Gordons' barracks at Selarang. This was located at the eastern end of the Johore Strait. Hamish attempted to contact local communists, who were continuing to resist the Japanese, but found they had recently left the area. However, the men were given shelter by some sympathetic Chinese. They laid up for a time but when Hamish returned to check the boat he was spotted by a Malay man who betrayed him to a Japanese patrol. They fired one shot at him which resulted in Artie Turnbull thinking his friend was hurt so he went to his aid and both were captured. The other two remained hidden.

After a short interrogation they were led up a path into a former quarry where the Japanese sergeant in charge told them to kneel. Hamish knew their situation was dire and was desperately trying to think how they could turn the situation around. The Japanese sergeant drew his sword and was ceremonially cutting the air just to their side. Artie appeared to have accepted their fate and was praying for all he was worth but Hamish was still shocked to see the severed head of his friend fall to the ground in front of him. Realising he was to be beheaded next, Hamish sprang up and made a dash for the jungle but he received a serious sword slash on his shoulder. While running away he was also shot at but fortunately the bullet was wide of its intended target. A search ensued by the Japanese patrol but Hamish remained hidden and evaded capture. Artie Turnbull's body was eventually recovered and is buried in Kranji War Cemetery. Hamish Johnston managed to get back to Changi by swimming across the Straits. This was very difficult with his wounded shoulder but fortunately the tide was in his favour. When he returned to camp he told the guard he had been swimming and had been bitten by a shark. This was a plausible story as parties of prisoners were sent out daily from Changi to collect sea water in drums for cooking rice. The Japanese did not provide any salt to the prisoners, so sea water provided an easily available alternative. Hamish was admitted to hospital and Battalion records show that Private James Grieve (2876720) acted as a blood donor for him on 18 July 1942. Hamish Johnston was never punished and the medical officers ensured that he was protected from Japanese interrogation as they did suspect something suspicious about how he obtained his wound. The two other NCOs also managed to return to Changi and got back through the wire unnoticed. They were sent to Japan as part of the first working parties to get them away from Singapore since the British knew they would be in serious trouble if the report from the Japanese patrol came to light and they were identified.

Meanwhile, British Army discipline continued as if nothing had changed. While one can appreciate the need for good order, one Gordon Highlander was charged with 'neglecting to obey Japanese Standing Orders for British and Australian Troops in the PoW Camp, Changi, in that he attempted to break through the barbed-wire fence of the Southern Area Boundary'. He was given eighty-four days detention, remitted to twenty-eight days. The full details of this are not known but his conduct would normally have been considered commendable and it may be that he was caught by a Japanese guard. In these circumstances, the British and Commonwealth command probably considered that their discipline had to be seen to be operating effectively so that the Japanese Military Police (the *Kempeitai*, widely regarded as the Japanese Gestapo with a reputation for brutality and ruthlessness which more than matched that of their German counterparts) did not have an excuse to get involved directly with the discipline of the PoWs. While it is understandable that order and morale had to be maintained, some clue to the mind-set of the 'top brass' can be discerned from the example of three Gordon Highlanders in March 1942. They were tried by District Courts Martial at Changi in April 1942 for failing to obey a lawful command given by a superior officer and, in two of these cases, using insubordinate language. In the early days of captivity it was obvious that proper discipline had to be maintained. It may be, however, that the long sentences passed by the court, of between fifty-six and eighty-four days' detention, remitted to fourteen to twenty-eight days by the Commander (Southern Area), were a warning to others. Another example is recorded in the contemporary notebook of Lieutenant Colonel Jack Stitt, held in the collection of Gordon Highlanders' Museum, which mentions another Gordon as being 'transferred to Detention Barracks, Changi on 23 June 1942' but his offence is not recorded. However, these examples clearly illustrate that the Japanese were still allowing the Army's internal administrative structure to continue virtually unchecked. These examples of indiscipline in the ranks and a loss of respect for their superiors was, in part, a reaction by some to the new situation in which they found themselves. Many of the men blamed their officers, especially the higher command, for this and they felt disillusioned. At Changi this level of discipline continued and in February 1943 another Gordon was charged with fraudulently misapplying property belonging to the regimental band, found guilty and given a sentence of eighty-four days' detention and a fine of $10. It is not clear how this man was expected to pay this, after a year of captivity without pay, and it is difficult to comprehend the mind-set in this instance, although the fine was remitted by a higher authority. In another example, a year later in February 1944, another Gordon was charged with stealing a pair of socks from an Australian PoW. He was found guilty and given six months' detention but the charges and sentence were eventually dropped.

As the Japanese became more organised they required working parties of men for clearing up the aftermath of the battle, for work on roads and loading and unloading ships in the docks. The Japanese could hardly believe their good fortune when they discovered the masses of food and other supplies they captured in Singapore. In addition, all the scrap from the damaged British equipment was also shipped to Japan to be ploughed back into their war effort. At this time the Japanese decided to build a memorial to their soldiers who died in the campaign and this was located at Butok Batok, just off the Bukit Timah Road, the scene of some of the heaviest fighting. Many Gordons were involved in the construction and Corporal George McNab (2885735) described it as a beautiful memorial. It was of a large two-tiered mound of earth with two flights of steps up to a twelve-metre pillar capped off with bronze. The ashes of the Japanese dead were housed in a marble shrine forming part of this memorial. When the tide of war had turned against them, the Japanese removed the ashes of their dead and transferred them back to Japan, fearing desecration by enemy forces after the war. The memorial was destroyed in 1945 and all that remains today are the flights of steps up the earthen mounds.

Many of the Gordon Highlanders were transferred to other camps in Singapore such as Havelock Road, Adams Road, Sime Road and Normanton. A few, some of whom had been seriously injured during the earlier fighting, were held in Roberts Hospital. In May 1942 the Japanese demanded that the British remove the minefield at Pengerang, which the Gordon Highlanders had laid in December of the previous year, as part of the defences of their battle station. This demand was wholly contrary to the Geneva Convention, which forbade the use of prisoners of war to carry out 'war work' for the enemy. However, Lieutenant V.I.D. Stewart (Derek) was instructed to carry this out. Derek Stewart commanded a small party of Gordons who were forced into the minefield by Japanese guards with machine guns. This was a highly dangerous operation for these men, as the mines were unstable and the mine-laying operation had already cost the lives of three Gordon Highlanders, with two others wounded. Now the anti-personnel mines were more unstable, having lain undisturbed in the warm moist earth of the tropics for eighteen months. In addition, the virulent jungle vegetation had taken back the area, so locating the mines and, more importantly, the trip wires, was extremely difficult.

Their mission went well and was almost complete but the last mine proved difficult to defuse. Lieutenant Derek Stewart took responsibility for this but, as he was defusing it, he accidentally triggered the mine. Realising it was about to explode, he bravely sat on it to smother the explosion and protect the men around him. He suffered multiple shrapnel wounds and was virtually blinded. He was taken to Roberts Barracks Hospital in Changi PoW Camp and had both legs amputated. In addition, he had numerous other minor operations to deal with his injured eye and multiple shrapnel wounds. For all this surgery to be carried out successfully in the difficult conditions of the PoW camp a call went out to his comrades in the Regiment to donate blood, in the hope that he might be saved. It is a true mark of respect that, despite these men suffering from malnutrition and disease, a total of seventeen Gordon Highlanders came forward, between 26 May and 28 August 1942, and donated their blood for his treatment.

After the war was over Lieutenant Derek Stewart's mother received the news of the death of her son and, in writing to a friend, relayed the information she had received from

Lieutenant Robert Fletcher (Battalion Adjutant) and Derek's best friend in Singapore. Mrs Stewart had not seen her son for some time as he had been at school at Ampleforth College, North Yorkshire, while their home was in Ceylon and he had been commissioned into the Gordon Highlanders on 31 May 1941 from the Officer Cadet Training Unit. He was posted to Singapore only a few months before the outbreak of war in the Pacific. The following is an extract from the letter she received:

> He was brought to Roberts Hospital where the medical staff, led by Col Julian Taylor (Surgeon to the King) Lt Colonels Houston, Neil, Major Doyle all of them surgeons, fought desperately to save Derek's life. Both [his] legs had to be amputated, one eye was badly damaged & he had multiple shrapnel wounds on his face & body, which necessitated several minor operations as well. For nearly three months he put up the most wonderful struggle, but he died on 29 August 1942.
>
> His courage in hospital was truly amazing and he won the admiration & affection of all his doctors & orderlies as no one else. Everything possible was done for him, he had a great friend in Major Massie, who went up to see him every day. Though rations were short, Massie got fried eggs, braised chicken – he even procured rubber soled shoes so that their boots would not disturb him. He was buried with full military honours. He was extremely popular with all as he had a natural facility for mixing with people. For relaxation he sketched, was able to recapture quite uncannily the spirit of life on the Scottish Moors. These sketches were divided among us there in his hopes that if one of us got through we would be able to give them to you at his request, many were stolen or lost when we were forced to work on the Siam Railway. The night before he was sent to Pengerang he had a premonition something

would happen to him and begged me to communicate with yourself if I escaped. I ridiculed his idea but he was serious about it.

After his operations he asked to see me. I was the only one allowed to see him every day and acted as liaison with his friends. He was blindfolded & swathed in bandages – I could scarcely believe he was alive. He spoke in that clear deep voice of his & apologised for looking so awful. I shall never forget his helplessness yet magnificent courage of a boy who realised the gravity of his condition yet [it] never ceased through terrible days of pain. His tragedy was known to all and daily I had to answer enquiries from people who had never met him, they had heard and admired his tenacity, cheerfulness & tremendous faith. I received many gifts in cash and kind for him, including collections made from other ranks. General Percival frequently visited him. I remember General Percival's farewell to Derek, just before he left for Japan on 19 August 1942. The General allowed me to be present. Derek was very weak and could not speak. The General saluted him & he and I walked the half mile back to camp. He did not talk except to tell me to spare nothing in Derek's aid.

He had his own personal orderlies and was moved into a quiet cool room for the last nine weeks. He loved books, and I read to him every day as he could not see, and music. We were able to arrange gramophone concerts & the entire Officers' Ward of over sixty officers would remain silent for Derek during two hours whilst we played his favourites. He died on 29 August at 8.15 am. Changi, with its thousands in the Singapore Area Camps, was in mourning. The Gordon Highlanders, commanded by his Company. Commander, Major Duke, carried out the burial at 3pm. Every Regiment in Singapore Area was represented. The military funeral with 'Last Post', 'Reveille' and 'The Flowers of the Forest' was watched by many of his fellow patients, medical staff and his friends. All of us who knew him had lost something immeasurable. A wreath was placed on his grave from you both and again on 6 February 1943, on his birthday.

After the war, on 12 September 1946, a notice printed in the *London Gazette* confirmed that Lieutenant V.I.D. Stewart had received a posthumous Mention in Despatches for his conduct during his short time as a prisoner of war.

This was not the only unfortunate incident involving live ordnance. While Private James Wilson (2876392) and Private Arthur Butterfield (2876898) were working under Japanese supervision at Kranji, Singapore, on 15 May 1942 a grenade was accidentally detonated. This killed James Wilson and Arthur Butterfield was severely wounded, losing one eye.

Meanwhile, the men got on with the day-to-day business of survival. They began to realise the nature of their enemy early on when they saw the atrocities being meted out to the Chinese members of the civilian population, apparently in retaliation for their support of China in the continuing conflict there. As the Gordons were marched into Singapore to work in clearing up the city they saw the heads of Chinese men stuck on poles at the side of the road, apparently their punishment for looting. In another incident, groups of young Chinese men, blindfolded and with their hands bound, were seen being driven to the shore area where they were massacred by the Japanese. The pretext for this was that they were part of a resistance movement which had fought against the Japanese in the battle for Malaya. After some days, when the tide had failed to disperse the bodies, a detail of PoWs, including Bill Young (2876638), was forced to recover these partially decomposed and bloated corpses from the sea and bury them at the top of the shore. This was a nauseating and truly traumatic task and they found the bodies tied together in groups of eight; they had been bayoneted to death.

Following the arrival of a new Japanese commander, General Fukuei, in Singapore he decided that the prisoners should all sign a pledge not to attempt to escape. This demand was made on 30 August 1942 but was contrary to the terms of The Hague and Geneva Conventions and also specifically forbidden by British Army Regulations, hence there was a general refusal to comply. This mass display of defiance enraged the Japanese authorities so they decided all of the prisoners should be concentrated at Selarang Barracks. Selarang Barracks had been the home of the Battalion since March 1937 so it was well known to them but conditions were very different on their return. Constructed to house only a single battalion of almost 1,000 men, it was now required to hold almost 20,000 men.

The overcrowding created an intolerable situation and a serious risk to the men's health. There was not enough room to get everyone under cover to protect them from the elements and some make-shift tents were erected. In addition there were insufficient toilet or washing facilities, made worse by the Japanese cutting off the water supply, a basic necessity for life, allowing only one tap to be used for everyone. Latrines were dug into the concrete of the parade ground and Private John (Murray) Melville (2888645) remembered that one Gordon Highlander achieved his long held ambition of relieving himself on the parade square – unthinkable under normal circumstances, where nobody could even set foot on the square unless properly dressed and on parade. Diseases like dysentery and diphtheria spread rapidly, which made conditions worse with the limited latrines. After a few days of deadlock, the Japanese threatened to cut off the water completely, reduce food rations and move the wounded patients from Roberts Hospital into Selarang. It was recognised immediately that, in their already weakened condition, this would result in many of their deaths and the medical officers warned the senior staff officers of this danger. After trying to negotiate with the Japanese, the officer commanding the British and Australian troops, Colonel E.B. Holmes MC, decided on 4 September 1942 that further resistance was not in the best interests of the men and gave the order that the pledges could be signed 'under duress'.

This pledge read 'I the undersigned, hereby solemnly swear on my honour that I will not, under any circumstances, attempt to escape.' The whole incident was farcical since escape was virtually impossible but, in any event, the Japanese were not familiar with any of the men so many wrote with their left hand to change their signature. Others changed or falsified their names, for example, Corporal Alistair Urquhart (2883851) signed himself Alistair Kynoch, using his middle name for his surname and many of the Australians reputedly signed as Ned Kelly, the famous Australian folk hero. The incident ended on 5 September 1942 and the men were allowed back to their original barracks but they now realised that the Japanese intended to enforce their demands ruthlessly.

In 1946 General Fukuei was tried by the Allies for the incident, including his ordering that during the protest four 'escapees' be executed by firing squad, forcing senior British and Australian officers to witness the execution. At the time it was fairly common for prisoners to leave their camps to forage for food and this was well known to the Japanese, who made little attempt to prevent them. In the circumstances, these four escapees were really harshly treated. Fukuei was found guilty by the court and sentenced to be executed by firing squad on Changi Beach, at the same spot as those men he ordered killed.

The Japanese eventually decided they were going to use the vast pool of manpower to labour on war works and everything changed. Men were formed up into forces (or 'battalions') of around 600 men drawn from diverse units and sent to various places in their newly-conquered Sphere of Co-Prosperity. Even in the early stages of their captivity, whilst in Changi, food rations were inadequate and the overcrowding, together with the insanitary conditions that sometimes occurred, led to debilitating diseases. When the Japanese required the British and Australians to produce working parties they painted a very rosy picture of new camps, in Thailand, where there would be plentiful food and a much kinder climate that would be beneficial to the sick. As a direct result of this, British sick men were included in the strength of these parties, which was to prove a disastrous decision for many. The Australians were more wary of the Japanese promises of better times and chose only to send fit men to Thailand, with less disastrous consequences.

A small number of men had been transported to Japan in August 1942 and at about this time all Allied senior officers, above the rank of lieutenant colonel, were removed to a Senior Officers' camp in Taiwan. Colonel Willie Graham MC was among these. The vast majority of the PoWs held by the Japanese in Singapore were sent to Thailand and for the Gordon Highlanders things were no different: 65 per cent of the Gordons who survived the earlier battle were taken to Thailand to work on the Burma-Thailand railway. Later, in November 1942, another group of men were taken to Taiwan and, in April 1943 another group, including Gordons, were transported to Sarawak and Borneo. In the main, the movement of large numbers of men to Japan did not get underway until 1944. Since all of these parties had slightly differing experiences, each area has been described separately in the passages that follow.

In October 1942 men were marched to Singapore Railway Station and herded onto goods wagons. These were made of steel, there was no window but each had one sliding door, which was chained shut. The men were crowded into these cars, at least thirty in each, with no room for them to sit down, let alone to stow their belongings. The car was airless, with little ventilation, and under the tropical sun the metal bodywork became too hot to touch but was freezing at night. The journey to Thailand took four days. The trains moved slowly, pulling into sidings to give priority to trains moving north with Japanese soldiers bound for the front line against the British forces in Burma. In addition, the steam engines were fuelled by wood which had to be replenished fairly often, so stops were made for this and at less frequent intervals to provide food. The food provided was unappetising, consisting of a sort of watery rice 'pap' with few vegetables but no meat. Local traders would offer to sell or trade for eggs, fruit, rice cakes and fritters, and those who had no money parted with watches, rings, or some items of their kit.

Many of the men were already suffering from dysentery and could not control their bowel movements. At each stop there was a mad dash as men ran to the side of the track to relieve themselves. This inevitably meant that the men in following trains would become filthy from the piles of excrement left by the men on the earlier trains, particularly those reaching these locations in the hours of darkness. In addition, the conditions attracted millions of flies and the situation which greeted these men is almost unimaginable. There was neither time nor facilities for the men to wash themselves and the medical officers became extremely concerned about the rapid spread of disease. The steam trains had to take on water as well as fuel and sometimes a friendly engineer could be persuaded to dowse the men with his water hydrant. The problems for the men with dysentery were not confined to the stops as their need for relief up to twenty times a day had to be accommodated while the train was moving. In order not to foul their car any more than absolutely necessary they were forced to try and defecate through the slightly open doorway. This was done by sticking their rear end out while two others held tightly onto their arms. The stink and the squalor for all the men were unbearable. Eventually they reached Ban Pong, a few miles west of Bangkok, and this was the starting point of the railway which the Japanese intended to construct to Burma. At Ban Pong, which was just a transit point, the scene that greeted the men was depressing in the extreme. Their accommodation was long bamboo huts with palm frond thatch (atap) and long split bamboo slatted benches all along each side, with a central earthen passageway. They arrived at the end of the rainy season and the floor of the huts was two feet deep in floodwater, which was contaminated with human waste as the latrines had overflowed. Their first night in Thailand did not bode well for the future.

The Japanese Army required this railway to supply their troops fighting the British in Burma as they pushed towards their dream of conquering India. These troops were originally being transported and supplied by sea but the success of British and American submarines, sinking Japanese merchant shipping in the Andaman Sea, forced the Japanese to change their strategy. The tide had turned on the Japanese Navy when they were heavily defeated at the Battle of Midway in June 1942.

The route for this new railway, over 400 kilometres long, was through difficult mountainous terrain, dense virgin jungle with high monsoon rainfall and in an area where tropical diseases, such as cholera, malaria and dysentery, among others., were endemic. The Japanese were fully aware that a British company had, at the request of the Thai Government, surveyed the route, essentially following the north–south river valley of the Kwai and Kwai Noi through the mountains in the north. After two years work, it was decided that the project was too difficult and wholly uneconomic. This meant little to the Japanese military as they now had a pressing need for the route and had at their disposal a vast unpaid labour force, for which they cared little if they lived or died, so long as their railway was built. The timescale, originally estimated by the British as taking some ten years, was compressed into an unbelievable ten months, requiring completion by August 1943. Thus the 'stage' was set for one of the greatest human tragedies of the Second World War.

The strategy the Japanese used to achieve their tight timescale was to construct the railway simultaneously along its entire length. This meant that camps were built at numerous points along the route from Ban Pong to Thanbyuzayat, Burma (now Myanmar) to connect to an existing line to Mouleim. A large number of Gordon Highlanders were assigned to the areas of Kanchanaburi, Tha Makhan (Tamarkan), Chunkai, Wang Po (Wampo) and the camps in the much more difficult terrain from Hintock to Kinsaiyok, including Kanyu (the notorious Hellfire Pass). Generally the men had to march from Ban Pong to these camps as no transport was provided and the journey was generally undertaken at night. There were no proper roads in this area, so when morning came and the men reached their destination they were exhausted. Among the Gordon Highlanders morale remained high and Major R.G. (Reggie) Lees is recorded as saying how proud he was of his men who, when they arrived at Tamarkan, were dismissed by the Japanese officer but they waited until the order was given by their own officer and NCO before they fell out. The British officer in command at Tamarkan was Lieutenant Colonel Philip Toosey, a thirty-eight year old Territorial Army artillery officer who was inspirational in the way he dealt with the Japanese, together with Reggie Lees, who was also held in high esteem by his men (and by all other PoWs by the time the war was over). Tamarkan was recognised as the best camp in Thailand, being clean, well run with the excesses of the Japanese punishments, such as gratuitous beatings, being controlled to a large extent. Toosey was reputedly the inspiration for the character Colonel Nicholson, played by Sir Alex Guinness, in the post-war film *The Bridge on the River Kwai* and this is now generally regarded as a travesty of the truth. Toosey knew how to deal with the Japanese and to get the best for his men but never collaborated with the enemy, as suggested by the film. (An excellent biography of Philip Toosey, entitled *The Colonel of Tamarkan – Philip Toosey & the Bridge on the River Kwai* has been written by his granddaughter Julie Summers, which sets the record straight.)

Initially the work to create the railroad track in the flat areas of the Thai lowlands from Bon Pong up through Kanchanaburi to Chungkai was relatively easy and progressed quickly. This is not to minimise the individual hardships for men. They worked long hours under the blazing sun with little protection while carrying out heavy physical labour with primitive hand tools. Excavation of the earth was with a large hoe, called a chunkel, and the spoil was shifted by two men with a piece of sacking tied to two poles, like a stretcher. In this way cuttings were excavated and embankments built up to form the level railbed for the track. The Japanese operated a form of quota system and each man had to move a fixed amount of material, initially a cubic metre, each day. Once completed the men could finish but if completed faster than expected then the quota was increased the following day. In the easy flat lands at the start of the railway's route the quota was initially easy but, as it increased and the going become more difficult, these quotas were becoming impossible and the Japanese did not take account of changing ground conditions. All of this hard physical labour, without any rest days or holidays, had to be undertaken on a meagre daily diet of three portions of rice with few vegetables and practically no meat or fish. The large natural barriers such as rivers and ravines were crossed by constructing wooden bridges, using trees cut down from the surrounding forest. These were felled by hand and although sometimes the trunks were hauled to the sawmills at the bridge sites by elephants, very often this was done by manpower, the PoWs having to carry the massive logs on their shoulders. The taller men inevitably bore more of the weight. However, there was always the danger of a man tripping, leading to the collapse of the whole gang, with the potential for injury as the heavy log crashed to the ground, possibly crushing a limb. At the bridge sites there was also great danger: falling from the structure and being swept away by the raging waters below when the river was in flood, or in the dry season, sustaining a life-threatening injury if the water was too shallow to break the fall. In addition work such as driving piles for the bridge supports was arduous and likened by many to the work of the enslaved Israelites under the ancient Egyptian Pharaohs. This entailed gangs of men pulling on ropes attached to pulleys which raised a heavy block of wood and, at the given command, was released to crash down on the wooden pile and drive it into the riverbed. This practice was repeated endlessly until it was considered sufficiently secure.

For the men who were in the up–country areas, the magnitude and inherent dangers of their task was immeasurably greater. Not only did they have the same punishing work schedule, working twelve or sometimes eighteen hours per day, the climate in the mountainous areas was much more extreme. Heavy rains, particularly in the monsoon season, meant they were continually wet and they never got the chance to dry their clothes, which in any event were rotting away on their backs in the steamy jungle heat. The terrain was more difficult with long deep cuttings to be excavated through solid rock, using only a hammer and chisel to drill a metre-deep hole for the gelignite. Water was poured into these holes and, as the drill chisel bit continued to be hammered home, the rock flour turned to mud and spurted out of the top of the hole. This had the unfortunate result of making the drill bit slippery. The fuses for this explosive were lit by a PoW who would be in great danger as the fuses were fairly short and there was little time to get round them all and run for cover. The blast was not controlled and rock shards flew everywhere. The only perk of doing this job was that there was less physical effort and the fuse was lit using a glowing cigarette supplied by the Japanese. Often these charges were detonated with little warning to the other PoWs and many injuries occurred. After the explosion the rock had to be removed by hand and, as the cutting got deeper, had to be manhandled up the sheer rock sides and dumped over the edge.

At sites like Wampo, where a long shelf, or rock terrace, had to be cut from the sheer cliff face above the River Kwai Noi, the rock was merely pushed over the side into the river below. At cuttings like Kanyu, which is in two sections, the first approximately 450 metres long and seven metres deep and the second seventy-five metres long and twenty-five metres deep, the Japanese did not want to waste time by allowing the rock to be carried out of each end. In any case, the whole cutting was filled with men digging and drilling so the path out to the ends was not clear for men in the centre to travel out with their spoil. Wide rock barriers to the progress of the line would conventionally be overcome by boring a tunnel but the Japanese were in too much of a hurry for that to be done. Apart from the almost complete absence of any mechanical equipment all along the railway, a tunnel was discounted as it could only be worked at from the two ends. However, by opting for a cutting they could have many men working along its entire length and with no shortage of captive manpower it was a way of speeding up completion.

The Kanyu cutting was christened 'Hellfire Pass' by the PoWs because they were forced to work eighteen hours per day which meant they had to continue in the hours of darkness. In order to provide light for the work to continue, the Japanese made them light large bamboo bonfires along its length and for the men looking down on the scene from the higher edges of the cutting it looked like the jaws of hell. This was not only because of the fires but the pathetic picture of toiling skeletal bodies that were being driven on regardless, in the flickering firelight by their merciless Japanese and Korean guards, which also resembled a vision from Hell illustrated in the medieval religious works of the old masters. A similar cutting was excavated at Hintock.

By the beginning of 1943 the Japanese engineers working on the railway began to realise that their target of August for completion of the railway could not be met and so determined that more manpower was required, although they conceded the deadline had to be extended to October, much to the annoyance of the authorities in Tokyo. The Japanese had already engaged the services of around a quarter of a million native Asian labourers (mainly Tamils, Malays, Burmese and others) who had been promised good conditions and high wages so, accompanied by their families, they had willingly entered into a contract to build the railway. These were termed K and L Forces by the Japanese. The additional manpower for the new impetus required could therefore, in terms of PoWs, only come from Singapore.

To meet this new need the forces known as F and H were formed and despatched to Thailand from April and May 1943. These men, both British and Australian, were some of the least fit who had not been selected to go to Thailand in October of the previous year. After a similarly difficult train journey to Ban Pong they were then force marched hundreds of miles to the up-country camps, among the most notorious along the railway. The urgency of the Japanese brought on the so called 'Speedo' period, where the Japanese ruthlessly drove these exhausted and diseased men beyond the state of physical exhaustion, and on a diet which was barely sufficient to keep the men alive even if they were not required to carry out physically demanding labour for up to eighteen hours each day. Up country at camps such as Kanyu, Nikki, Konkoita *(*Conquita*)*, Prang Kasi and Sonkurai, the supply of food reduced below even these inadequate levels as the rough tracks, which passed for roads in the dry season, were converted into muddy pools by the rains. This meant that supplies had to be delivered by river barge. If these could not get upriver because of river-flow conditions the men starved. Also at this time cholera struck. This disease was known to be endemic in the region and it is believed that the first to be affected were the Asian labourers. Their conditions were possibly worse than those of the PoWs who had in their favour the presence of medical staff, although their impact was limited by the lack of any medicines. However, they had a good knowledge of the importance of hygiene and disinfection, such as the need to boil drinking water and keep flies off food. Good hygiene was also recognised by the Japanese and at Kinsaiyok CSM Frank Knight (2874564) received a beating in front of his men from the Japanese gunzo (sergeant), because overnight men had been relieving themselves near the huts instead of going to the latrines. The Gordons knew they were not at fault, so the next night a picket was mounted and an effective Gordon boot in the backside soon discouraged the offending Javanese Dutch PoWs caught in a compromising position.

The railway was eventually completed on 16 October 1943 when the two tracks from Ban Pong in Thailand and Thanbyuzayat, Burma met at Konkoita. The Japanese celebrated the occasion with a ceremony and a golden spike being driven into the track to symbolically mark the completion of the project. PoWs were given new uniforms and a celebration dinner held by the Japanese, and the whole proceedings filmed for propaganda purposes. However, the largesse was short lived with the prisoners having to hand back their new garments when the filming finished and once again stood up in only their 'Jap-happy' or *fundoshi* (a strip of cotton cloth tied round their waist and through their legs to preserve their modesty when their uniforms had become totally unserviceable). The men were now gradually withdrawn to the larger base camps, where there was slightly more food and basic medical help but it was too late for many of them.

Of the Gordon Highlanders who are known to have gone to Thailand just under 30 per cent died there. As a percentage this is slightly lower than the average for a British Army unit but for the Asian labourers it was considerably higher. This was not the end of their ordeal, however, as their captivity was still not at an end and the railway had to be maintained. Men were picked for this and since the numbers required were much reduced, there was less pressure on the sick. Angus Cassie (2878447) began to recuperate and wondered what it would be like to see the railway in its entirety, so volunteered to go with a maintenance party as far up as Prang Kasi. He told the story that on one occasion there was a guard who was reprimanding him constantly and he (Angus) hit his hand with an iron bar and burst the guard's fingers. Nothing came of this as it was at the end of the war. He said that

> in any event we knew their rifles wouldn't fire as the guards made us clean their rifles and we filed down the firing pins. Soon afterwards we had a feeling that something was happening but nobody told us the war had ended but the guards left. We went to a nearby railway station and we joined a Japanese train which took us back to Bangkok and we eventually joined back up with the Regiment.

However, the Japanese had more projects to complete during 1944 and 1945. In Thailand this included the Mergui Road, in the south of the country. In Singapore, a new airfield was constructed at Changi and, in Japan and Taiwan, PoWs were used to replace their own manpower, which was being sucked up by their armed forces.

The Mergui Road was carved out of almost virgin jungle across the Kra isthmus, in the south of Burma (Myanmar) and Thailand, with the aim of linking the Gulf of Siam, in the east, with the Andaman Sea, in the west. Not only was this virgin terrain but the isthmus has a mountainous spine that had to be crossed. For these veterans of the Burma-Thailand railway it was deja vu. Conditions were equally harsh but now, in 1945, disease and malnutrition had taken an even greater toll and the men were very weak. A number of Gordon Highlanders were unfortunate enough to be included in the men working on this strategic project for the Japanese war effort. The road was built to link the two seas and helped them in the evacuation of their troops from Burma, where they were now suffering heavy defeats. Seven Gordons died on this road project, all in the closing months of the war. This was a horrific task, calling for a staggering feat of endurance but, by this time, the men had no physical reserves left.

The Japanese were keen to exploit the resources of their newly acquired colonies and in addition to Thailand men were being sent from Singapore to work in other areas. At the end of March 1943, after a year held in Singapore, a large working party, including thirty-one Gordon Highlanders under the command of Lieutenant P. G. Symington and two former Gordons in the Intelligence Corps and the Corps of Military Police, was sent to Sarawak, on the island of Borneo. They arrived at Kuching on 1 April 1943 and the other ranks and officers were immediately segregated. The men were sent to Dahan to work on a road and Band Sergeant Percival Bent (2865598) was then the most senior Gordon in the party, which returned to Kuching in June 1943. Just after the war a detailed account of their time in Sarawak was prepared by Lieutenant Symington. It appears that, when in charge of a working party in and around Kuching, Sergeant Bent, a talented musician and fine all-round sportsman, made contact with local Chinese and obtained food from them. He was, therefore, already displaying the bravery which was later to cost him his life. Shortly after this, the Japanese alleged Bent had been acting as a messenger between Chinese civilian internees and Chinese outside the camp, although his actions mainly involved the transfer of local newspapers which were translated by the internees and news circulated among them and the PoWs. Since the newspaper reports were already heavily censored and full of propaganda they could not be regarded as secret. The Japanese were, however, paranoid about such things. He was charged with organising sabotage and espionage and taken to Kuching Gaol where he was interrogated and, in Lieutenant Symington's words, 'put through it' by the Kempeitai. It is believed he was subsequently taken to Jesselton with six other civilians where they faced a court martial. Sergeant Bent was believed to have been executed but there is also the small possibility he was killed in an air raid. The Japanese failed to properly record Sergeant Bent's cause of death.

This group of Gordon Highlanders was perhaps the most unfortunate of all their comrades and suffered the highest casualty rate (85 per cent) of all the working groups sent from Singapore. Only five of the thirty-two men survived. The majority of the men were sent to Labuan, a small island just off the coast of north Borneo, in August 1944 to work on the construction of an airfield. Eight men remained at Kuching as they were already too sick to join this working party. All of those who went to Labuan died and none has a known place of burial. They are consequently commemorated on the Singapore War Memorial. Of the nine who remained in Kuching seven survived until the Japanese surrendered, but conditions were so bad by the end of their captivity there that two of these, Charles Robertson (2879166) and David Thom (2568691), died within two weeks of their liberation, while three others died in the preceding three months. The cause of death given by Lieutenant George Symington was starvation, although the immediate cause was malaria and dysentery. These high casualty figures, which were not confined to Gordon Highlanders, are not unconnected with the successes the Australian Army was having in the area, with landings in Borneo in May 1945. The Japanese were hell bent on preventing PoWs falling into Allied hands and brutally dealt with their defenceless captives, in many cases marching them into the mountainous interior, away from the coast. In these 'death marches' anyone falling behind was callously murdered by the guards. It is not known how these twenty Gordon Highlanders, who have no known place of burial, died but there is the clear possibility that they were the victims of some Japanese atrocity.

If the men who were sent to Borneo were in the most unfortunate party, possibly Albert Lawson (3597764) and Henry Tavendale (2881341), the only two Gordon Highlanders who were sent to Korea, were far more fortunate. This was because the Korean camps were essentially 'show camps' for propaganda purposes to show the world how well the Nipponese Empire treated its prisoners. Perhaps, this was one of the cruellest ironies of the war. Journalists, photographers and the International Red Cross were allowed access to the camps and, while there was a shaky start, the conditions for the men settled down and, provided they accepted the strict disciplinary regime, they were relatively well treated and received sufficient food, including Red Cross parcels which were rarer than hen's teeth in other areas. In all, there were relatively few prisoners of war held in Korea but they were paraded in public in a sort of triumphalist gesture to underline the Japanese victories over Europeans (including Australians, who at this time were mainly of British extraction). Albert and Henry, in the company of about 1,000 other PoWs, left Singapore in mid-August 1942 sailing in convoy, via Taiwan on the Japanese transport ship the *Fukai Maru*. Like all the hellship voyages, of which there will be a greater consideration later, this was extremely unpleasant, with the men being held like mere cargo in an airless hold, in filthy conditions. They reached their first camp at Jinsen, (now Incheon, a major South Korean city) on 25 September 1942. They both remained there until 1943 when, in July, Henry was moved to Kobe in Japan. Albert stayed on until September when he was also moved but only to Konan in north-eastern Korea, where he stayed until liberated. Both survived the war as did the majority of their fellow prisoners held in Korea, a marked contrast to other areas.

Another party of Gordon Highlanders who left Singapore in 1942 was bound for Taiwan (Formosa). As mentioned earlier, Colonel Willie Graham left with all the high-ranking officers, including General Percival, aboard the *England Maru* on 20 August 1942. Also on board were twenty-one Gordon Highlanders of other ranks (i.e. no officers). They arrived on 29 August and all were taken to Heito Camp, in the south of the island, near the modern day city of Pingtung. A week later Colonel Graham accompanied the high-ranking officials and senior officers to Karenco, on the east coast of Taiwan, while the enlisted men remained at Heito. On 20 October 1942, another party, including fifteen Gordons, left Singapore aboard the *Dainichi Maru*, and docked at Keelung Takao on 14 November 1942. They reached their PoW camp at Taichu a day later by train. Only six more Gordon Highlanders spent any time in Taiwan. Five arrived in November 1944, survivors of the sinking of the hellship *Hofuku Maru*, and one in January 1945, who transferred off the *Enoura Maru*, luckily just before it was bombed by American aircraft, from the carrier USS *Hornet*, while in Takao (Kaohsiung) harbour. All six left for Japan in January 1945 aboard the *Melbourne Maru* (four) and the *Enoshima Maru* (two). In all only forty-two Gordons spent time in PoW camps in Taiwan although several more visited the island en-route from Singapore to Japan, although they never spent time in the PoW camps ashore.

Initially the work at Heito involved clearing land in preparation for sugar production and at Taichu the PoWs were employed in the excavation of a flood diversion channel near the camp. In both locations the men spent long hours in the strong tropical sun without protection and it was hard, exhausting labour compounded, as in the other areas where the Japanese forced the PoWs to work for them, by the inadequate diet provided, both in quantity and nutritional value. For almost half of these men things were to become much worse over the course of 1943. From May men began to be moved from Taichu and Heito to work in the copper mine at Kinkaseki. This mine was located on the north-east tip of Taiwan, which is a mountainous part of the island. Getting to the mine for work each day involved a long march over difficult terrain, with a steep gradient, but once inside conditions were primitive in the extreme. The copper ore was extracted by hand and acidic mine water dripped down on the men all day. It was hot and dirty and the work extremely hard and dangerous, with rock falls, slippery surfaces and little light in which to work. Needless to say, health and safety was never a consideration. If this was not enough to endure the guards were brutal and used any excuse to inflict terrible corporal punishment on the helpless PoWs, who were weak from exhaustion, lack of food and debilitating diseases like malaria and dysentery. At Kinkaseki there was a fairly large contingent of men from the 155th (Lanarkshire Yeomanry) Field Regiment, Royal Artillery, Scots who mostly hailed from just south of Glasgow. A strong bond of friendship developed between the Gordons and their fellow countrymen with Michael Dougan (2885055), Archie Hume (3244946) and John Young (2883928) all natives of this same area of Lanarkshire. Many years after the war Michael Dougan's son married the daughter of a Lanarkshire Yeoman (John McEwan).

Kinkaseki Mine was closed in March 1945 and in May and June all the PoWs were transferred to what they called the 'Jungle Camp' at Kukutsu, where they remained until the end of the war. The situation was very difficult at this camp also, with primitive living conditions, lack of food and medicine, and savage beatings from the guards. Basically this was an extermination camp designed to eliminate the PoWs. Sadly Lance Corporal Robert Milne of the Gordon Highlanders died of beri-beri in this camp, on 22 August 1945, seven days after the war ended. He was waiting to be returned to Taihoku for evacuation but was too weak to hold on for another few days when intervention by fully-equipped medics might have saved him.

Despite the brutality and harsh conditions the death rate of Gordon Highlanders was less than the average for PoWs held in Taiwan. Of the forty-two men who were in Taiwan only three died, and after the war their remains were transferred by the Commonwealth War Graves Commission to Sai Wan War Cemetery, Hong Kong. In addition, James Summers (2875032) died in New Zealand, just a month after he was evacuated, following the Japanese surrender. Eleven men were sent to Japan in January and February 1945, two of them dying there. Willie Graham left Taiwan on 4 October 1944 and spent the rest of the war with other senior officers in Manchuria.

Despite the dense population of Japan the demands of the Japanese military for manpower for the war effort meant that, for the first time, Japanese women were brought into the workforce. However, a decision was made fairly soon after Singapore's surrender to send prisoners of war to Japan to bolster the workforce there. The majority of PoWs who were told they were bound for the Japanese 'home' islands were filled with dread at being sent to the heart of this alien empire. When telling the PoWs that they were going to Japan, the Japanese themselves spoke in reverential tones about their own homeland, often including a note of envy at their 'good fortune'. Movements of men to Japan were, however, initially slow as the Burma-Thailand railway was seen as the top priority. After the railway was completed in October 1943, the shortage of manpower in Japan had become much more critical and many men were selected to travel from many locations of the newly acquired territories, not just Singapore. Large numbers of 'fit' men were moved from Thailand back to Singapore in June 1944 for onward transport to Japan in September 1944.

The mode of travel was always by ship in vessels universally referred to as 'hellships'. This term was not applied frivolously as any voyage aboard any of these ships was truly a living hell for most men, although many also died on the voyage. The men were, as one Gordon put it, 'packed like sardines' into the holds and the hatches immediately battened down. These ships were generally cargo vessels and the holds were dark and usually filthy from the previous cargo. Sometimes this was just inert dust from coal or some metal ore which, although unpleasant, was not in itself harmful. On other occasions livestock may have been transported and the hold was filthy with dung and urine. However, no matter how clean the PoWs found the hold when they boarded, conditions soon deteriorated because of the manner in which they were treated. Many of the PoWs were very sick, despite being classified as 'fit' by the Japanese. They generally all had malaria and many were also suffering badly from dysentery and, with some, the many involuntary bowel movements meant that they were not physically capable of climbing the narrow ladder to the deck to visit the perfunctory *benjo* (toilet - generally just a sort of seat slung over the side of the ship at the after end of the deck). This inevitably meant that men were forced to relieve themselves where they were sitting and the bottom of the hold became a stinking soup of faeces and urine and the airless holds became fetid and stank. Sometimes, after some lobbying by the officers, a few men at a time would be allowed on deck and if they were lucky they would occasionally be hosed down by the crew. Crowded as they were the men could not find a place to lie down and food and water rations were even more scarce than usual. Drinking water was habitually just lowered through the open hatch in a bucket with no means of sharing it around the crowded hold. Similarly rice was distributed randomly, sometimes formed into ball and thrown to the wretched prisoners like a snowball. These voyages were often weeks long and getting enough food and water just to survive was a deadly lottery.

In the midst of all this misery one Gordon Highlander showed a great strength of spirit and stood out from the crowd. Private William McShane (2875960), from Aberdeen, left Taiwan where he had endured double pneumonia and physical brutality from the guards at Kinkaseki mine. Sailing from Taiwan on 21 February 1945, he was on the eight-day voyage to mainland Japan, on the hellship *Taiku Maru*. Despite all he had endured he gave an impromptu concert on board to lift the spirits of the other PoWs, singing three old-time favourite songs. This worked wonders and men 'at the end of their tether' brightened up and for a brief moment the sufferings on board the hellship seemed a little less. William had some theatrical blood in his veins as he was the son of Billy McShane, the famous music hall comedian known as the 'Sheeny Man'. William originally joined the Royal Scots in 1935 but in 1936 opted to transfer to the Gordon Highlanders, joining them in Gibraltar. He moved to Singapore with the 2nd Battalion in 1937. His destination in Japan was Sendyu PoW Camp, on the north-west coast of Kyushu near Nagasaki. Here he was forced to work in a coal mine. He survived the war and was liberated by American forces and taken to Manila in the Philippines, where he transferred to the British aircraft carrier HMS *Implacable* and was repatriated to Britain via Vancouver.

As the tide of war turned in favour of the Allies, control over the Pacific Ocean was being consolidated after a large build-up of the United States submarine fleet that operated in the South China Sea. This did not bode well for the PoWs who were being transported on unmarked merchantmen in convoys escorted by

Japanese warships. US submarine wolf-packs sailing from Pearl Harbor and Midway Island operated freely in 1944 and Japanese losses were colossal. During the Second World War US submarines created a stranglehold on Japan by sinking almost five million tons of merchant shipping, well over half of the Japanese merchant fleet, together with around one third of the Japanese Navy, which provided the escort protection for the convoys.

From April 1944 the Japanese High Command had been assembling a large number of 'fit' prisoners in Singapore, drawn from the camps in Thailand, with the aim that these would further serve the Emperor by working in the Japanese home islands. At the beginning of June, therefore, a party of twenty-five Gordons left Singapore in a convoy bound for Japan and arrived safely and were held at Funatsu, Nagoya Camp 3. However, the majority did not leave until later and while these men awaited their onward journey they were held in Havelock Road and River Valley PoW Camps and forced to work loading and unloading ships and in the 'godowns' (warehouses) at the docks. In July the second group of PoWs learned they were about to sail and were marched to the docks. Among this group were fifty-nine Gordon Highlanders, under the command of Lieutenant James Lawrence. As they were boarded, with some 1,300 other British and Dutch PoWs, the Japanese ordered each man to pick up and carry onboard a pillow-sized piece of raw rubber. They were told this was their life preserver but by now the prisoners knew all too well that the Japanese never had their welfare in mind so were surprised by this regard for their safety at sea. As they lined the dock waiting to board one man inadvertently dropped his 'pillow', which fell into the water and sank like a stone. The men's faith in their original assessment of the Japanese character was reinstated, realising they were just being used as unwitting stevedores. Their ship was the *Hofuku Maru* (also known as the *Toyofuku Maru*), an old cargo ship. As usual the PoWs were crammed into the dark holds with insufficient room to lie down. Being principally a cargo vessel, not designed to carry large numbers of passengers, there were also no proper toilet facilities and this was overcome by a makeshift structure which was slung over the side so that the waste could simply fall into the sea below.

The *Hofuku Maru* set sail on 4 July as part of Convoy SHIMI-05, which included four other ships carrying almost 4,000 PoWs in total, the largest movement of PoWs by sea undertaken by the Japanese during the Second World War. This was not to be a straightforward journey for the men aboard the *Hofuku Maru*. The ship developed engine trouble after only two days at sea and limped on to North Borneo where she stopped to carry out repairs. It was too dangerous for the whole convoy to remain stationary so the rest carried on. Over the next nine days engine repairs were carried out and during this time the PoWs remained aboard the ship. This led to a serious problem as water to cook the rice for the prisoners was drawn up in buckets from the sea. However, there was very little current where the *Hofuku Maru* was anchored so, close to the ship, the sea water became polluted by the human waste discharging from the crude toilet arrangement. Dysentery spread like wildfire and by the time the ship reached Manila in the Philippines on 16 July 1944, 104 men had already died from dysentery. In Manila further engine repairs were carried out and the Japanese decided to offload the ballast to let the ship gain more speed and create some more space for the PoWs. After two months in Manila, over 150 PoWs were seriously ill with beri-beri, dysentery and other diseases. Among these were four Gordon Highlanders. Kenneth Petrie (2884113) and Anthony Smith (2876481) who both died and two bandsmen, Hector Lovie (2876624), who had severe dysentery and Peter Wood (2883945) who was completely incapacitated with elephantitus.

They finally set sail again on the evening of 20 September

1944 as part of Convoy MATA 27 but weighed anchor overnight in a bay behind Corregidor before sailing again early next morning. The PoWs were allowed on deck to have breakfast but no sooner had they got on deck but they were herded below and the hatches battened down. John Macrae (2876679) felt a vast explosion at around 10.00am and the ship shuddered violently with the wooden stairs to the deck disappearing. After a second explosion, sea water rushed into the hold and there was total confusion in the holds, but John Macrae found himself in the sea and on reaching a life raft climbed onboard. Looking up he could see American carrier-based planes circling above with aerial torpedoes slung under their fuselages and they continued to attack and sink most of the other ships in the convoy. Sharing his raft were three other men, including another Gordon, Lance Corporal Bob Peart (2879172). A Japanese destroyer was ploughing through the water picking up survivors but with no regard for the PoWs; only Japanese personnel were rescued. The shore was within sight and, using pieces of wreckage for paddles, they vainly tried to reach it but the strong tide prevented them. They were eventually picked up and taken to Bilibad Prison, Manila where they joined the other survivors, fifteen in total. Thirty-nine of their comrades had perished, including Alfred Dick (2875875) who had been one of the Gordon Highlanders marching so proudly at the head of the column during the ceremony held to celebrate the return of the drums in 1934. John Willox (2876280) was one of those rescued but died only four days after the attack. On 3 October 1944 six of the surviving Gordons were taken to Taiwan and later on to Japan. After the war a Japanese sergeant major, Kitaichi Jotani, was tried for the war crime he committed aboard the *Hofuku Maru* when in charge of a draft of British and Dutch prisoners of war. This concerned the ill-treatment of the PoWs, resulting in the death of about ninety-eight of them and the physical sufferings of many others.

Meanwhile, back in Singapore, a second group had been informed of their departure and like their predecessors, who left earlier in the month, they knew their destination and marched to the docks for the final time. On the way there George McNab (2885735) saw an old Chinese woman standing by the roadside watching the column pass. She called out to them, 'don't go, don't go, you'll be torpedoed' (a warning to the men that their ship would probably be sunk by American submarines). In an instant a guard went for her and smashed her in the face with the butt of his rifle then stabbed her with his bayonet. She slumped to the ground, clearly dying, but the PoWs could do nothing to help her.

On 6 September 1944 another large convoy, MI-72, of approximately thirty ships, including the *Rakuyo Maru* and the *Kachidoki Maru,* left Singapore bound for Japan. On board were a party of forty-seven Gordon Highlanders crammed into the holds along with 2,200 other British and Australian PoWs. As has been illustrated earlier, the close bonds linking many of the Gordons coincidentally produced among this group two brothers, Allan (2876877) and Henry (2876671) Elder, and three unrelated men from the small fishing village of Portsoy, on the Banffshire coast of the Moray Firth, Charles Bruce (2876269), John Campbell (2884170) and Jim Ingram (2876257). Eventually boarding commenced with the inevitable excited shouting and screaming by the Japanese guards who drove the PoWs up the gangplank, beating and prodding them with sharpened bamboo canes, just like herding animals.

The convoy set sail and several days out the men began to hear rumours, soon confirmed, of other ships in the convoy being attacked and sunk by submarines. George's mind immediately went back to the old woman they had seen on the way to the docks back in Singapore. In the very early hours of 12 September 1944, torpedoes from the US Submarine *Sealion* ripped into the *Rakuyo Maru*. After some initial panic it was realised that the ship was not sinking quickly and the Japanese started to deploy liferafts, mostly taken by the crew and the other Japanese on board. The PoWs improvised rafts from hatches and other pieces of wreckage and took to the water. The Japanese escort destroyers attempted to depth-charge the submarine and the men aboard the *Kachidoki Maru* soon became aware of their plight and increasingly nervous as they feared they would be next. The hours passed and they began to relax thinking that the submarine may have realised they were on board or, alternatively, it had lost the convoy in its own attempts to escape the counter-attack by the Japanese escorts.

At 10 o'clock that night, however, their worst fears were realised when torpedoes struck home, this time from the US Submarine *Pampanito,* and the ship started to sink. Not only was there the explosive impact of the torpedoes but the boilers exploded in a blinding flash and there was chaos aboard. Unlike the *Rakuyo Maru*, the ship sank quickly which, combined with darkness, inevitably meant there were bound to be more casualties. A large number of Japanese war wounded from the Burma front, who had been receiving medical treatment in Singapore, were also aboard, on their way home to Japan. A Japanese officer started shooting some of these men, 'mercy' killings of those he considered were so badly wounded they were incapable of surviving in the sea. The PoWs didn't know why he was doing this and became alarmed and fully expected that they were to suffer the same fate. The PoWs had to save themselves any way they could but there was the problem of exiting the dark hold through the small exit hatch to the deck as the ship took on water and so developed a steep list. It was literally every man for himself and the survivors jumped blindly into the sea in the inky darkness, although some found themselves floating in the sea with no idea how they got out, forced like a cork out of a bottle as water rushed into the holds from the massive holes in the hull. Here, their miserable state became instantly worse as they became covered in thick, sticky, black crude oil which had escaped from an oil tanker in the convoy that had also been a victim of the submarine wolf pack. Struggling for their lives, the lucky ones found a liferaft but more often a piece of floating wreckage to cling onto, but these men were in the minority and many drowned.

At daylight one of the Japanese convoy escort ships came back to the scene to pick up Japanese survivors. The captain knew it would be too risky for him to stop in the water as he would then be an easy target for the submarines which were obviously operating in that vicinity. His way of getting around this danger was to throw a cargo net over the sides and steam slowly around the area and survivors had to grab this and scramble up onto the deck. William 'Archie' Brown (2876375) was in the water and realised this was probably his only chance of survival but fully expected that, even if he could get on board the ship the Japanese would throw him back overboard. As the ship slowly passed him he managed to get a hand to the net and, with his last remaining reserves of strength, pulled himself up on to the deck. To his relief he was taken on board and, in a remarkable display of civilised behaviour, in the midst of this scene of misery and carnage, he asked to be allowed onto the bridge to thank the captain for saving his life and permission was granted by the guards.

Fate dealt each man a different hand. None of the PoWs had lifejackets but at daylight some of those still alive managed to take lifejackets from dead Japanese floating in the sea with them. George McNab and his friend Alistair Paris (2876571), who were both survivors of the Thai Burma Railway, got out of the *Kachidoki Maru* and managed to scramble onto separate pieces of wreckage which drifted together for a period, their spirits sinking. Sharks were in the area and they saw them circling and occasionally they felt them bump their 'rafts', which was a grave worry to some men who were swimming in the sea just holding on to floating wreckage for support. In some ways this was a slightly preferable way to survive the sun beating down on them mercilessly in the open ocean with not a morsel of shade. The saving grace was that the large oil slick helped to discourage the sharks from attacking. Some of these remaining survivors in the water just could not go on and, after a time, just gave up and slipped away below the waves. The actions of the tide and wind slowly began to separate George and Alistair, who was known by the nickname 'Madam Paris' and originally from a rural area of the Highlands just north of Inverness. As they were almost out of earshot Alistair shouted to George, 'Dod' (a colloquial form of George's name) 'if I survive this, I will never leave the Black Isle again!' and with that he was gone.

George was not alone. Sharing his raft was a sergeant from another regiment and after three days and nights without food or water they were jubilant when they spotted a Japanese ship which was picking up the few remaining survivors. However, as the ship came alongside the crew's attitude was in stark contrast to that experienced by Archie Brown. They callously told them that they were already overloaded and only one of them would be allowed on board. The sergeant implored George to go as he was still a single man he was prepared to take his chance while he knew George was married with a young daughter. Thankful, but with a heavy heart, George climbed aboard and when his hands reached the deck the Japanese guard stood on his hand. George gritted his teeth and struggled onto the deck and was safe but his finger was broken. The fate of his companion is not known but this brave and compassionate man was facing almost certain death. Alan and Henry Elder were separated and only Henry was saved but he suffered so badly as a result of his ordeal that he died only a month later.

The three Portsoy men all fared differently. Jim Ingram drowned, Charlie Bruce was rescued by the Japanese and ended up at Fukuoka Camp 25B, near Nagasaki but John Campbell had a truly amazing rescue. Three days after the attack, on 15 September 1944, the USS *Pampanito* returned to reconnoitre the area where it had sunk the *Kachidoki Maru*. The skipper, Paul Summers, gave the order to raise the periscope and when he surveyed the scene above he saw a lot of wreckage and, here and there, survivors in the water floating on improvised rafts. Entirely unaware that there were Allied PoWs on board any of the ships they had sunk, Summers assumed these survivors were Japanese. He decided to take a closer look and, after checking that there was no danger lurking from Japanese escort destroyers, gave the order to surface. He brought his crew to action stations and they made themselves ready to deal with any enemy threat they might encounter. As soon as they surfaced they trained automatic weapons on the men in the water and were incredulous when they heard a voice shouting in English for them to be thrown a line. At first they thought this was a trick but soon realised most of these men were Australians whom the crew immediately started to haul aboard. Some of the crew dived into sea to rescue those too weak to haul themselves on-board. These were survivors of the *Rakuyo Maru*, sunk by the *Pampanito*'s sister submarine USS *Sealion*. Paul Summers realised he could not take all the men on board and, after saving seventy-three men, broke radio silence and asked for assistance. The USS *Sealion* and two other subs, the USS *Queenfish* and the USS *Barb*, came to the scene and rescued another eighty-six survivors. Despite the best efforts of the USS *Pampanito*'s crew, who gave up their bunks for the survivors and worked tirelessly, treating them for exposure, cleaning them up and removing the thick film of oil, John Campbell died the following day and was buried at sea. In this action the Americans saved 159 men while the Japanese rescued 656 PoWs but the total lost to the sea was almost 1,400 Allied POWs, among them twenty-six Gordon Highlanders.

Those rescued by the Japanese were taken to the nearby

Hainan Island, just off the southern tip of the Chinese Vietnamese border, near the Pearl River. It was here George met his old friend Dr Ken Matheson, who had treated him for temporary blindness in Thailand. Both had been shipwrecked and hugged each other. After a few days they transferred to a Japanese whaler and were taken to Taiwan mainly on the *Hokusen Maru*. Arriving in Taiwan the PoWs did not disembark but were briefly allowed on deck to get some air, while the ship refuelled and took on supplies. While George was taking his turn on deck he was surprised and delighted to see Colonel Willie Graham on the quayside, among a group of the high-ranking officers captured at Singapore who, after being held in Taiwan for the previous three years, were now on their way to Manchuria. September 1944, with the sinking of the *Hofuku*, *Rakuyo* and *Kachidoki Marus*, was the month with the greatest loss of life for the 2nd Battalion during the entire war, all the result of, the somewhat ironic modern day term, 'friendly fire'.

For those who made it to Japan, the PoWs generally found their treatment a little better than it had been in the newly captured territories. They did, however, find the country was suffering badly from the ravages of war. The American submarine blockade was having a huge impact and the Japanese civilians were almost as hungry as the PoWs. The PoW camps were located widely over the Japanese home islands, although the Gordon Highlanders were mainly around Fukuoka (Nagasaki), Nagoya, Osaka in the south and Sendai in the north. The type of work they were required to do varied greatly, including coal mining, smelting zinc, carbide manufacture and various heavy industries. The working conditions in these plants were terrible and, in the foundries, the heat was often so intense that George McNab could barely tolerate it, with the floor almost impossible to walk on. Bill Young complained about the weight of the ingots of zinc and seriously injured his foot when he accidentally dropped one of these, which was fairly serious as medical

Colour Sergeant Dick Pallant (2867720),
with the 2nd Battalion Nominal Roll.
(*Courtesy of Gordon Highlanders' Museum*)

Mrs Irene Lees. (*Courtesy of Major
Malcolm Ross*)

Mrs Lees' scrapbook. (*Courtesy of Gordon Highlanders' Museum*)

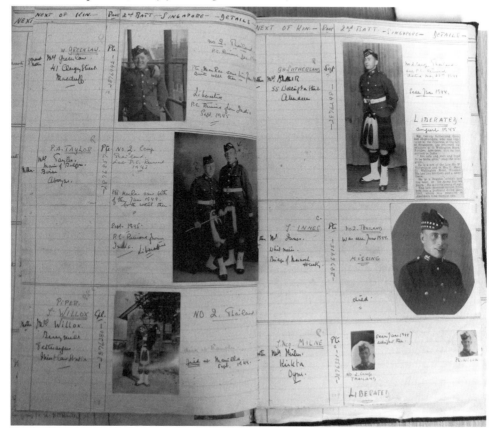

## India Squad Passing Out Parade at Castlehill Barracks, Aberdeen 1933

*Back Row.*—Pte. Sutherland.  Pte. McRobbie.  Pte. McInnes.
*4th Row.*—Pte. Laing.  Pte. W. Christie (82).  Pte. Buchan.  Pte. R. Sangster (48).
*3rd Row.*—Pte. W. Mollison.  Pte. Young.  Pte. Dingwall.  Pte. G. Campbell.  Pte. Pirie (51).
*2nd Row.*—Pte. R. Fyvie.  Pte. Christie (96).  Pte. W. Moir (97).  Pte. C. McHardy.  Pte. A. Dick.  Pte. V. Nisbet.
*Front Row.*—Pte. D. Bowman.  Pte. Quirie.  Pte. Scroggie.  L./Cpl. C. Watt.  Sergt. E. Clark.  Cpl. T. Robertson.  Pte. J. Elphinstone.
Pte. R. Hall.  Pte. W. Jappy.

'India' Training Squad 1933 at Castlehill Barracks, Aberdeen. (*Courtesy of Gordon Highlanders' Museum*)


General Sir Ian Hamilton, Lieutenant Colonel S. R. McClintock with Colonel von Hindenburg (son of the German President) and German ADCs, Berlin 1934. (*Courtesy of Gordon Highlanders' Museum*)

Ceremony of the Drums – February 1934. [Private Alfred Dick (2875875) marked with X].
(*Courtesy of Gordon Highlanders' Museum*)

Postcard commemorating the departure for Gibraltar aboard HMT *Somersetshire*. (*Courtesy of Gordon Highlanders' Museum*)

The very tall drum major William Low (2870244) leading the 2nd Battalion Pipe Band in Gibraltar. *(Courtesy of Mrs Jenny Low)*

Private Harry Johnston (2876156) feeding the Barbary apes, Gibraltar, circa 1936. *(Courtesy of David Ross & Gordon Highlanders' Museum)*

Gordon Highlanders embarking for Egypt aboard HMS *Repulse*. (*Courtesy of Gordon Highlanders' Museum*)

Gordon Highlanders farewell parade, Gibraltar, 1937. (*Courtesy of Gordon Highlanders' Museum*)

Selarang Barracks, Singapore, with the Gordon Highlanders on parade. (*Courtesy of Gordon Highlanders' Museum*)

The Gordon Highlanders, led by the Pipes & Drums, marching through Singapore 1937. (*Courtesy of Gordon Highlanders' Museum*)

Gordon Highlanders on exercise in Malaya, circa 1941. (*Courtesy of Gordon Highlanders' Museum*)

2ND BATTALION CRICKET TEAM, COMMAND WINNERS, MALAYA, 1938.

*Standing.*—Sergt. Topp. Cpl. Bent. Pte. Yeats. Cpl. Milne. Bdsn. Darby. Pte. Cross. Pte. McNally.
*Sitting.*—Lieut. Elsmie. Major Steel. Capt. Duke. Lieut.-Col. Burney. Lieut. Macmillan. Lieut. Bell. Lieut. Findlay-Shirras.

2nd Battalion Gordon Highlanders cricket team, Malaya Command Winners, Singapore 1938.

Signalling course at Selarang Barracks, Singapore, circa 1940. (*Courtesy of Rod Smart*)

Anti-gas training exercise at Selarang Barracks, Singapore, circa 1940. *(Courtesy of Gordon Highlanders' Museum)*

An afternoon siesta – barrack room at Selarang, Singapore. *(Courtesy of Gordon Highlanders' Museum)*

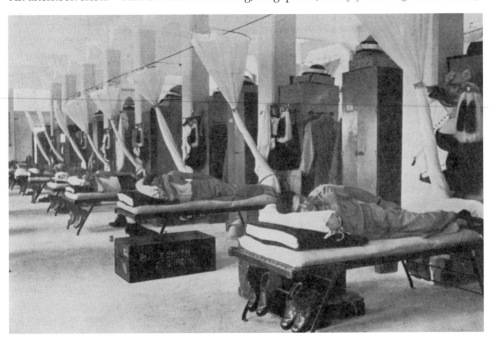

Swimming pool at Roberts Barracks, Changi, Singapore, circa 1938. (*Courtesy of Gordon Highlanders' Museum*)

Corporals' Club carnival dance, Selarang, 1937. (*Courtesy of Gordon Highlanders' Museum*)

Captain & Mrs Roper-Caldbeck (left) together with Major & Mrs Duke in an Amateur Dramatics Production in Singapore. *(Courtesy of Mrs Bridget Boyle)*

Draft of Gordon Highlanders en route to Singapore in 1941. *(Courtesy of Gordon Highlanders' Museum)*

Kanyu Cutting known as 'Hellfire Pass', Thailand. (*Author's collection*)

Gravestone at Kanchanburi War Cemetery. (*Courtesy of Bobby Davidson*)

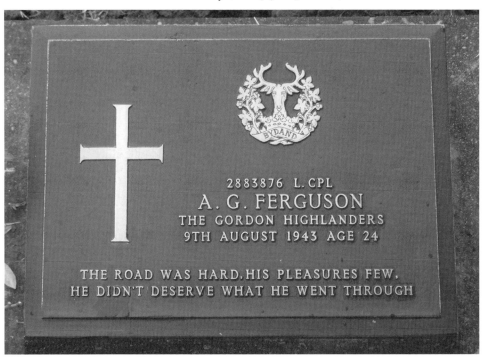

2883876 L.CPL
A. G. FERGUSON
THE GORDON HIGHLANDERS
9TH AUGUST 1943 AGE 24

THE ROAD WAS HARD. HIS PLEASURES FEW.
HE DIDN'T DESERVE WHAT HE WENT THROUGH

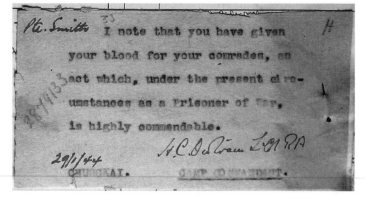

Death Certificate for Sergeant Robert Spence (2871799) who died 19 February 1943. (*Courtesy of Gordon Highlanders' Museum*)

Blood donor's certificate presented to Private Alex Smith (2879133) at Chungkai, Thailand on 29 January 1944. (*Courtesy of Gordon Highlanders' Museum*)

Silver Wedding card given to William Mackie (2882556) at Tamuang PoW Camp, Thailand, 1944. (*Courtesy of Eileen McIntosh*)

Private Albert Middleton (28769710). A sketch by Jack Chalker. (*Courtesy Michael Laing & the Middleton Family*)

Major W.D.H. Duke, a sketch by Josh Old. (*Courtesy of Mrs Bridget Boyle*)

'Peggy', the battalion mascot. (*Courtesy of Gordon Highlanders' Museum*)

'Donald' the duck with Corporal William Gray (2876971). (*Courtesy of Gordon Highlanders' Museum and Aberdeen Journals*)

POWs, shortly after liberation at Nagoya 3 PoW Camp, Funatsu, Japan. (Private Alexander Smart (2877319) shown with 'A' below his feet with fellow Gordon Highlander Corporal David McMaster (2876507) by his side, centre of the front row). (*Courtesy of Rod Smart*)

Bandsman James Johnston (2879289) (wearing his Glengarry) with patients and Australian medics in 1945. (*Courtesy of Mrs Jean MacClymont*)

Lieutenant Colonel Jack Stitt showing the recovered colours to his son and daughter. *(Courtesy of Aberdeen Journals)*

Memorial plaque in The Presbyterian Church in Singapore. *(Courtesy of Christina & Stephen Brand and Orchard Road Presbyterian Church)*

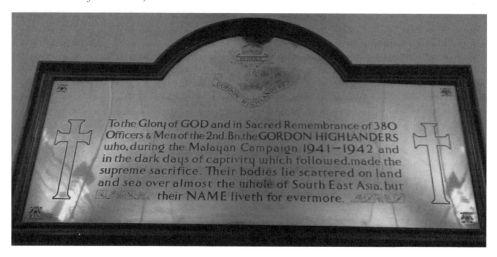

To the Glory of GOD and in Sacred Remembrance of 380 Officers & Men of the 2nd. Bn. the GORDON HIGHLANDERS who, during the Malayan Campaign 1941–1942 and in the dark days of captivity which followed, made the supreme sacrifice. Their bodies lie scattered on land and sea over almost the whole of South East Asia, but their NAME liveth for evermore.

Wampo viaduct, still in use at the present day. (*Author's Collection*)

Hamish Johnston (2876288), on the left, at home in north-east Scotland in 1949, with his friend Paul Gibbs Pancheri, a Straits Settlements Force Volunteer FEPOW. (*Courtesy of Michael Pancheri*)

treatment was somewhat rudimentary. The winter was very cold and the PoWs suffered badly because their clothing was inadequate, their accommodation was poor and food was scarce. As the PoWs were surviving on a ration of only two or three bowls of plain boiled rice daily, the Medical Officer at Omuta complained to the Japanese Camp Commander that they desperately needed meat. His solution to the problem was simple and pointed to the PoWs pet Alsatian. The unfortunate animal ended up in the soup served that evening. George McNab was in this camp and remembered that many of the PoWs couldn't bear to eat their four-legged friend, but for the majority it was just a matter of survival. Some of the camps had a lot of Americans who had been captured in the Philippines and this was generally a new experience for the Gordons. Bill Young considered the Camp Leader, who was an American, favoured his own men over the other PoWs. Many of the female civilian population had been drafted in to work in the Japanese heavy industry and worked alongside with the PoWs. They got on reasonably well with them, helping each other rather than displaying any deep hatred. Bill Kellas (2876651), who was a prisoner at Osaka, noticed that many of the houses were draped in black, signifying they had lost a family member in the war and it was obvious from this that the war was going badly for the Japanese.

Another party of PoWs to leave Singapore late in the war were those bound for Saigon. These men were under the impression that they were also bound for Japan since, like many of those who left for Japan in September the year before, they were being held in the River Valley Camp, located near to the docks and within Singapore City itself. This camp was a mosquito-ridden place with a fresh-water stream close by and regarded as a transit camp for Japan. At the beginning of February 1945, over 2,000 PoWs, a mixture of British, Australian and Dutch, including around ten Gordon Highlanders, all veterans of the Burma-Thailand railway, were herded onto the *Haruyasa Maru*. Archie Black (2879290) hoped that she was too small for an Allied submarine to waste its torpedoes on. The hold was divided into layers to increase the storage capacity giving only three or four feet vertical space between the layers. As more and more men were crammed in, the PoWs ended up sitting in a crouched position, leaning against each other. Loading went on all through the heat of the tropical afternoon and it became more and more uncomfortable for the men on board, who huddled motionless in the fetid atmosphere created by hundreds of sweat-soaked men, all panting for breath and parched with thirst. Eventually, come evening, the ship moved away from the dock but only to the outer harbour where she remained for three days. This was a tense time for the PoWs, cooped up in the hold, as there were Allied air raids on Singapore going on. The sound of approaching planes gave rise to a great deal of tension and as the noise of each plane receded the relief was palpable. Fortunately the three days passed without incident as a direct hit would have created panic and confusion in the crowded hold and it is likely that few would have got out safely. The convoy of five ships finally set off and once at sea the PoWs were allowed on deck which was a massive relief after the dark dank hold. The guards relaxed a little as there was now no likelihood of escape attempts in mid ocean so the voyage became more bearable. Escape had not been an option for the PoWs for over three years so it is hard to understand the paranoia of the guards in this respect. Time on deck was permitted and the PoWs were allowed to haul up buckets of seawater to wash. The danger from Allied forces was not over, however, and one night the PoWs clearly heard thudding noises and panic set in as the rumour went round that torpedoes had hit the ship. The thudding noises did indeed turn out to be torpedoes finding their target but fortunately for them it was two other ships in the convoy which were sunk and, after five days at sea, they made it safely to Saigon on 9 February 1945.

After disembarkation they were marched to former French Foreign Legion barracks which were positively palatial compared to some of their accommodation over the preceding three years. Initially work was in the godowns (warehouses) at the docks in Saigon. Over the next few months a total of twenty-three Gordon Highlanders would be transferred to Indochina, some going there directly from Thailand. Private Eddie Strachan (2876326), an Aberdonian, was among this party and in a letter written home, after his liberation, he described how they had to endure a 300-mile march from Bangkok. This took two months to complete. They had eleven handcarts and stretchers made from bamboo poles and empty rice sacks on which they carried the Japanese sick, their own sick, all of their kit and their rations of rice. Eight PoWs died on this march. Work in Saigon was followed by the construction of an airfield at Fumi (or Fukui), which was some distance inland. The journey upriver was by barge and in the evening the PoWs were allowed to swim in the river. One PoW got into difficulties and had to be rescued by Archie Black and Bandsman John Milne (2876223). There was a problem with mangrove roots below the water in which it was possible to get tangled. Together with the strong river current and the underwater danger this proved to be a difficult and risky operation, but eventually a rope was thrown to them from the barge and they all managed to get aboard safely. By comparison with other camps the PoWs had endured, conditions were reasonable in Saigon but during construction of the airstrip it was like being back on the railway construction in Thailand. The engineers had started from opposite ends of the runway and had a competition to see which team would get to the middle first. This meant they pushed the PoWs harder and harder, just like the days of Speedo. In addition, working on a site at altitude meant that the nights were often very cold. Blankets were scarce and conditions were miserable but the men tried to keep their spirits up by singing, although silence was enforced by the guards, subduing their mood. One day a Gordon Highlander was crossing the airfield with his precious ration, a bowl of rice and some pumpkin juice, when a US B-24 Liberator bomber flew over them and strafed the airfield. Realising the danger he dropped to the ground and protected his meal with the topee he was wearing. Later when Lieutenant Charles Gibson, who had seen the whole incident, asked him why he had done this, he replied in broad Doric, 'Och it was jist instinct sir, I didna wint tae lose ma denner'.

Once work at the airfield was completed, in April 1945, a number of the PoWs were travelling to their next camp by train when it was attacked by another Allied bomber. George Moffatt (2879284) saw the plane following the train and initially thought it was Japanese. It began 'spitting fire' and people were jumping off the moving train to escape and immediately after it passed overheard he heard a loud explosion and saw a blinding flash as a bomb scored a direct hit on a number of the carriages up ahead. Private Henry Campbell (2879498) was killed, Private Simon Forsyth (2876183) was mortally wounded and fellow Gordon, 'Big' John Smith (2875926), comforted him in his last hours. Sadly another two Gordons were lost to 'friendly fire' and Jim Murch (2876243) recorded that there were also many Japanese casualties. In another bombing raid in Saigon, some Gordon Highlanders witnessed a group of French nurses tending the wounded, with no regard for their own safety and only stopping their mercy work when pushed away by the Japanese guards.

# CHAPTER 5

# 'Their Road Was Hard and Their Pleasures Few' Life as a Prisoner of the Japanese

The British and Allied troops who surrendered at Singapore endured three and a half years of captivity under the control of the Imperial Japanese Army. This was a very difficult time and the clash of cultures created situations which at best led to simple misunderstandings but often even these had dire consequences for the PoWs. The title of this chapter was inspired by the epitaph requested by the family of Lance Corporal Alex Ferguson who died in 1943 in Thailand while working on the Burma-Thailand railway. This is inscribed on his headstone which is in Kanchanaburi War Cemetery, Thailand. The actual inscription reads:

> 'The Road Was Hard, His Pleasures Few,
> He Didn't Deserve What He Went Through'

Despite Japan signing the Geneva Convention in 1929 this was never ratified. Japanese soldiers were specifically forbidden to surrender and were indoctrinated to believe this would be a great dishonour for their family. As a direct consequence, the Japanese High Command saw little point in treating prisoners of war with any degree of respect or decency as they knew that there would not be the likelihood of any retaliation against their troops, simply because there were unlikely to be many Japanese prisoners held by the Allies. In respect of the treatment of prisoners, this was directly contrary to the promises made by General Yamashita to General Percival in the surrender talks, at the Ford Factory in Buket Timah Road on that fateful day in February 1942. In addition, the Japanese claimed mistreatment of Japanese PoWs by the Allies, citing an incident at Cowra PoW Camp, Sydney, Australia. This camp held Italian, German and some Japanese prisoners of war.

Here the Japanese PoWs staged a riot and attempted a mass breakout in August 1944. The Australian guards lost control of the situation for a short time and fired on gangs of prisoners charging the fence shouting 'Banzai'. A number escaped but many others committed suicide or inflicted fatal injuries on their fellow PoWs, all because they considered it shameful to be held as a prisoner of war. It appears this camp was complying fully with the Geneva Convention but, nevertheless, the Japanese authorities chose to view this incident out of all proportion to the reality and cited it as an excuse for their own behaviour.

From the outset, the Japanese made it clear that no display of insubordination or lack of respect would be tolerated. Prisoners, of all ranks, were required to bow before addressing any Japanese soldier and their flag (the Rising Sun, known to the PoWs as the 'poached egg') had also to be saluted. In addition there was a requirement for a prisoner to salute every Japanese guard and while the PoWs tried, although perhaps grudgingly, to comply with this demand they would often be caught out by guards looking for trouble. Even if an obvious guard had been saluted another, more distant and less visible, would deliberately take issue with not being saluted as well as his counterpart. The standard response of a Japanese soldier to express his displeasure was to use physical violence against any unfortunate prisoner who was considered to have shown even the slightest disrespect. In the mildest form this would be face slapping but could develop into a severe beating or 'bashing' which could easily result in broken bones or even death. In such an event, the men knew it was important not to fall to the ground as this seemed to get the guards' blood up and the Japanese would continue the beating and kicking without mercy. Death or permanent injury was a real possibility in these circumstances.

There was also a requirement to learn a certain amount of the Japanese language. Every roll call, or *Tenko*, used Japanese numbers given to each PoW. When the PoWs first started work in Thailand, the Japanese soldiers laid out all the tools on the ground and named them in Japanese, which the PoWs then had to learn. After about three attempts, if they picked up the wrong tool when instructed in Japanese they were punished with a beating. Sometimes the rules enforced by the Japanese made little sense to the prisoners. Whilst at Fukuoka Camp 17B, in Japan, Bill Young (2876638), having acquired a cigarette butt, was discovered by a guard having a fly puff. The problem was not that he was smoking, which was allowed when the men were not at work, but that he had no ashtray. He was taken to the guardhouse, stripped naked and beaten unconscious with rifle butts. This was not the end of his ordeal. He was revived with buckets of cold water and then made to kneel on sharp stones and a heavy iron bar was placed on the back of his legs, behind his knees. Two guards then bounced on the ends of this and this treatment went on, with additional beatings, until darkness fell when he was more or less left for dead. Fortunately Bill survived the night and his fellow prisoners looked after him but his health was severely affected for a long time after this. In another incident at Tamuang, Thailand, Alistair Urquhart was working at the construction site of the bridge to cross the River Kwai. He was drilling holes through thick teak planks, newly cut from the forest, in preparation to take bolts used in building the bridge. His problem was that the boring awl he was supplied with was too short to go all the way through the plank so he had to bore from each side and hope that the two holes met. This had to be done by eye and no mechanical aid was provided to ensure the holes were aligned. When talking to the Oral Historian from the Gordon Highlanders' Museum, Alistair recalled that, on one occasion, the two holes did not meet and when the Korean guard noticed this he went berserk. He smashed his rifle butt into Alistair's face, splitting his tooth which subsequently had to be removed by the medical orderly without any form of anaesthetic.

The Japanese, being generally small in stature, often picked on tall men to humiliate as they were now in a wholly defenceless position. This was a significant problem for Colour Sergeant William Low who was a giant of a man, standing six foot eight inches tall. His striking stature was ideal while he was the Drum Major of the Battalion Pipe Band, especially when they performed at a public ceremonial occasion, but as a PoW it made him vulnerable to be singled out by malicious guards for mistreatment.

The 2nd Battalion Gordon Highlanders, a Regular Army unit, was one of the best acclimatised, disciplined, trained, and close-knit forces in Singapore. The decision to surrender was forced upon them by the General Staff in Singapore. As a consequence, they did not begin their time as prisoners of war feeling they had been defeated, either in a personal sense or as a unit. One example of their esprit de corps was given by Captain Francis Moir-Byres who cited the example shown by Regimental Sergeant Major Alexander Milne (2869674). He had been badly wounded in the right shoulder during the Malayan Campaign and required eleven operations on his wounds while a PoW. With the sympathetic medical officers treating him, he could have stayed in Singapore, in a reasonably good camp, but he insisted that he continue with the major part of the Battalion sharing their trials of bad living conditions on the Burma-Thailand railway. Captain Moir-Byres stated that Milne's 'continued devotion to duty, unselfishness and fine bearing did much to retain the morale of the men'. After the war, Alex Milne's conduct was recognised as extraordinary by the King when he was appointed OBE. During their entire time as PoWs the Gordon Highlanders displayed, time and again, courage, a defiant spirit and a capacity to overcome and win through. Their individual and collective deeds are recalled by many personal accounts by men from many other units but not least of all by their own comrades of the Battalion.

One such brave act took place early in their captivity by Private Campbell, who carried a wireless set into Havelock Road Camp, Singapore. This was disguised as a bundle of firewood. In addition, during the period from November 1943 to March 1944, at Kinsaiyok Camp, Thailand, Company Sergeant Major Angus W. Collie (2874524) was involved with a group of men from the Royal Artillery (RA) in concealing and operating a wireless set. This set was concealed in the bunks occupied by Regimental Sergeant Major Mannion (RA) and Angus Collie. The set, which fitted into a water bottle, and ear phones were kept underneath Angus Collie's bed and the batteries (100 torch batteries all linked up) were kept under Mannion's bed. Numerous searches were held by the Japanese and the sentries kept close watch and there were several narrow escapes. Their luck prevailed but this was a very nerve-racking time. This same wireless set was safely taken to Tamuan, Thailand and operated again. These were extremely brave acts and if caught these men would almost certainly have been executed. The Japanese were absolutely paranoid about spies and appeared unable, or unwilling, to distinguish between a radio receiver, which could only listen to external broadcasts, and a radio transmitter which would let them talk to another party. Both Colour Sergeant William Low (2870244) and Lieutenant William de Meir assisted Captain Max Webber, of the Loyals (the Loyal Regiment (North Lancashire) Regiment) and his brother (Lieutenant Webber) to operate a wireless set in Chungkai, and

Kanchanaburi, Thailand. William Low was a member of the camp police force and had fairly free movement in and out of the camp without guards. He was, therefore, in an ideal position to obtain batteries and smuggle them back into camp, though certainly not without great risk. The main aim of maintaining the operation of the wireless set was to raise the morale of the PoWs through the dissemination of bulletins to the rest of the PoWs. However, the release of information had to be done in a very careful and controlled way, e.g. by delaying the news release to the men. The most important thing was to ensure that nobody could inadvertently give away the existence of a radio in the camp, which in any case was only known about by those directly involved and the senior Allied officer in the camp.

In many instances Gordon Highlanders took the chance to strike back at the enemy any time they could. The risks, however, were great. Bill Kellas recalled that he broke into a food store at Conquita, Thailand, in August 1943 with Andrew ('Dinger') Bell (2876858) and another man but they were discovered. Bill and Dinger got away from the guard but the third man was caught. He was tortured to get the information out of him as to whom his accomplices were but he bravely remained silent. Their own officer came to them and asked that they give themselves up as, otherwise, the man would be tortured to death. They came forward, as requested, and were immediately beaten up and then a rope was tied round their necks and hands and then to a wall where they were left for days in the sun. Bill Kellas was then 'tried' and expected to be beheaded but the Japanese Camp Commander left before his sentence was carried out and for some unexplained reason he was spared. However, things did not always work out so well. Corporal Benjamin J. Morgan (2875814) recorded that Private William Martin (2876659) was given six months' rigorous imprisonment for removing and selling wheels and electrical equipment from a car in a Japanese car park at Tamarkan. His actions were entirely selfless as he gave the money he earned from his exploits to the camp hospital funds.

Bill Young (2876638) operated a profitable scam while in Singapore. Again, all his 'ill-gotten gains' were passed onto Major Reggie Lees to buy food on the black market for the benefit of the rest of the men. Shortly after the fall of Singapore, Bill, unaccompanied, was driving a road tanker, ferrying water for steam-rollers working on a road being built at the golf course. There was an emergency reserve petrol tank bolted to a cradle at the side of his vehicle and this was detachable. Bill realised the average Japanese soldier had little mechanical knowledge so didn't know how much petrol was required for the short trips he was making. He could, therefore, fill up the two tanks without provoking any suspicion from the guard. The local Chinese paid a high price for petrol on the black market and, when loading water at the hydrants, Bill would unhitch the reserve tank and roll it down an embankment to his Chinese accomplices, who were waiting below. The tank would then be emptied and left in position for Bill's next trip. Bill did have a couple of narrow escapes when challenged by passing guards but was able to fool them into believing he was simply going about his business, drawing water from a hydrant, and on another occasion, that he was fixing a water leak in his radiator. All this was at great personal risk to Bill as two Australians, who had also been involved in stealing petrol, although not with Bill, were beheaded by the Japanese.

Stealing was always risky and Private William Merchant (2879026) was nicknamed 'Rice-bag Willie' because he developed a technique of stealing rice from the Japanese cookhouse and secreting it in a little bag which he hid in his 'Jap-Happy'. He would smuggle the rice out to prisoners who were sick and in the camp hospital. One day he was caught and threatened with execution but the Japanese guards decided instead to have some 'fun' at his expense. After a severe beating, they tied him up, with his hands up behind his back and the rope around his neck in such a way that as he tired and dropped his arms the rope would tighten around his throat. He was left like this, out in the tropical sun, for three days but lived to tell the tale. George McNab (2885735) recalled another incident at Kinsaiyok, Thailand, where his friend, Bombardier Blackner (Royal Artillery), who was also working in the Japanese cookhouse, stole some pork crackling to give to him and some others. The Japanese found out and, after beating him up, he was made to stand in front of the guardhouse holding a large stone over his head. However, being weak after his beating, he tired quickly and lowered the stone, which resulted in another beating and was then forced to continue his punishment. A variation on this, described by Archie Black, was the unfortunate PoW singled out for punishment who was forced to stand with arms outstretched sideways holding a large stone in each hand while sharpened bamboo sticks were wedged under his armpits. As the man tired he dropped his arms, causing the sharp canes to pierce his skin. The only relief was to force the arms upwards but this dislodged the sticks which fell to the ground, resulting in a beating from the guards and then the process was repeated until the guards lost interest.

John ('Nellie') Wallace (2888398) found a novel way to inconvenience his Japanese hosts. He had a spell working in the Japanese cookhouse at Takanun, a job allocated to him by the medics in an attempt to let him regain some weight as he had just recovered from cholera. He was told he was being moved to Chungkai, so that morning he incorporated a laxative with the breakfast he prepared for the Japanese. On his journey back down the line, he was relishing the thought of the effects of the adulterated meal on his unwitting victims when the vehicle he was travelling in broke down. He waited nervously for the repairs to be effected worrying that an angry party of Japanese soldiers was in pursuit but he got away safely. Perhaps the guards were preoccupied by numerous visits to the latrines.

The men had always to be on their guard and Bill Young recalled that the camp commander at Conquita, Thailand, was a psychopathic madman. He was nicknamed 'Speedo', due to his constant urging on of the PoWs to work faster. His idea of fun was to creep up on a prisoner when he was working high up on the bridge under construction and catch him by surprise. He would then push him off the bridge where he fell to his death or became severely injured. On one occasion Jock Ross, a Gordon Highlander originally from Insch, Aberdeenshire, became aware of Speedo's approach. When he pounced he grappled with him and, while swearing profusely, in broad Doric, that he would not fall alone, he foiled Speedo's fun.

In February 1943, at Bankow, Thailand, there was a slight altercation between Captain Ludovic G. Farquhar and a Japanese sentry. The sentry lost his temper and attacked Farquhar with his rifle and fixed bayonet. Captain Farquhar succeeded in parrying several thrusts with his hands, receiving superficial wounds. Luckily, Lieutenant John B.H. Leckie saw what was happening and, at great personal risk to himself, went to Captain Farquhar's assistance and prevented the sentry from doing further damage. As a result both men were made to stand in front of the guardroom for a long time but were eventually allowed to go. It was widely considered by other witnesses (Majors Walter Duke and William ('Waddie') Innes, that, if it hadn't been for Lieutenant Leckie's intervention, Captain Farquhar would have been seriously injured. Captain Farquhar himself concluded that Lieutenant Leckie had literally saved his life. In the same camp at about the same date, another misunderstanding occurred over some work to be done. This involved Captain George Moir-Byres, along with Major Buchan (1st Bn Manchester Regiment). They were made to kneel while a Japanese officer and NCO (Lieutenant Kuriyama and Sergeant

Higuchi) made cuts and passes at them with drawn swords for about an hour. As an eye witness, 'Waddie' Innes stated afterwards that he could not tell whether the final intention was to behead the men or not. Moir-Byres and Buchan showed the greatest courage throughout their ordeal and, fortunately, sustained no injury but afterwards were made to stand for several hours in front of the guardroom.

Lieutenant Colonel John (Jack) Stitt MC, who had taken over command of the Gordon Highlanders from Colonel Willie Graham on 31 December 1941, at the height of the battle for Singapore, kept a notebook during his captivity. He recorded a number of incidents that he headed 'War Crimes', which included incidences of severe beatings, such as that of Private Charles English (2876675) by a Japanese Guard named Fukowa, at Wang Po (Wampo) in March 1943. Private English died of dysentery within three months of the incident. He singled out a number of other guards for special mention such as Motiyama and Keohara, but also used the nicknames given by the PoWs to some of the more notorious, often Korean, guards, The Mad Mongol, Silver Bullet and The Singing Master, who all gained notoriety along the railway.

In his book, entitled *Nemesis, the Battle for Japan 1944–45*, Max Hastings describes an incident which took place in Thailand during the construction of the Burma-Thailand railway. This involved an officer of the Gordon Highlanders who protested to the Japanese about sick men being forced to work. The account states that the officer 'was taken into the jungle and tied to a tree, beneath which the guards lit a fire and burnt him like some Christian martyr'. The Regimental Museum does not hold any information about this incident but only eight officers of the 2nd Battalion Gordon Highlanders died during the war and, of those, five were killed in action or died of wounds during the battles in Malaya and Singapore. Of the remaining three, the causes of death, by disease, are held by the Museum and the Commonwealth War Graves Commission confirms a place of burial for two of these men. This leaves only one other possibility, who died in 1943, as the single possible victim. His ashes are buried in Kanchanaburi War Cemetery, Thailand and he is commemorated on a memorial rather than an individual grave. His official cause of death is listed as cholera but it is debatable if the Japanese authorities would record the actual cause of death in a case such as this. Dr Robert Hardie did cite instances in his book, (*The Burma-Siam Railway the Secret Diary of Dr Robert Hardie 1942-45*) where the Japanese would insist on a change in the death certificate if they considered it embarrassing. In this officer's case the actual cause of death remains unclear; his body would have been cremated if he had died of cholera, so there is no conclusive evidence to support either. In another incident in 1943, at Tarsao work camp, 125 kilometres up country on the Burma-Thailand railway, a group of men of the Lanarkshire Yeomanry (155th Field Regiment Royal Artillery) escaped. However, with a bounty on their heads, they were soon betrayed by local Thais and recaptured. The other PoWs, including George McNab, were assembled and forced to watch these men dig their own graves and then their execution, each one bravely waiting in turn for his fate.

There were very few occasions when direct physical retaliation against Japanese personnel was possible and only one report of such an action by a Gordon Highlander has been found. Private Walter R. French (2819143) recorded 'So far as I can give you any details we killed three Japs and a lot more was done by our soldiers'. At first sight this claim to have killed three Japanese guards appears incredible, particularly when the penalty for any form of open dissent against the Japanese was severely punished. However, Arthur Lane states in his book, *When You*

*Go Home*, 'Many Japanese guards, officers and engineers went missing, officially reported as deserters when in fact they were no longer alive. I can quote two examples which I witnessed personally plus another in which I was involved.' On this basis it appears that French's report can be accepted as factual. In another incident, Bill Young had a life and death struggle with a guard whilst on a 'hellship' transporting him from Singapore to Japan in 1944. The ship had been hit by a tropical typhoon and Bill was lying on the deck trying, with some difficulty, to get some sleep with little cover from the rain and sea spray. For some reason he was kicked by a guard and Bill, a man with a quick temper, instinctively retaliated, then realised that he was now in desperate trouble. He had no choice other than to try and kill this guard as he would certainly kill him, without mercy, for showing disrespect. After a desperate struggle Bill eventually managed to push the guard overboard and, fortunately, in the noise and confusion of the storm, the incident went unnoticed. In the morning Bill was mightily relieved when it appeared to be assumed that the guard had been accidentally swept overboard by the heavy seas washing over some areas of the deck.

There were very few ways that the PoWs could strike back at the Japanese but one way in which they could was to employ the tactic of sabotage. There were many examples where men punctured oil drums, poured sand or mud into oil drums or the fuel tanks of motor vehicles. Stealing and selling tools and batteries to the local Chinese or Thais raised much-needed funds but, on a more trivial but perhaps more personally satisfying sense, Private John Stewart (2819471) stole documents from Japanese offices and used the paper to roll his cigarettes. Paper was at a premium and could also be bartered with other PoWs. In working parties the men would work as slowly and act as stupidly as they could get away with. In addition, when working on the Burma-Thailand railway, where they had to build up large embankments with excavated soil, they buried tree trunks, branches, sleepers and even oil drums when the guards were not looking. This action had a number of advantages. In addition to keeping up their morale, it allowed them to reach their height quota more easily and they knew the wood would inevitably rot fairly quickly in the warm, wet climate, or possibly be eaten by white ants and so cause subsidence in the embankment. This collapse then disrupted railway traffic. This was a direct blow to the enemy's war effort in Burma. Another example that brings this into context comes from Sergeant Douglas Hepburn (2876059) who stated that sabotage was carried out as often as the opportunity was presented. In particular, whilst he was in charge of a bridge repair gang at Rin Tin, Thailand, where five bridges were constructed, he and his men damaged and lost tools. They misinterpreted orders, found non-existent damage to repair and worked slowly in repairing major damages, thereby hindering trains of troops, ammunition and other supplies en route to Burma. Most of the sabotage was on a small scale as the guards were generally vigilant. However some acts were very successful. While working at Otami Industries Ltd, Amagasaki, near Osaka in Japan (September 1944 to May 1945), Private Sydney Shulman (2889889) continually put large planing machines out of action. In addition, at Camp 6, Nagoya, Japan, from May 1945, he put the wrong mixtures of metal ores into the furnaces and the resultant molten metal was useless.

Although their daily contact with the guards put them under tremendous mental strain with the constant threat of physical abuse at the merest whim, their greatest challenge, by far, was the danger of some debilitating or life-threatening disease. As a general case, food was inadequate in terms of the quantity provided and its poor nutritional quality. This was particularly the case when the men were perpetually required to carry out hard physical labour. They were driven on, almost to the point of exhaustion, during the construction of the infamous Burma-Thailand railway, various airfields and roads. Unsurprisingly, therefore, food was constantly on men's minds and for those men who were too sick to work their rations were stopped by the Japanese, whose maxim was 'no work no food', so the sick men relied on the rest of the men to share their already inadequate rations. The Japanese had an unshakable belief that sickness was all in the mind of the PoWs, a philosophy which they held on to despite the stark evidence of starving and gravely ill men all around them.

It is not surprising, therefore, that the men resorted to every means possible to get food. Initially, when they still had possessions such as watches, rings and items of clothing, they would barter with the locals. Such was their desperation that they would resort to trading items of great sentimental value for a few morsels of food. The Japanese paid the prisoners but this was a pittance of ten cents per week for enlisted men. However, up country, in northern Thailand, most men never saw any money at all. If they were paid, the camp senior officer would often arrange for this money to be used for the good of everyone, including the sick. Trading with local people, for duck eggs and vegetables, was permitted and the extra rations would go to the cookhouse for general consumption. The officers did receive more pay than the men (one dollar per week) and most shared this, either through the general fund or directly. Willie Niven (2880078) recalled, when he was working on the Burma-Thailand railway, Lieutenant Charles Gibson sneaking out of a camp at night and going to the local village to buy food, which he shared with his men. Any chance of extra 'free' food was also grabbed. Whilst up-country in Thailand, where rations were always short, George McNab persuaded the Japanese guards that they should try to catch lizards which were living in burrows near the camp. This was accepted and they caught a number of them which they shared with the Japanese. George commented that the piece of meat down the animal's back was just like a piece of fillet steak!

In September 1943 Murray Melville (2888645) was on a march from Kinsaiyok and while along the trail near Konkoita they came across a bullock, apparently left behind or a stray from a herd being driven by another group of PoWs ahead of them. The PoWs did not disclose their find to the Japanese guards as they were also driving a few head of cattle and concealed it among their own charges. As soon as darkness fell and before any questions could be asked, the bullock was killed, skinned and butchered by a Gordon Highlander who had worked in the abattoir in Aberdeen before the war. The offal was consumed immediately, for their evening meal, and the rest of the meat boiled up and stuffed into any container they could find. This was a welcome additional supply of protein and served to sustain them for several days. On another occasion meat became available to Bandsman James Johnston (2879289) and a group of Gordons when working deep in the jungle of Borneo. An orang-utan appeared on the edge of the camp and the Japanese guards were taking 'pot shots' at it. The Japanese were notoriously bad shots and they succeeded only in wounding the animal which was then crying out, obviously in great pain. A Gordon grabbed the rifle from the guard saying, 'If you are going to shoot it for Christ's sake kill it' and despatched the wounded animal, with a single shot. He paid dearly for his compassion and was badly beaten by the Japanese guards. The men were allowed to eat the meat of the animal but the pleasure of a rare decent meal was ruined by the plaintive cries of the orang-utan's mate, which continued to haunt them for several days afterwards.

The death toll of the men through malnutrition and disease was high. After the battle for Singapore and the resulting deaths of those men killed in action, or died of wounds, together with those evacuees who perished at sea when the SS *Rooseboom* was sunk, a total of 925 men of the Battalion remained to become prisoners of war. It is these whom we are considering here. At the end of the war 30 per cent of these men were dead through injury, disease, malnutrition and exposure. This is a lower percentage overall for British PoWs than the accepted average of 40 per cent and is perhaps a testament to the character and training of the men as well as the leadership of their officers. With regard to the latter, Major Reggie Lees was seen as inspirational and as second in command to Lieutenant Colonel Toosey, at Tamarkan, they set a benchmark in camp hygiene standards by digging proper latrines, which were covered to control flies and did not overflow in the monsoon rains. They also worked at developing an understanding of correct behaviour by the Japanese towards the Allied prisoners. The commonly quoted death rate was around five per cent for prisoners of war held by the Germans, who largely complied with the terms of the Geneva Convention. This serves to highlight the vast difference in their treatment of their prisoners of war, although their treatment was also very hard and should not be confused with the Hollywood myths.

The climate and the environmental conditions in South East Asia in the 1930s and 1940s were, as a whole, unhealthy and serious tropical diseases were always a risk. For example, in May 1939, Captain Lawrence (Battalion Adjutant) contracted malaria while on leave on the island of Bali. Captain McPherson developed dysentery in Java and during 1941 four men of the Battalion died after they were hospitalised with various conditions, including malaria. The risks of these diseases were, therefore, high even in peacetime but became significantly higher when in captivity as the men had no protection from mosquitoes while they slept, and medicines were either unavailable or in short supply. In the jungle areas malaria was endemic and medical staff were extremely concerned by the lack of precautions to prevent mosquito bites. The PoWs had no mosquito nets and no quinine for prevention, so the only possible action they could take to improve the situation was to remove the mosquito's breeding grounds. These were the stagnant pools of rainwater in the jungle around the camps, and parties were formed to drain these. Where the Japanese would not release men from the railway construction, or other project on which the PoWs were engaged, officers, who did not normally engage in physical labour, volunteered to carry out this task. They fully realised the importance of this work for the health of themselves and their men. The other solution was to pour oil on the surface of the ponds which prevented the mosquitos from laying their eggs there while their larvae, which hang just below the water's surface using the surface tension film, were killed.

Although 248 men died in the PoW camps, there are only 194 specific causes of deaths recorded but these give a clear insight into the risks they ran from the poor diet and unhygienic conditions they were forced to suffer. A rare example of a Death Certificate for Regimental Quartermaster Sergeant Robert Spence (2871799), who died at Chungkai PoW Camp, Thailand, is held by the Gordon Highlanders' Museum in Aberdeen. This small flimsy piece of paper, measuring only nine by eight centimetres, details that he died of 'Acute Bacillary Dysentery Haemorrhoidectomy', at 13:30 hours on 19 February 1943. The certificate also gives his age and shows he had been admitted to the hospital Dysentery ward (D Ward) twenty-six days earlier.

The biggest single killer, however, was dysentery, accounting for thirty-seven per cent of the deaths where the cause was recorded. Dysentery is a highly contagious disease with constant diarrhoea, often resulting in the discharge of blood, with the loss of fluids and general debilitation being a real problem for the victims. The medics had no medicine with which to treat dysentery and often the only thing they could prescribe was charcoal, which they produced themselves, burning bamboo in the absence of air in a clean environment, then grinding it into a fine powder. However, other diseases of poor hygiene, such as cholera, typhus, diphtheria, scabies, septicaemia and jaundice accounted for a further twenty-seven per cent. The crowded conditions of the bamboo huts, where the men slept, had a sleeping platform giving each man only about 18 inches (45 centimetres) of space. Bed bugs were a nuisance but, more seriously, infections spread rapidly, particularly when, as so often was the case, there was no adequate means of ensuring personal hygiene. During the rainy season, campsites and huts often became inundated by the rivers bursting their banks, resulting in human waste from overflowing latrines flooding into the huts and ponding a few inches below where the men had to sleep. Jimmy Scott (2880277) caught diphtheria at Brankassie and was being treated for a septic throat. Fortunately for him he was examined by a Japanese doctor who told him that he had a practice in Australia before the war and apparently hated the war. He diagnosed diphtheria and arranged for him to be sent back to Roberts Hospital in Singapore, which saved his life. He readily acknowledged that it was the Japanese doctor who had saved him. He had developed a hole in his throat and couldn't swallow, so had to lie on his side to eat the rice polishings and palm oil given to him to provide the essential vitamins and increase his weight, which had dropped to a mere six and a half stones (forty-one kilos).

The graph (right) illustrates very well the periods when the highest numbers of deaths of Gordon Highlanders occurred. There were the initial casualties from December 1941 to March 1942, during the battle for Singapore, and those who were lost at sea or died of wounds after the surrender. Then there were fourteen months when the casualty rate was relatively stable, at fewer than five per month. The Speedo period, when the Japanese increased the pace of work to try and meet their already unrealistic deadline for completion of the railway, and cholera epidemic, which was visited on those working on the Burma-

Thailand railway between May and December 1944, created conditions leading to huge loss of life. This amounted to over fifty per cent of all Gordon Highlander Far East prisoners of war who died. The next tragic period was in the month of September 1944 when there was a large loss of life following the sinking of hellships carrying PoWs to Japan and of the 105 Gordons who made this journey only thirty-three survived.

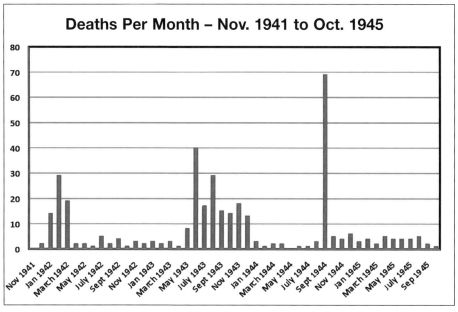

Deaths of Gordon Highlanders from November 1941
to October 1945

In addition, their meagre diet of boiled rice and watery soups, with few vegetables or proteins, led to conditions such as beri-beri, pellagra and polyvitaminosos, and this serious level malnutrition was the cause of death for twenty-four per cent of those where a cause was recorded. After their release in 1945 many of the men were still suffering from beri-beri and Private Willie Niven (2880078) told the author that he was released just in time. He was in the hospital hut and in a critical condition at the time the Japanese surrendered. Charles Robertson (2879166) was not so lucky. Although he knew he was a free man, his liberation came too late and he died just twelve days after the Japanese surrender. Similarly, James Summers (2875032) never made it home as he was still so weak that, even after evacuation from Taiwan to New Zealand and a large degree of medical care, he died on 8 October 1945. Another problem with the vitamin deficient diet was that it could lead to temporary blindness. One such case, at Kanyu Camp in Thailand, was George McNab (2885735) who became blind for four months. He knew that if he didn't work his rations would be cut but, fortunately for him, he was helped by his friend and fellow Gordon Highlander, Sergeant James ('Tibby') Burnett (2874727). Tibby tied a line to George's wrist and they worked together in Hell Fire Pass. George held the chisel while Tibby wielded the heavy hammer to drill holes for the explosive charge. When George's sight returned unexpectedly one day, while working in the rock cutting, they began to hug each other in celebration but the Japanese guards fell on them for stopping the work and gave them a brutal beating. George's sight reappearance proved permanent but he bore the scars of that attack for over fifty years. Charles Taylor (2881760) was also blinded but his condition proved permanent.

In 1943 cholera was a big killer in the jungle camps in Thailand. The Gordon Highlanders had thirty-eight recorded deaths from this disease. The first of these was 28 May 1943 at Tarkanung, where many of the recorded cases affecting Gordon Highlanders occurred. Those in F Force, working near the border with Burma at Nikki and Kami Sonkurai, were also badly affected. The last cholera case affecting a Gordon was on 25 August 1943 and this brief three-month period had been terrifying for those in the affected camps. The situation was exacerbated by the monsoon as the constant rain made it difficult to get dry fuel to keep the fires burning, so hampering sterilisation techniques to limit spread of the disease. These included boiling all drinking water, isolation of the victims and cremation of the dead. The disease first broke out in the camps of the numerous Asian workers whom the Japanese had shipped into the area, with their families, promising high wages and good conditions. These were dreadful places with no hygiene precautions, where the river was used for everything from drinking water to washing and defecation. When cholera started claiming victims among this group of people they were suddenly and totally overwhelmed. Corpses were not cremated or buried and the disease spread like wildfire, with the rainwater washing the deadly bacteria into streams, carrying the disease downstream.

To try and combat the spread of the disease to the PoWs, orders were issued to drink only boiled water and forbidding the men to bathe in the river. These instructions proved difficult for the men to comply with, even though they understood they were for their own safety but it was just another burden, adding to the constant anxiety about the threat of contracting this terrible disease. Where men were slaving for long hours every day in the humid heat it was very tempting to take a drink from any source, particularly on long marches and this was often the cause of their downfall. Bill Young (2876638) remembered that Company Sergeant Major Frank Knight died of cholera after he drank some river water. Although generally fatal, two Gordons are recorded as having recovered from this deadly disease. They were Corporal Alistair Urquhart (2883851) and Private John ('Nellie') Wallace (2876354). Death was a consequence of severe dehydration, following the rapid and uncontrolled loss of body fluids through constant diarrhoea and vomiting. Treatment was rudimentary and saline drips were improvised, using water distilled in the camps, but this was rarely an option in the remote, smaller, camps up country, where the disease first struck.

The jungle itself also harboured many dangers such as snakes and scorpions while tigers were even reported to be in the remoter areas. The Japanese were particularly terrified by even the rumour of a tiger in the area and built large campfires to ward them off. However, perhaps one of the most ubiquitous but nevertheless most dangerous forms of wildlife was the tiny malaria mosquito. Malaria was endemic with most men contracting the condition because the Japanese did not provide any mosquito nets or quinine for protection. Malaria is caused by a microscopic parasite which is carried by the mosquito and enters the victim's bloodstream when the insect bites. Normally only the rare cerebral form is fatal but the disease causes severe debility, with a raging fever and other symptoms. In the situation in which the PoWs found themselves, being unable to work meant reduced rations and this, together with the absence of any drugs for treatment, resulted in a general physical deterioration to a point where the affected man died. The first recorded death from malaria occurred in June 1943 but was cited as either the primary or secondary cause of death of thirty-one Gordons, with deaths still occurring right up until the end of the war. Many are recorded as having malaria attacks on over twenty occasions and Private John McRae (2876679) recorded that he had thirty-two bouts of the disease (an average of one episode every month during his time as a prisoner). On his release in 1945 Willie Merchant had a dangerously enlarged spleen as a result of malaria. He was very ill and spent many weeks in a hospital in Calcutta before he could travel home to Aberdeen, where he was also hospitalised for many months before recovery.

Jungle ulcers also occurred, from the infection of wounds from bamboo thorns or cuts from flying razor-sharp shards of the crystalline limestone rock during blasting operations. These ulcers were alarming and bacteria rapidly ate through flesh to expose bone. The treatment was rudimentary in the extreme, usually involving scraping out the rotting flesh and puss with a sharpened metal spoon or introducing maggots to eat the affected tissue to clean the wound. Private Edward Gallacher (2876625) and Corporal James Grant (2876752) each had a leg amputated in Thailand as a result of tropical ulcers, the former at Nong Pladuk in 1944 and the latter at Chungkai in 1943. Many prisoners were afflicted to a greater or lesser degree and one of the causes of death given for Privates James Chisholm (2877911) and James Napier (2876793) was tropical ulcers. In charge of Tarsoa Hospital Camp, Thailand was Doctor Ernest Edward 'Weary' Dunlop, an Australian Army doctor, who was knighted by the Queen in 1969 in recognition of his work in treating and saving the lives of hundreds of PoWs and his post war work assisting Far East PoW organisations. When he examined Bandsman Percy O'Donnell (2876690) in 1943, both his legs were a mass of tropical ulcers and Weary Dunlop recommended a double amputation but Percy emphatically refused to allow this. Death would follow quickly if gangrene set in, so this was very brave, or very foolish, depending on the outcome. Scraping out the rotting flesh daily was excruciatingly painful and after each treatment he was left totally exhausted. A new treatment became available about this time, which was the application of a mixture of potassium permanganate, borax and zinc (PBZ), which had the effect of chemically cleaning and disinfecting the wound. This was even more painful than the traditional mechanical method but it did prove more successful. Percy O'Donnell received this new preparation and his bravery and fortitude were rewarded as he retained full use of both his legs.

After their release in 1945 many of the men praised the courage and ingenuity of the medical staff who helped them. Since the men were dispersed they had different medics attending them in different camps. However, at the beginning of the railway construction period there was a fairly large contingent of Gordon Highlanders who were initially with Lieutenant Colonel Stitt at Wampo. Their doctor was Captain Stanley Septimus Pavillard, an officer from the Straits

Settlements Volunteer Force. The Gordons had had a close friendly relationship with this regiment prior to hostilities so this bond was strengthened as a result of his treatment of them. This extended beyond mere medicine, looking after their welfare as he himself recounted in his memoirs *Bamboo Doctor*. On one occasion Private Charles English (2876675) laughed at a Japanese guard who was being reprimanded by his superior. This loss of face provoked the guard, nicknamed Silver Bullet, to go straight to him and strike him with his rifle butt, splitting his skull. (Silver Bullet was so nicknamed as he was syphilitic and went to the doctor for an arsenic preparation which was referred to as a 'silver bullet' because, at this time, it was the only known treatment for this disease.) While his wound was being cleaned Silver Bullet reappeared and Charles English went berserk trying to get at him. This would have been suicidal and Dr Pavillard saved the day by injecting English with morphine, causing him to lose consciousness. He then told the guard that the blow to his head had caused him to go mad and he was now in a coma. This turned the tables and the Japanese guard then became fearful when Doctor Pavillard explained that, if Charles English died, he would have to report it to the senior Japanese officer, in which case Silver Bullet would again be in trouble. On another occasion, he also saved Angus Collie who had an adverse reaction to a treatment for malaria and had to be held down by two others as he shouted and screamed that he was going to kill the Japanese; again morphine was administered, averting a serious situation. Doctor Pavillard was a doctor in private practice in Singapore prior to the outbreak of the Pacific War and returned to this after the war ended. He was appointed MBE for his services to the PoWs. After the war, in an address by Major (by then Lieutenant Colonel) Reggie Lees to a Gordon Highlanders' Far East PoW reunion in Aberdeen, the affection and respect in which Dr Pavillard was held by the Regiment was highlighted. (Doctor Pavillard was attending.) His address was as follows:

I have been asked to pay a short tribute to Doctor Pavillard. At one stage on the Railway, I arrived with my working party at Hell Fire Pass where we were pitchforked into a combination of Japanese Speedo and a cholera belt, with no doctor. Fortunately for us, we were able to get the services of Doctor Pavillard. We ourselves had no experience of cholera, but he, from the moment he came to us, taught us all the precautions we had to take, and by his skill, initiative and cheery manner was instrumental in saving many of my men's lives, and we all owe him a great debt of gratitude.

I am glad to have this opportunity of saying on behalf of us soldiers, thank you to him and all the other doctors who worked so selflessly and ceaselessly for the sick and the dying. They had practically no weapons or medicines to fight with. Their skill and categorical sense of mission was their only armoury. If it had not been for them many of us would not be alive today.

Another doctor who came in for specific praise both by George McNab and Alistair Urquhart was Dr Kenneth Matheson from Paisley, south-west Scotland. He was an officer of the Royal Army Medical Corps who had been posted to Singapore in early 1940. Both Gordons were treated by him while they worked on the Thai–Burma Railway and again in Japan. In addition, Captain Malcolm Fuller remembered that Private Derek Barr-Sim (2889970) of the Gordon Highlanders, an untrained medical orderly, through his unselfish and devoted work saved many of his comrades' lives during the cholera epidemic in Thailand in 1943. Derek Barr-Sim, the son of an RAF group captain, had been in the London Scottish, a Territorial Army Battalion of the Gordon Highlanders, and only arrived in Singapore at the end of November 1941, just ten days before the Japanese attack on the city. The work done by the medics was truly amazing, matched only by the courage in adversity of the men. For example, whilst at Kinkaseki Camp in Formosa (now Taiwan), Michael Dougan (2885055) had to have an operation to remove his appendix. This was done successfully by the two camp doctors at Kinkaseki, Captain Peter Seed (RAMC) and Dr Ben Wheeler, a Canadian who had been working in Singapore for the British Indian Medical Service when it fell in 1942. This difficult procedure was carried out, without any anaesthetic, using a razor blade for a scalpel. Many years after the war, at the age of seventy, Michael Dougan had to have another operation and told the surgeon that no anaesthetic was necessary. On this occasion his surgeon decided otherwise.

It was not only Allied doctors who helped the PoWs. After a 400-kilometre march through Thailand, many of the men were exhausted and mostly in bare feet after losing their boots in the sucking, cloying mud of the rain-sodden tracks. They were forced to sleep in the open in rain-soaked paddy fields and consequently were also suffering from exposure. Private Edward Strachan (2876326) was in a party which found itself near Tak City, Thailand, near the border with Burma, where a local doctor, Doctor Yarnyong Lauhachinca, allowed the sick PoWs into his hospital and treated them. He persuaded Eddie Strachan to break out of the PoW camp and meet him at his house that night where he gave him a sack of medicines and surgical instruments. This operation was repeated on several occasions and was highly dangerous for both Eddie and the Thai doctor.

When the vulnerable position these men were in is considered, with an ever-present and imminent risk of injury and disease, combined with their declining standard of health, the donation of blood to their comrades or fellow prisoners has to be seen as an act of selfless bravery. Whilst in captivity, no less than forty-four men of the Battalion gave their blood on a total of fifty-five occasions. This was both while they were in

Singapore, in 1942, but also much later in the war when they were in Thailand and their physical condition had deteriorated significantly. In Singapore the donations were mainly to men who had been wounded in some way, such as Piper James Johnston (2876288) who received a sword wound when making his escape from the Japanese and Second Lieutenant Derek Stewart, who received multiple shrapnel wounds while forced by the Japanese to clear mines at Pengerang. Piper Johnston received blood donations from two of his comrades but over a three-month period, Lieutenant Stewart received a staggering seventeen donations, all from different Gordon Highlanders. However, Private David Gallacher (2876625) also received two donations of blood from two Gordons, on 6 September 1942, but unfortunately died of dysentery four days later. A further twenty-one blood donations were made at Chungkai, Thailand, by men of the Battalion, with five Gordons each giving multiple donations, e.g. 2876331 George Crichton, from Cruden Bay, Aberdeenshire, gave blood four times at Chungkai from 25 September 1943 to 23 September 1945. These blood donations would have been to assist with operations, such as amputations, as described above, when the medical facilities would have been the most basic. Possibly direct transfusion was practised, where the donor is linked directly to the recipient. Jack Jamieson (2877746) gave blood at Chungkai, on 27 July 1944, and in a conversation with the author, indicated that his blood was simply removed using a hypodermic syringe.

These selfless acts were recognised at the time and an example of a certificate for such a donation is held in the collection of the Gordon Highlanders' Museum. One such example is the small flimsy scrap of paper (measuring twelve by six centimetres) presented to Private Alexander Smith (2879133) on 29 January 1944. It is signed by the Senior British Officer at Chunkai, Lieutenant Colonel Henry Outram, Royal Artillery.

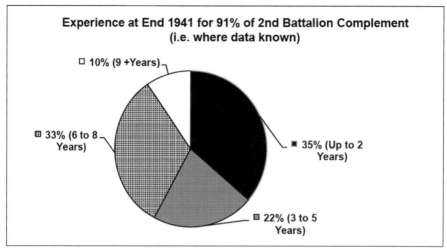

**Experience at End 1941 for 91% of 2nd Battalion Complement (i.e. where data known)**

☐ 10% (9 +Years)

⊞ 33% (6 to 8 Years)

■ 35% (Up to 2 Years)

▨ 22% (3 to 5 Years)

**Pie Chart showing Length of Service Distribution of the Men of the 2nd Battalion in 1941**

When considering the chances of survival of the PoWs, the obvious assumption would be that the young and fit would be the best able to survive the rigours of PoW life, where nutrition was poor and inadequate for the forced hard physical conditions they had to endure. On the other hand, it is equally conceivable that the Battalion's experienced Regulars, with good training and discipline and not unaccustomed to physical effort had the best chance of survival with perhaps only the oldest men being the most vulnerable. However, if we consider the makeup of the Battalion in detail, the results are a little surprising. If we first consider the length of service across the age ranges they are fairly evenly spread, although only ten per cent had served for ten years or more. (The age ranges were chosen to make each group of a similar size, so far as was possible, to make the comparisons between ages more valid.) It can be seen that prior to going into action against the Japanese, in January 1942, that only a third were wartime conscripts with two years or less service. The majority of the Battalion were Regular soldiers and a significant proportion (fifty-nine per cent) had been together as a unit since they left Gibraltar in 1937 and just under half (forty-three per cent) had six years or more service, so were experienced and highly trained.

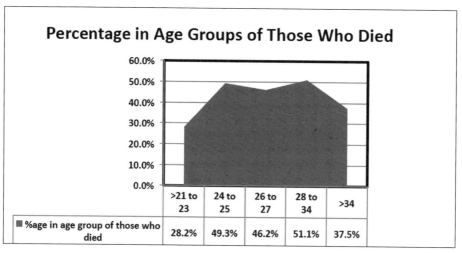

## Percentage in Age Groups of Those Who Died

|  | >21 to 23 | 24 to 25 | 26 to 27 | 28 to 34 | >34 |
|---|---|---|---|---|---|
| ■ %age in age group of those who died | 28.2% | 49.3% | 46.2% | 51.1% | 37.5% |

**Relative Numbers of Men of the 2nd Battalion Who Died in Each Age Group Shown**

After the battle for Singapore there were 925 men who became prisoners of war and of these 299 died (thirty-two per cent). However, the death rate differed across the age ranges. Originally it was believed that the youngest (say twenty-two years old and under) did not have the mental resources or experience of life to survive the harsh regime of the Japanese PoW camps, while the oldest (say thirty-four years old and above) were more likely to have succumbed to the hard work, poor diet and were less able to fight off disease. Those over twenty-two and under thirty-three years old were in the prime of their lives, mostly experienced soldiers and fit and so should have had the highest proportional survival rate. The statistics,

133

however, paint a different picture. Between the ages of twenty-three to thirty-three a more or less uniform rate of death occurs across these age groups, but average death rate for this group, of forty-nine per cent, greatly exceeds the overall average. The over thirty-fours died at a much lower rate of thirty-eight per cent, only a little above the overall average. This is completely at odds with a long-held view. Only three men who were under twenty years old died and the three youngest Boys, William Bremner (2890085), Frederick Brind (2890780) and Patrick Brind (2890744), all survived while, of the seven oldest PoWs, all born before 1900, only two failed to survive the war.

Although the three and a half years of captivity was a horrific experience the collective camaraderie of the Gordons did much to help individuals get through. They looked out for each other in so many ways, such as favouring vulnerable comrades for light jobs. One such example was Sergeant Tom Skene, who was the Battalion cook and was pressed into service by the Japanese who put him in charge of their own cookhouse at Tarsao. On seeing George McNab was exhausted from his physical work, cutting and collecting bamboo, he arranged for him to have an easier job in the cookhouse, where the opportunities for extra food were greater and allowed him to build up his strength and probably saved his life.

Entertainment, an important morale booster, could only be organised on any significant scale in the large camps and where there were men with the talent to put on a show. John ('Snuffy') Craig (2876114) was very productive in organising performances and even arranging some impromptu sing-songs up in the remoter areas of Thailand. This did much to lift the men's spirits in these hell holes. He was a keen amateur performer in pre-war Singapore and had produced numerous shows for the Battalion, often drawing in family members including children and other Gordons into the cast. During the early years in captivity there was a fairly regular troupe of performers, including Bandsman Henry Campleman (2874252), Sergeant William Stark (2876554) and 'Paddy' (Frank) Quinn, who were considered to be the best sword dancers in the Regiment. Angus Collie was the stage manager and Charles English (2876675) provided the props. After the war Snuffy Craig received a glowing testimonial from Colonel Harold Lilley (Sherwood Foresters) who was the Senior British Officer in charge of most of the camps Snuffy was in, while working on the railway in Thailand. He wrote to Snuffy saying, 'I will always remember the way you got things going at Wampo and how you carried on all through those desperate years'. This is all the more remarkable when it is known that, at the end of 1943, while at Kinsaiyok, Snuffy was near to death. His weight dropped to a critical level of around four stones (25 kilos) and Dr Pavillard had diagnosed amoebic dysentery. By some miracle he had pulled through by Christmas that year. He received a small card from some of his fellow PoWs, with 'Merry Christmas Snuffy' written on it, which gave him a terrific boost. Other 'thespians' in the Battalion included Lieutenant Charles Gibson, a graduate of Aberdeen University where he was well known in the University artistic spheres, graduating with an MA and becoming a minister of religion before joining the Gordon Highlanders. In addition, Lieutenant William Ferguson Hogg ('Fergie') was a friend of Captain Ronnie Horner, an officer in the Royal Army Service Corps, with whom he shared a Batman. Ronnie Horner was also prolific in arranging entertainment for the PoWs. In his Memoirs, entitled *Singapore Diary*, there are several references to 'Fergie' and an illustration of a programme for a show entitled 'A Bird in the Hand' which was produced by Fergie and staged at Sime Road Camp, Singapore in April 1944. At Chungkai, Thailand, it had been possible to gain permission to build a permanent stage in a corner of the camp and 'Nellie' Wallace appeared in the cast of the show, 'Wonder Bar', also featuring Ronnie Horner and staged in May 1944.

A number of Gordons kept their artistic spirit and were able to marvel at and appreciate the spectacle of nature around them in other ways. Lieutenant John Leckie marvelled at the spectacle of the partial eclipse of the sun at Kanchanaburi, Thailand, in the summer of 1945. The small holes in the atap roofing acted like a pin-hole camera throwing a perfect image of the event onto the earthen floor of his hut. Similarly Snuffy Craig was not the only Gordon Highlander to receive a greetings card and a hand-drawn New Year's card, believed to have been given to Frank McKimmie (2876477), forms part of the collection of the Gordon Highlanders' Museum.

Private William Mackie (2882556) received a silver wedding anniversary card from his fellow patients when in Tamuang Camp Hospital, Thailand, in 1944, which he managed to bring home and is still treasured by his family. There were other men who were unsung artists. Piper John Willox (2876280) had a simple exercise book in which he wrote music, songs and poetry, all of which was colourfully illustrated. Watercolour portraits were done for at least five Gordon Highlanders while they were in PoW camps. Colour Sergeant William Low was painted at Chungkai, Thailand, in February 1944, by I. Franz and Albert Middleton (2869710) was painted by Jack Chalker, a well-known PoW artist who captured many scenes of everyday horrors of the prisoners. Another PoW artist, Ashley George ('Josh') Old, painted portraits of at least three Gordons' officers, Lieutenant Forbes Sandison, in Singapore during 1942, Lieutenant Colonel Jack Stitt and Major Walter Duke, at Chungkai, Thailand in 1944. The officers sometimes had money and for Josh Old, a trained artist, this was certainly a means of generating a few cents to buy extra rations to improve the meagre diet provided by his captors.

In these seemingly Godforsaken places in which these men were forced to exist, some took comfort from their Christian faith. One obvious example was Lieutenant Charles Gibson, who was an ordained minister in the Church of Scotland and had been called up to serve as an infantry officer with the Gordons, rather than the more logical deployment as an Army chaplain. Charles Gibson was a charismatic young officer. He was nicknamed 'Hoot' by the men on account of his heavy rimmed spectacles, which gave him an owlish appearance. He gained a reputation as a hard drinker following an incident recalled by Murray Melville (2888645). While the Battalion were on a route march, on a very hot day in pre-war Singapore, Hoot offered Murray a drink from his water bottle, which he readily accepted. He drank thirstily but gasped and spluttered when, to his dismay, he discovered the water bottle contained neat gin. However, he had a much deeper, more sympathetic, side: when in Saigon, near the end of the war, he comforted a soldier who was not a Gordon Highlander and wrote an inspirational passage in the man's bible, which he treasured until his dying day, long after the war was over. On another occasion at Chungkai, Thailand, late one evening in 1943, he was comforting a dying man, a young Scot from Argyll. When everything seemed lost, unseen, came the long low notes of the bagpipes being played by Piper Sam Robertson. The dying man's eyes lit up and he said it reminded him of home. He told Charles Gibson, 'if it is the last music I hear, I will be happy.' He died next morning. Lieutenant Gibson was critical of the Japanese for not providing facilities or allowing prisoners time for religious services, which would undoubtedly have provided great solace to many.

Other men drew great strength from reading the scriptures but bibles were, unfortunately, very scarce. Sergeant Jock Webster (2865818) had recovered his daughter's bible from the gymnasium at Selarang Barracks, where the Battalion's personal belongings had been stored. He used the blank pages of this bible to make a simple calendar to keep track of the date and also to record a roll of honour of those men who died. He treasured and read his bible thoroughly and particularly noted Chapter Four of First Corinthians, Verses 11 and 12. This reads:

> *11 Even unto this present hour we both hunger, and thirst, and are naked, and are buffeted, and have no certain dwellingplace;*
> *12 And labour, working with our own hands: being reviled we bless; being persecuted, we suffer it;*

There can hardly be a more fitting passage from the Bible which more accurately described the situation in which he found himself. Jock Webster survived the war and brought home the bible, which he had gifted to his daughter, Phyllis, for good attendance at Sunday School in 1941, before the war in the Pacific began. This now forms part of the collection of the Gordon Highlanders' Museum after the family donated their treasured possession for safe-keeping and to allow others to appreciate just how much it meant to Jock in the desperate circumstances he faced as a prisoner of the Japanese. Bill Hunter (3318210) was another man with a strong faith which no doubt kept him going when starvation and disease reduced his weight to a mere four stone (about 30 kilos). After the war he became a lay preacher in Motherwell and went on to become Chairman of the Scottish Catholic Lay Apostolate Council, but the effect of his time as a PoW meant that his health remained poor and he suffered two heart attacks and died at the relatively young age of sixty-one.

Links with home and reminiscences were also an important way of maintaining some hope. Although in the 1930s it was very unusual for a private soldier to have a camera, James Taylor (2875631) had been a keen photographer and kept a photo album with 'snaps' of all his friends taken during much of his service, spanning his time in India and Gibraltar as well as pre-war life in Singapore, the happy times. Jim Taylor was nicknamed 'Dherzi', which he had been given when serving with the 1st Battalion Gordon Highlanders in India. Apparently Dherzi can be translated to 'tailor' in the Indian language which matched his surname, though not his occupation. While a PoW in Changi, Singapore, a Japanese officer saw him with his album and as the Japanese considered keeping a diary or holding any document a serious matter he grabbed the album from 'Dherzi'. It fell to the ground and lay open at a page with a large photograph of Colonel Burney, who had been the Battalion Commanding Officer up to 1939, in full-dress uniform. The Japanese officer asked who it was a photograph of and thinking quickly but without hesitation Dherzi said it was his father. This greatly impressed the Japanese officer who relented and let him keep his album. Realising that his album might not survive his captivity, he wrapped it in a groundsheet and buried it and was able to take it home when he was liberated. His family retain and cherish it still.

The PoWs were issued with postcards to send home to their families. In most cases the distribution of these was limited to a maximum of five cards for the entire duration of their captivity. These normally had a list of standard phrases to tick or score off but sometimes it was possible to write a message but this was limited to twenty-five words. The PoWs knew that they had to paint a rosy picture of life in the hands of the Japanese or the card would not make it past the censor. In addition, they did not wish their families to worry about them and the most important message to give was that they were still alive. The Japanese did not give much priority to this mail and if it ever arrived back in the UK it was often over twelve months old. Unfortunately, sometimes this gave false hope to a family as, by the time it reached them, their loved one may already have died as life was precarious for a PoW, particularly in the terrible conditions of the camps in northern Thailand. In turn, if a PoW did receive letter from home this was truly a 'red letter day' for him. It was more likely that mail would get through in the larger camps than the small up-country ones and if letters were received they would appear in batches, obviously being held back somewhere in the Japanese system.

The experience of Corporal Jimmie Simpson (2877045), a PoW in Taiwan from November 1942 until his liberation, illustrates this well, although he was exceptional in the number of cards he sent. He sent postcards home to his mother in Portsoy, Banffshire, on an almost monthly basis throughout 1943 and 1944. But despite his perseverance, he had not received any replies. In a postcard he sent at the end of June 1944 he mentions this, appearing to believe that no letters were being sent to him, rather than they were being held back by the Japanese. He did, however, receive three letters together in August 1944. His confidence in the system that his letters were being sent away and received as normal was, nevertheless, not diminished. In his postcard home in August 1944, immediately after he received the three letters from home, he stated 'I hope to be able to write a letter soon'. His hopes were realised when he was permitted to send a letter which was dated 23 October 1944, which he started quite jubilantly, 'Dear Mother, I told you to expect a letter and here it is, the first we have been allowed to write. I received six letters from you ... ' His letter is written in a way that is obviously pitched to comfort his mother and to ensure she will not worry; kindly misleading her into thinking his situation is much better than it was in reality. He continues:

> We are kept pretty busy here and the time passes quickly. Our food consists of rice and vegetables and we are looking forward to eating some good bread and butter and potatoes. We've had three lots of Red Cross parcels and can't tell you how much we enjoyed them.

His unbroken spirit shines through as he ends on a rather optimistic note about the end of the war, writing:

> I am certain that it won't last much longer, In fact I hope it will be over before this reaches you. Don't worry, look

after yourself and I'll be with you before long, keep smiling, love to all, Jimmie.

He kept up his optimism and even in February 1945, when there was, in reality, still little prospect of the war in the Pacific ending soon, he wrote:

Dear Mother, I've received six more letters from you. ... Am keeping well and just waiting for the great day ... Don't worry, get my bedroom ready – I'll be using it soon. Cheerio, Jimmie.

It would, however, be another nine months before Jimmie saw his bedroom, which he had left almost twelve years earlier.

Two unconventional PoWs were included in the Gordon Highlanders' numbers while in Thailand. These were the Regimental mascot 'Peggy', a bull terrier, and a local conscript, Donald Duck.

Peggy was a pedigree Staffordshire bull-terrier bitch who was found at Pengerang, Singapore, before the Pacific War began and adopted by the men of the Battalion. While most of the men would pet and spoil her with titbits she was nominally in the care of Company Quartermaster Sergeant Jim King (2876113) and her status within the Battalion had the full backing of Major Reggie Lees. When the Battalion was ordered up to Johore to engage the Japanese, in January 1942, Peggy went into action, travelling in one of the Bren-gun carriers. She remained with the unit right throughout the fighting and became a PoW with the men. Her first move from Changi was to Adam Park, Singapore, living at Watten Park within that camp. Whilst here she mated with a 'native' mongrel and was pregnant when the Gordons moved to Tamarkan, Thailand, where she gave birth to two black pups. Whether these survived or not is unclear as it has been suggested that they were killed and eaten, but in the autumn of 1943, a young black bull terrier was seen by Murray Melville at Tamuang and was likely to have been one of her offspring. Major Lees left Tamarkan in May 1943 with a plate-laying party, laying rails all along the railbed far up-country to Konkoita and the pup may have gone up-country with them.

Peggy soon learned to eat rice and spent a lot of time round the cookhouse, where she could scrounge food, but also went with the men to the work sites along the railway. The Japanese guards did not like her and she bore the scars of several bayonet wounds. However, this gave her a healthy respect for her enemy, which proved useful to the Gordon PoWs. For example, she could smell a Japanese guard well before any of the men could see or hear him and would alert them of the danger. This doggy olfactory skill was useful when the PoWs went on nocturnal breakouts to trade with the native Thais for eggs and other fare. The favour was reciprocated and if the men said 'Nips' to her (referring to their Japanese 'hosts') she made herself scarce and disappeared in a flash to keep out of trouble.

As a prisoner of war at Chungkai, Thailand, in 1944, Corporal William Gray (2876971) spotted two ducklings floating on a branch of a tree being swept down the adjacent river, which was swollen with flood waters. He dived in to try and save these two birds and, despite the strong current, successfully brought them to the bank safely. Unfortunately, one of the ducklings died shortly afterwards but one survived and was christened 'Donald', after the famous cartoon character, and the name was also considered appropriately Scottish.

Donald thrived under the care of Willie Gray and soon rewarded his owner with the present of an egg proving that Donald was actually female. The Japanese threatened to kill Donald for their own consumption but Gray was equal to the challenge by telling them that she was in fact a sacred duck, which, to his surprise, did the trick and Donald was saved. Because Donald gave a steady supply of eggs, when all other forms of rich protein were virtually unavailable to the prisoners, Donald was safe from harm and survived to the end of the war.

All these various morale boosters were invaluable in keeping the PoWs going but these would all have been surpassed by far if only the exploits of one of their own officers had been known to them. In September 1943 Ivan Lyon, now a major, returned to Singapore. The city's name originated from Singapura the Malay for Lion City but after their victory in February 1942 the Japanese renamed it Syonanto meaning 'Light of the South'. Ivan Lyon was about to metaphorically reclaim the original name and if not 'Lyon City' possible 'Tiger City' from the large tattoo of a Malayan tiger on his chest. In an undercover raid, codenamed Operation JAYWICK, launched from far off Western Australia, Ivan Lyon led the British and Australian Commando unit codenamed Z, which penetrated the defences of Singapore Harbour. Their voyage to Singapore was undertaken in a former Japanese fishing boat named the *Krait* after a small highly venomous snake of the cobra family and common in the jungles of Asia. This was a very risky venture as the seas were largely in enemy hands, so they sailed under the cover of a Japanese flag to escape detection. On arrival in the waters off Borneo and Singapore they finally dropped off the attack teams in the Riau Archipelago on 18 September 1943. They stole in silently, in two-man collapsible kayaks (known as folbots), and sank seven ships, some 50,000 tons of Japanese shipping, without any loss and got away completely undetected. They returned to Australia after forty-seven days at sea, thirty-three of them in Japanese-held waters. Ivan Lyon was awarded the Distinguished Service Order (DSO), to add to his MBE. As an award for valour, the DSO is, for an officer, second only to the Victoria Cross, the highest and most prestigious award for gallantry that can be awarded to British and Commonwealth forces.

Unfortunately, there were serious repercussions in Singapore. The Japanese could not conceive of Ivan Lyon's boldness so believed the sabotage had been organised and mounted by local guerrillas. The Kempeitai rounded up over fifty innocent civilians, tortured and then executed many of them in what was known as the 'double tenth massacre', so called as the arrests occurred on 10 October 1943. After the war the Kempeitai commanding officer, Lieutenant Colonel Sumida, and twenty-one of his men were accused of torture and killing of fifteen of the suspects. Sumida was one of eight sentenced to death, by hanging, while six others received various terms of imprisonment. Incredibly, just a year later, Ivan Lyon, now promoted to lieutenant colonel, led another daring attack, codenamed Operation RIMAU (Malay for tiger and deriving from Lyon's tattoo). This was a larger and more sophisticated operation, using midget submarines to enter Keppel Harbour and place limpet mines on the Japanese shipping anchored there. The force included six veterans of the JAYWICK raid. Unfortunately, the build-up to the raid did not go well and they were forced to open fire on a police patrol boat that challenged them and their cover was blown. However, Ivan Lyon pressed on undeterred and succeeded in sinking three ships before escaping. They were not able to shake off the Japanese this time and, on 16 October 1944, on the tiny island of Soreh in the Riau Archipelago just south of Singapore, Ivan Lyon was killed after a prolonged firefight in which around sixty Japanese soldiers were killed or wounded by the smaller force of just three. Most of the remaining men in the force were either killed or captured and eventually executed by the Japanese. The *Krait* was returned to Australia in 1964 and, now restored, rests in Darling Harbour, Sydney, as a permanent memorial to the bravery of the men who undertook the JAYWICK and RIMAU missions.

# CHAPTER 6

# Liberation

The Japanese did everything they could to prevent the PoWs knowing what was going on in the wider world and, as time went on, especially when the war was not going well for them. However, they could not hide the sight of Allied planes in the skies overhead and, with the aid of some clandestine radio receivers, there was some knowledge of the progress of the war in most camps. For example, the end of the war in Europe in May 1945 was known about. Where there was contact with local people, who generally did not have much time for the Japanese, they confirmed the situation by surreptitiously whispering to the PoWs 'Hitler finished'. The ordinary Japanese soldiers appeared to have little information on the progress of the war and were totally convinced that things were going well and had no conception of defeat. For example, in 1944, Murray Melville encountered some Japanese soldiers on a train at Nong Pladuc, Thailand, who firmly believed they were in India. Archie Black had a similar experience when he was working in the docks at Saigon in 1945, where a group of Japanese soldiers became very aggressive when he tried to convince them that they were not in India either. Both groups were almost certainly deceived by their own propaganda. India was the goal and expected great prize after their swift and early victories, but denied to them by the dogged resistance of Allied forces, who had regrouped on the India-Burma border, under General Bill Slim and deep penetration offensive actions by the

'Chindits', commanded by the charismatic but eccentric Major General Orde Wingate. These eventually pushed the Japanese back and Burma was successfully held, although it was a close-run thing.

The sight of Allied planes overhead was a beacon of hope for the PoWs but these planes also spelled real danger. The Burma-Thailand railway was the supply route for Japanese troops fighting against the British in Burma and so was a prime target for the RAF, operating from its bases in British India. The bridges at Kanchanaburi and Tamarkan, together with the long trestle carrying the railway around the cliff face at Wampo were weak points. Bomb damage here had a longer-term effect than just cratering the line, although the large sidings at Nong Pladuc were also a frequent target. The Japanese used the PoWs as human shields and despite repeated pleas by senior British and Australian officers, they would not relocate the PoW camps away from the railway line nor, shamefully, would they allow markings to highlight to the airmen that the camps held PoWs. The jubilation of seeing the RAF bombers screaming in to attack was tempered by the fear of injury or death as the pilots generally considered the camps fair game, mistakenly believing these were camps for Japanese soldiers who were being rested from the Burma front. Privates Richard Entwhistle (2879489) and William Martin (2876659) were injured in air raids at Nong Pladuc and Tamarkan respectively while Private John Sangster (2877014) was killed in a raid at Kui Yae (Kwiye), and initially buried in the jungle by the line, near the 190-kilometre mark, but after the war reinterred at Kanchanaburi War Cemetery. Despite the dangers, the PoWs still saw these attacks as bitter blows being inflicted on their enemy and they even used them as opportunities to hit back themselves, where they could. For example, when air raids were in progress at Wampo, Thailand, in November and December 1944, Company Sergeant Major Angus Collie gave encouragement to the Indian engine drivers to

146

leave their locomotives exposed in the open and blowing off steam. This made them more obvious and inviting targets.

As the end of the war appeared to be near, the PoWs started to become apprehensive. They believed that their captors had every intention of exterminating them and wondered how they could possibly be liberated by Allied troops, recapturing the enemy-held territory they were in without terrible reprisals against them. They would not have known about the successful liberation of just over 500 American PoWs held in Cabanatuan PoW camp in the Philippines in January 1945, but in any case this was a bit of a one-off and it was probably best that they did not know about the enforced 'death marches' in Borneo, where the Japanese moved the PoWs away from the coast to prevent liberation by Australian forces, resulting in the death of almost every PoW. One of the things that bothered them most was that in 1945 the Japanese forced the PoWs to dig large trenches around many camps. The Japanese passed these off as anti-tank defences but the PoWs believed them to be preparations for their mass execution and burial. After three and a half years of experience of the Japanese, they knew they were ruthless and wholly capable of such an atrocity.

During 1945, the PoWs in Japan were exposed to numerous and intense raids carried out by American B-29 bombers, each carrying a full load of incendiary or high-explosive bombs. These wreaked havoc on civilian, military and industrial targets, causing terrific destruction in cities where most of the buildings were constructed of wood. PoWs were engaged in heavy industry and witnessed this almost daily destruction with the planes clearly visible above them. These raids frequently occurred in daylight as the Japanese air force had been almost completely destroyed by the summer of 1945. In July 1945 George McNab was being marched with a group of PoWs to the carbide factory where they worked and the area around was completely devastated by previous bombing raids. There was a shout from one of the guards of 'scouki, scouki' (the Japanese for aeroplanes) as they heard the noise of incoming dive-bombers. They ran for the beach and lay hugging the ground while the planes attacked and flattened the surrounding factories, without any apparent opposition. In August 1945 Bill Young was in Fukuoka Camp 17B, near Nagasaki, and heard of rumours emanating from the Japanese guards, that some major catastrophe had occurred in a city up north but little was known, due to official censorship. However, the Japanese authorities were unable to block out all news of the terrible destruction of the city of Hiroshima, on Sunday 6 August 1945, by the world's first atomic attack. US bombers had been dropping leaflets on all the major Japanese cities but, inevitably, most ordinary Japanese civilians dismissed the news as Allied propaganda.

The morning of 9 August 1945 was a fine day and Bill Young (2876638) was at this stage in a very bad physical shape, suffering from beri-beri and his abdomen and legs were swollen up with the retention of fluid. He was unable to work and so dependent on his friends for scraps of food as the Japanese refused to feed men unfit for work. He was sitting in the sun overlooking Nagasaki Bay while other Gordon Highlanders Billy Burns (2881921), George McNab (2885735) and Alistair Urquhart (2883851) were working as normal in the same area. All were survivors of the Burma-Thailand railway and shipwreck in the South China Sea but were now at Fukuoka Camp 25B. George was working to clear up rubble and other debris from previous air raids and Alistair was tending the Japanese officers' vegetable garden. All were taken by surprise by a blinding flash, which they initially thought was lightning, followed by a terrific clap of what they thought was thunder. Billy Burns saw the colossal cloud of smoke rising up from the city and thought that an oil dump had been hit. Bill Young, from his vantage point above the city, also saw the cloud of smoke and thought an Allied plane had been hit but noticed the cloud began to connect to the ground until a huge black mushroom-like cloud grew and grew and, quite quickly, day turned into night as the cloud blotted out the sun and overshadowed his camp. An eerie silence descended, there was no bird or insect song and the only sound was the distant drone of aeroplane engines, and everything for miles around became coated in black fallout dust.

This was a totally new weapon, the atomic bomb, unknown to the PoWs or for that matter the Japanese. A single bomb was capable of destroying an entire city with the explosion creating a huge fireball, which, within a fraction of a second of the detonation, reached temperatures of over a million degrees at its epicentre. The explosion sucked all the air in from the surrounding area, creating a towering mushroom cloud. Meanwhile a blast wave raced outwards, destroying everything in its path for miles around. The destruction and the death toll were enormous, with tens of thousands of people killed and injured. The mutterings earlier by the guards, about a terrible weapon that had been deployed by the Americans in the north of Japan, now made sense, this being at Hiroshima only three days earlier where a similar scene of devastation had occurred.

Although they were unable to comprehend fully the event they had just witnessed, it was soon apparent to these men that the war was almost over as the Japanese guards disappeared quickly to escape the immediate area and to check on the fate of their families. The more able PoWs could now get out of the camp and forage in the villages nearby. Although the Japanese surrendered on 15 August 1945 it was not until 20 August 1945 that the PoWs were paraded and given the news they were anticipating that the war was over and they were free at last. Within a few days an American B-29 Superfortress flew low over the camps dropping leaflets confirming they were free, but informing them that it would take some time to liberate them but not to worry as food and clothing would be air-dropped to them.

Jimmy Mowatt and Willie Morrison had transferred from Taiwan in January 1945 and were at Camp 3 Sendai, near Tokyo, where the PoWs could see Mount Fuji, sacred to the Japanese. Jimmy had been working underground in the lead mine while Willie was working above ground casting ingots of lead. They had a feeling the war was coming close to ending and knew something was happening. One day a Japanese officer came up and spoke to the guards in Japanese, so they didn't know what was going on but were told to stop work and go back to the camp. Later that evening the lights came on, which was a surprise as there was normally a strict blackout since there had been a lot of American planes carrying out air raids in their area. There were rumours that the war was over and eventually, after a couple of days, they had to assemble and a Japanese officer announced 'The war is over and I hope you get back soon to your loved ones'. Soon after this all the Japanese left. One man was determined to get some revenge on the Japanese for the mistreatment he had had over the previous three years, but he never found any of the guards. The Americans dropped white sheets with instructions to lay them on the ground in a large white cross. They then dropped food and other items like tee-shirts, using this cross as their target. The air drops came in 40-gallon drum-like containers and some crashed through the roof of the camp. One man was on the roof and jumped off and broke his leg, and two others died. They were told not to overeat as they were not used to rich food but, unfortunately, some men ignored this advice and made themselves very ill.

The Japanese, who had made the surrender in 1942 the excuse for the mistreatment of the PoWs, could not bring themselves to admit they were now in that same position, with inevitable loss of face. The delay in breaking the news to the PoWs that the Japanese Empire had been crushed and the war was over was commonplace. In August 1945 Archie Black was with a group of PoWs who had left Saigon and was on a river barge, moored just north of Pnom Phen, Cambodia, being taken to Dien Phen Phu to work on another airfield. Local people passing by all appeared very cheerful and called out 'boom, boom, finish'. After a short time the barge turned about and started making its way back to Saigon. Nothing was said to the PoWs and they became very edgy about their situation and wondered whether the war was really over and if they should take a chance and try to overpower the guards, thinking there was little chance of the Japanese allowing them to survive and tell of the atrocities they had endured. They decided, however, to wait to see what happened. On reaching Saigon they were amazed to see that the city was no longer blacked out and French civilians called out to them from the riverbank, but they were still not sure if the war was over. When they disembarked, the guards were as belligerent as usual, slapping people for being slow or out of place which made them wonder further if there was some brutal reprisal in store for them. When they reached their barracks an armed guard with fixed bayonet was on duty at the gate as usual but they noticed that, strangely, the weapon slits in the adjacent bunkers were all closed with turfs. Distrustfully, they entered the narrow entrance in the barrack wall expecting the worst but, as soon as he entered, Archie was grabbed by an Australian who said. 'It's OK, the blue is over' and he had to repeat this several times before Archie could take it in.

Over the next few days the men began to exploit their new-found freedom and started to leave the camp and enter the town, often receiving the hospitality of the local French population, who had previously been unwilling to even acknowledge them for fear of reprisals. To their credit the British and Australian PoWs rarely took revenge on individual Japanese guards but one amusing incident involving Gordon Highlanders occurred in Saigon. One evening, on returning from the city, Archie and a group of friends found a British sergeant, entirely on his own and well under the influence of drink, presumably after an enjoyable evening with some hospitable French. He was inspecting the Japanese guard who were on duty at a large building. The guards with rifles and fixed bayonets were standing rigidly to attention as the sergeant, swaying from side to side, carried out his inspection and finding many faults was none too complimentary. Apparently this had all started when a guard had failed to salute him as he passed by, so he decided they needed smartening up a bit. Archie and his friends took the sergeant under control and dismissed the relieved guard but this served to underline the Japanese soldier's culture of blind obedience, even to former PoWs, as they accepted their new situation. Lord Louis Mountbatten, Supreme Allied Commander in South East Asia, a cousin of King George VI, realised that, after the Japanese surrender, it would take time to reach and liberate all the Allied PoWs but, in the meantime, they had to be looked after, ensuring that no harm came to any of them. He instructed that the Japanese Army would continue to keep their weapons until relieved by Allied forces and maintain order in the local area they were in at the time of surrender. The Japanese guard in Saigon had obviously been issued with this order, which was why they were so compliant.

Back in Thailand, in areas where there was closer contact with local people, some of the PoWs became increasingly confident that the war was coming to an end and, realising that the Thais were now more openly sympathetic to them and the Allies, decided to risk everything and take matters more into their own hands. On the night of 29 July 1945 Corporal Charlie Anderson (2876693), with Lance Bombardier D. McGee, of the Royal Artillery, escaped from a rest camp at Raheng by slipping past the Japanese guards. They intended making for the nearest Thai barracks and after walking for three hours they came across a Thai soldier who took them to his officer. After questioning they were given food and clothing. News of their escape became known and they received instructions from Major Bryce-Smith, a British Special Forces officer working undercover, to proceed to Nabod aerodrome, where they met the major and, a few days later, joined up with other PoWs on their way to Takki. Corporal John Donald (2876568) was also at Raheng and had already broken out of the camp several times and had been obtaining food and medical supplies from friendly local Thais for the sick PoWs in the camp. He made contact with a Thai major and intended to break out permanently on 4 August 1945 but the Japanese knew of other escapes and doubled the guard. He finally escaped on 13 August and linked up with other undercover British forces in the area.

In Sumatra Hugh McGurk, like many of his comrades in other areas, had to endure appalling conditions. An Australian NCO had managed to procure radio components from some Chinese who were friendly towards the PoWs and had built a radio receiver and they knew how the war was progressing. In the last few months of his imprisonment Hugh, along with five other men decided to escape by motor launch down the Musi River from Pelembang, They had helped to build this craft under the supervision of the Japanese, but their plans were foiled. When finally prepared to leave, having already amassed some stolen food and medical supplies, their leader (Leading Seaman W. Branny) discovered that the Japanese took the sparking plugs out of the motor launch every evening to disable it. This discovery was very fortunate for them as, if caught in the act of trying to steal the motor launch to escape, they would have faced certain death at the hands of their captors.

Escapes from PoW camps, even this late in the war, were exceptional as most PoW camps were remote from population centres with only limited contact with local people who could give the PoWs any clue that their ordeal might be at an end. Murray Melville, together with a number of other Gordons, was at Pratchai in August 1945. (Prachai or Prachinburi, located just north-east of Bangkok and known to many Gordons as the 'Tunnelling Camp'.) This camp, like many others in Thailand, had a large dry moat dug around the perimeter, six metres wide and five metres deep, with guard posts and machine guns at each corner. This place, more than many others, was certainly a place for the PoWs to feel nervous about their fate if there was any armed attempt to liberate them. Immediately adjacent to their camp an entire division of the Japanese Army was encamped. These soldiers had been driven out of Burma and were now preparing to hold this position to protect their newly-held territory of French Indochina. They employed the PoWs to dig bunkers, or tunnels, into the side of the adjacent hills to store ammunition and other supplies. On 17 August 1945, even though in reality the war had ended two days earlier, unknown to the PoWs, Murray and his fellow P0Ws were put to work as normal until 6.30p.m., when they were ordered back to the camp. On arrival, Murray couldn't believe his eyes as there was no guard on duty at the gate and a large group of PoWs was standing around laughing and talking. On seeing Murray and his group, they shouted 'it's all over, we're free'. Despite the apparent signs that the situation was as described, Murray, a Londoner, sat soberly that evening with a group of Gordon Aberdonians, naturally dour in nature, as all were a little sceptical about the sudden turn in events. They took their meal quietly, waiting for some more formal acknowledgement that the war and their three and a half year ordeal really was all over. It began to look as though they were right to be anxious when, around midnight, there was the rattle of machine-gun fire but then silence. In the morning it became known that some local Thai guerrillas had approached the camp and the guards fired at them. It was not only at Pratchai that the PoWs found the sudden capitulation of the Japanese hard to believe. At Ubon, Thailand, where Willie Niven and other Gordons were constructing a runway on another airstrip, Willie was in a bad way and knew he wouldn't survive much longer, having had malaria over twenty times and his stomach was swollen up with beri-beri. He also heard rumours of the Japanese surrender but only believed it when one day a truck stopped at the gate of the camp. An American officer got out and went to the earth mound used as a makeshift stage for camp entertainment, addressed everyone and announced the war was over. Strangely one of the first things he said was 'there is a Labour Government in power in Britain', which Willie didn't care about in the least although he was pleased to receive a gift of razors and cigarettes.

Over the next few days the Thai Army came to their aid and they were given better food and new clothing issued, all dropped onto a nearby airstrip. At the beginning of September arrangements had been made to fly them to Rangoon, Burma. They made this trip in Douglas Dakotas and, once on board, the men could truly believe they were free. For most this was the day they had dreamed of for three and a half years but for Sergeant Ernest Edwards (2876670) it was the worst possible. The RAF Dakota III of 117 Squadron, in which he took off, crashed en route from Bangkok to Rangoon and the crew of four and all of the twenty-four PoWs on board were killed. His body was never recovered and he is commemorated on the Singapore Memorial. For the others, however, Rangoon was luxury and they received proper medical care and a rice-free diet. A welcome letter from the Indian Red Cross and St John's War organisation was issued to all the PoWs welcoming them. This message was most apt and almost an apology by them for their impotence in the face of Japanese obstruction and failure to provide access. This read:

> At last the day has come. Three years of darkness and agony have passed and a new dawn is here, bringing with it deliverance for all from danger and anxiety, and for you above all freedom after bondage ...

Through these long years we have not forgotten you ... We of the Red Cross have tried every way of establishing contact and relieving your hardships. Some provisions have been sent and messages despatched; but we do not know how much has reached you, for the callous indifference of the enemy has made the task nigh impossible.

But now the enemy is beaten and you are free once more, we are doing all we can to give you the welcome you richly deserve and to make your homeward path a pleasant and joyful one ...

The journey home was determined by the state of each PoW's health and for most travel was by sea, via the Suez Canal, but Willie Niven, who was in a very poor state of health, went initially by aircraft carrier to Madras and on by train to Poona, from where he was flown home and was one of the first to arrive.

Charlie Bain (2876169) another who flew home at the same time, got on the last bus from Aberdeen to travel the fifteen miles to the village of Pitmedden, where he grew up but, with his overseas service with the Regiment and subsequent captivity, he hadn't been seen there for over eleven years. His mother had died before the Pacific War began and his father was elderly, so Charlie, not having heard from his family during his captivity, didn't know if his father was still alive. Charlie hadn't contacted his family when liberated. He had sent four postcards whilst a PoW in Thailand but none of these had made it home. His family now believed him to be dead, having had no news of him since he was posted missing in 1942. Arriving at a very late hour, he knocked on the door of his father's house but everyone was already in bed. His sister woke, alarmed that someone was calling so late, didn't care to open the door. She called out asking who it was knocking at the door when the house was in all in darkness. When the answer was 'Charlie' she retorted scornfully, 'Charlie who?', thinking someone was playing a trick on her and not even dreaming it could be her long-lost brother. When the surprise reply was 'Charlie from Singapore' she now became very angry at this apparent sick joke. With all the commotion, Mr Bain Senior awoke and went to investigate. He got the biggest surprise of his seventy years when he found his missing son on the doorstep. He had three sons and one of these had been captured in 1940, while with the Gordons at St Valéry en Caux, France. He had been a prisoner of the Germans for five years, and so their father was delighted to have them both home again safely.

George Brander's wife (Jean) also had no idea if her husband was dead or alive, having received no news of him since 1942, when she was told he was listed as a prisoner of war. In August 1945, when the war was over, she wrote a poignant letter to George telling him that she and their children were longing for his return and that his young son, George, had been expecting him to return every day after he had watched the fireworks display on VE Day in May 1945. Their hopes were, however, tragically dashed when they received a letter, in December 1945, confirming George had in fact died in Thailand on 31 May 1943.

Murray Melville's homeward journey started from Rangoon, aboard the SS *Orduna*. He was with a large number of Gordon Highlanders liberated from Thailand and Indochina. The Gordons who were in Singapore at the time of the Japanese surrender, like Andrew McIntosh who had returned there from Thailand, like all the survivors of the hellish torment as members of F Force, left for home on the SS *Monowai*. She docked at Liverpool on 11 October 1945, the first large contingent of Far East PoWs to arrive back in Britain. Andrew, who had been conscripted in 1940 and had wanted to join the

RAF with his two pals, was saddened to discover that neither of them had survived.

Peggy, the pedigree Staffordshire bull-terrier bitch and the Battalion's mascot with the PoWs in Thailand, gave birth to another litter of pups at Ubon PoW Camp in June 1945. After the Japanese surrender, when the men were to be flown to Rangoon, the RAF was not prepared to let the dogs travel. Major Reggie Lees stepped in and persuaded the RAF to look after the pups and let Peggy fly. Peggy was again barred by the Captain of the SS *Monowai*, but Reggie Lees once more worked his charm and she made it back to Liverpool. After her obligatory period in quarantine, she re-joined the Battalion at the Bridge of Don Barracks in Aberdeen. Peggy was awarded the same four medals as the men, the 1939–45 Star; the Pacific Star, the War Medal and Defence Medal, all of which are now in the Army Museum in London. She lived happily with the men at Gordon Barracks and Bill Kellas commented that he was sure that Peggy knew all the former Far East PoWs as she would come into their beds on cold nights in the barracks but never went to men who had not been in the Far East. The former FEPoWs delighted in playing a game with Peggy to impress non-FEPoWs. During a conversation they would say the word 'Nips', completely out of context, and to the amazement of the others, she would disappear. Peggy died on 9 July 1947 and was buried at Gordon Barracks. Reggie Lees erected a grey Aberdeen granite headstone in her honour. This was later moved to the gardens of the Gordon Highlanders' Museum and given pride of place, just inside the main entrance gate.

As with Peggy the authorities at Rangoon would not permit Donald the pet duck to travel. Corporal Willie Gray was undeterred so her wings, beak and legs were bound and she was smuggled aboard the SS *Corfu* inside Willie's kitbag. On their voyage back to the UK, Donald was discovered and after a short period, when she was again under the threat of being put into the pot. Willie pleaded for her to be spared and, as it was clear one duck could make little impact on the ship's dinner menu, the captain relented. As the SS *Corfu* left the warm latitudes, Donald started to feel the cold, so some of the men knitted a woollen pullover to keep her warm.

Eventually they arrived in Southampton, in early October 1945, and travelled home to Aberdeen by train, where Willie Gray was reunited with his family, which he had not seen for eight years. Willie's family lived at Forgue, near Huntly, Aberdeenshire, and a short time after his repatriation he travelled by bus the few miles to Aberchirder to visit relatives of Alexander Gibb, who had died in the Far East. Willie's own brother, Robert, had also died from wounds received during the battle for Singapore so he could empathise with the Gibbs in the loss of their son. Locals were surprised and delighted to see Willie getting off the bus with Donald waddling down the street after him. Later, Willie took Donald to the pub where they both had a glass of beer which Donald clearly loved as much as her master.

For the men in Japan and Taiwan their route home was rather different. They were generally taken to Manila in the Philippines, those from Japan passing through Okinawa. When the sick and emaciated PoWs boarded the ships in Manila some of the American sailors who were lining the decks in a welcome salute, fainted. The PoWs were generally given the option of some recuperation leave in Australia, America or Canada. Jimmy Mowatt was one of those who opted for Australia and spent some time in the town of Yass, New South Wales. Back in Britain he took up his hairdresser's business once more, which he ran successfully until he was over seventy years old. Eleven Gordons were evacuated from Taiwan on 6 September 1945 on the USS *Block Island* and taken first to Manila; others were onboard the destroyer USS *Brister* and the carrier USS *Santee*.

Aircraft carriers such as HMS *Glory* took them across the Pacific to Hawaii and on to San Francisco or Vancouver Island. They desperately needed to build up their strength prior to going back to the UK and Canadian and American families took these men to their hearts and some became lifelong friends. Canada had a large expatriate community and the Gordons received an especially warm welcome there. At the beginning of November the time to go home had arrived and the PoWs crossed the entire continent of North America from west to east by train, They converged on New York where some 4,500 PoWs boarded the RMS *Queen Mary*, the ship Bill Young had been so impressed with as he left the shores of Great Britain eight long years before. After a stormy crossing they docked in Southampton on 18 November 1945. Following a short stay in a transit camp they made their way by train to Aberdeen and home. Although most of the survivors made it home by the end of 1945 some others, such as Piper Hamish Johnston, spent quite a long time recovering in India and didn't make it back to Britain until February 1946. By an amazing coincidence his voyage home was aboard HMT *Somersetshire*, the ship on which the Battalion, which included Hamish, had sailed from Britain to Gibraltar in 1934, an episode that now felt like it had happened a hundred years before.

After the war some Gordons emigrated to Australia, the catalyst perhaps being that they had made lifelong friendships with Australian PoWs and a close bond had developed in the POW camps. Among these were Lieutenant Charles Gibson and Jimmy Hardie. Others, such as William 'Snuffy' Craig chose Canada and William John Bremner chose the United States, where they made new lives.

The Commanding Officer of the 2nd Battalion, Lieutenant Colonel Jack Stitt, was a prisoner in Thailand when the Japanese surrendered and, on his release, was anxious to recover the Battalion's property which had been put into safekeeping during the hostilities. On 10 February 1942, just before the capitulation, the Battalion silverware and Colours were lodged in the vaults of the Hong Kong and Shanghai Bank in Singapore. Under normal circumstances these would have been sent home to the UK for safekeeping, but the rapid advance of the Japanese had created the situation where this had not been possible. Jack Stitt sought and received permission to fly from Bangkok to Singapore to recover the Battalion's property and, miraculously, these items were found to be still intact when the British returned to the city on 2 September 1945. The Japanese had ransacked the bank but had obviously failed to recognise the value or significance of their find as they would certainly have taken them back to Japan as a war trophy or, at the very least, have displayed them in the museum they opened in Singapore to glorify their victory. The Colours came back safely to Britain aboard HMS *Nelson* and were returned to the Battalion.

After the war the majority of the PoWs were 'demobbed' and returned to civilian life. For those wartime conscripts, this was their expectation as they had not chosen an army life but had it thrust upon them through international circumstances. For many of the Regulars their seven years with the Colours was at an end and many had been away from Britain since 1934 and so were pleased their service was over and they could catch up with their families and settle down. Some still saw the Army as their vocation but not all were able to remain in it. The three and a half years of captivity, ravaged by various tropical diseases, malnutrition and mistreatment had taken their toll and many were no longer considered sufficiently fit for army service. Archie Black was one of the lucky ones. Although he was not considered fit enough to continue in the infantry he was allowed to transfer to the Royal Army Pay Corps and rose to the rank of major before retiring. Some, like brothers Charlie and Geordie Michie, stayed in the Gordons and had distinguished careers, both rising to the rank of major, before retiring. By a strange twist of fate, Charlie Michie returned to Singapore in the spring of 1954 when serving with the 1st Battalion Gordon Highlanders. He was billeted in Changi overlooking the very spot where he had spent his first few months of life as a prisoner of war. The Gordons' Commanding Officer for most of the time they were in Malaya, from 1950 to 1954, was Lieutenant Colonel Walter Duke, affectionately known by his men as 'Dukie', a fellow PoW. He was one of four of the Far East prisoners of war to go on to attain the rank of lieutenant colonel with the Regiment. The others were Reggie Lees, Moubray Burnett and George Elsmie. Lieutenant Jim Sandison, who had been a rubber planter before he was commissioned into the Gordon Highlanders while in Malaya in 1941, returned to that profession after the war and remained in Malaya, although he retired back to Scotland. The comradeship of the shared hardships produced lasting bonds of friendship. Hamish Johnston maintained his friendship with the Straits Settlements Force volunteer Paul Pancheri. Although Hamish lived in north-east Scotland and Paul in south-west England, Hamish was Paul's best man and piped for them when he was married in September 1946, and many years later Paul attended the celebrations for Hamish's daughter's wedding in 1970.

Bill Kellas, like a lot of men continuing to serve their country, went on to serve in the Military Police in Palestine. After leaving the army, he joined the staff of world famous River Dee Salmon Fishery Board, where he rose to become the superintendent. The River Dee flows through the Balmoral Estate where the Royal Family take their summer holiday, so, in a sense, he continued to serve the crown. Sandy Smart transferred into the Military Provost Staff Corps and effectively became a military prison officer and again served abroad in Germany and Egypt before retiring from the Army in 1956. Perhaps a close substitute for some, still wishing to retain the disciplined life but stay in 'civvy street', was the police force. Bill Young and Andrew McIntosh both had successful careers in this area. In other walks of life Captain, later Professor, Frank Pantridge went on to be eminent in the field of medicine, not only in his native Northern Ireland but gaining worldwide reputation. He became known as the 'father of emergency medicine' after he brilliantly invented the mobile defibrillator, a lifesaver for thousands of heart attack cases and now carried in virtually every ambulance worldwide. Murray Melville went on to practise law. Alistair Urquhart, after a successful career in business, published his memoirs to outstanding success which made him a bestselling author with his debut book. Jimmy Scott was appointed OBE for his contribution to the Royal British Legion and Norman Catto received a British Empire Medal for services to the North East Branch, Far East Prisoners of War Association. Alistair ('Madam') Paris, who did survive the sinking of the *Kachidoki Maru* in September 1944, was true to the vow he made to George McNab as they drifted apart on the South China Sea. He returned to his beloved Highland home in the Black Isle, Ross-shire, never to leave again, except once, when persuaded by George to attend a Gordon Highlanders' Far East Prisoner of War Reunion Dinner, in Aberdeen in the 1970s.

Unfortunately the mental scars, following their traumatic existence in captivity, resulted in some having psychological problems with recurring nightmares disturbing their sleep. Almost all of them had a feeling of isolation as they generally felt they couldn't talk about their experiences, not even to their wives or other close family, and so bottled it up. With their continuing health problems, many of the men died at a very young age as, even if they were able to cope with the mental aspects of their ordeal, their physical health was never good. Bill Hunter married in 1948 and with his wife, Rosina, brought up a large family but, after a lifetime of public service, both professionally and as a Lay Leader in the Catholic Church, he suffered massive heart attacks in his late fifties and died when only sixty-one. As a testament to the high regard in which he was held in his local community of East Kilbride, the parish church was packed at the reception of his remains and the Bishop of Motherwell presided at the solemn Requiem Mass along with twenty-one other priests. Many years after his death, Bill's son, Kevin, who had emigrated to Canada, was attending a concert in Toronto where the star was the popular Scottish Canadian singer John McDermott, also originally from Glasgow. He introduced one of his songs, entitled '*The Gift of Years*' by telling the story of his uncle, Mick Griffin (3322234) who had been a prisoner of war and forced to work on the Burma-Thailand railway. He told his audience that when on a long march his uncle and a friend came across a fellow Gordon Highlander, who turned out to be 'wee' Bill Hunter, lying exhausted by the roadside. The two of them helped Bill on to the next camp, where he was able to rest and recover. Unfortunately neither John McDermott's uncle nor his friend survived the war. Bill Hunter went on to raise a large family so their act of kindness resulted in a total of 750 years of new life for Bill and his offspring, hence the song title. Kevin Hunter was dumbstruck realising that the singer was talking about his father and how strange the coincidence that he was present, over 3,000 miles from home, listening to the story. At the intermission Kevin went backstage and introduced himself to John McDermott. At the start of the second half of the show, the singer asked for the lights to be brought up in the auditorium and introduced Kevin to the audience where he received a rousing reception.

The collective story of the men of the 2nd Battalion Gordon Highlanders is truly remarkable and so many seemingly ordinary men met the greatest of challenges and came through to lead meaningful lives and bring up families, which would help them forget. Their own country failed these men in so many ways, as when they eventually returned home the war, for most people, had been over for six months and they just wanted to move on and forget it. In this way they became the forgotten army and, seventy years on, with so few of these brave men still alive, it is a privilege to set the record straight and honour their courage. A few men were honoured for their brave services to their comrades while prisoners of war. These were Major Reggie Lees and Regimental Sergeant Major Alexander Milne (2869674) who were both appointed OBE. In addition, Captain George Moir Byres, Lieutenants Robert Fletcher, William de Meir, John Leckie and Derek Stewart, together with Sergeant Dick Pallant (2867720) and Private Edward Strachan (2876326) were Mentioned in Despatches. (Lieutenant Fletcher, a language teacher in civilian life before the war, had taught himself Japanese and was therefore a key man in the PoW camps in liaising with the Japanese authorities in the camps.)

For many their lives were cut dramatically short, dying in desperate conditions at the hands of an uncaring and malevolent enemy. For those brave young men who were caught up in the Pacific War and did not return, their mortal remains 'lie scattered on land and sea over almost the whole of South East Asia'. While many lie in well-tended war cemeteries in Thailand, Singapore, Burma, Indonesia and Japan, many others have no known grave. A great many were lost at sea and others lie in unmarked graves in the jungles of Malaya, Thailand, Burma and Borneo, their final resting places known only to God. These men are commemorated on the Singapore and Rangoon Memorials. In addition, a plaque, dedicated to the Regiment's fallen, was also erected in the Presbyterian Church, Orchard Road, Singapore, where a service of remembrance was held on 20 February 1949. (The Gordon Highlanders returned to Singapore in 1949 and on this occasion were involved in the successful campaign in dealing with the communist led insurgency.) The plaque was unveiled by General Sir Neil Ritchie KCB KBE DSO MC, Aide-de-Camp General to the King. A fitting tribute was paid to the men who had battled with their cruel and ruthless captors, displaying dignity, compassion and tenacity throughout. One of the hymns sung at this service was Hymn 223 with the appropriately worded verse five, which reads:

> Hunger and thirst are felt no more
> Nor suns with scorching ray;
> God is their sun, whose cheering beams
> Diffuse eternal day.

# Appendix

## The Men of the 2nd Battalion Gordon Highlanders

| Name | Photo | Number |
|---|---|---|
| **From** | | **Rank** |
| **Adams, George** | | 2876456 |
| Edinburgh | | Private |
| **Adamson, W E** | No Photo | 3318953 |
| Newcastle On Tyne | | Private |
| **Aitken, Alexander** | | 2876833 |
| Gartly, Aberdeenshire | | Private |
| **Aitken, George** | | 2876325 |
| Kineff, Kincardineshire | | Private |
| **Aitken, Victor** | | 2867159 |
| Balmedie, Aberdeenshire | | Lance Corporal |
| **Alexander, Norman** | | 2869663 |
| Aberdeen | | WO3 PQMS |
| **Alexander, William.** | | 2876167 |
| Ellon, Aberdeenshire | | Private |
| **Allan, David** | | 2876583 |
| Edinburgh | | Private |
| **Allan, James** | | 2876278 |
| Pitmedden, Aberdeenshire | | Private / Bandsman |
| **Allen, Mark** | | 2875307 |
| Sheffield, Yorkshire | | Corporal / Bandsman |
| **Anderson, McDonald** | No Photo | 2885220 |
| Elgin, Moray | | Private |
| **Anderson, Alex** | | 2876386 |
| Turriff, Aberdeenshire | | Private |

| Name | Photo | Number |
|---|---|---|
| **From** | | **Rank** |
| **Anderson, Charles** | | 2876693 |
| Motherwell, Lanarkshire | | Corporal |
| **Anderson, Douglas** | | 2876341 |
| Banchory, Aberdeenshire | | Private |
| **Anderson, Francis** | No Photo | 2879194 |
| London | | Private |
| **Anderson, Frederick** | | 2879163 |
| Edinburgh | | Private |
| **Anderson, George** | | 2877521 |
| Turriff, Aberdeenshire | | Private |
| **Anderson, George** | | 2878340 |
| Tarland, Aberdeenshire | | Private |
| **Anderson, Harry** | | 2880438 |
| Tarland, Aberdeenshire | | Lance Corporal |
| **Anderson, Harry Greig** | | 2877571 |
| Fordoun, Ellon, Aberdeenshire | | Private |
| **Anderson, Lewis** | | 2879103 |
| Farnborough, Hampshire | | Private |
| **Anderson, Robert** | | 2882177 |
| Whitehouse, Aberdeenshire | | Private |
| **Anderson, Walter** | | 2876356 |
| Aberdeen | | Sergeant |

| Name | Photo | Number |
|---|---|---|
| **From** | | **Rank** |
| **Andrews, Raymond** | No Photo | 2889835 |
| Tooting, London | | Private |
| **Angus, John** | | 2876378 |
| Fyvie, Aberdeenshire | | Private |
| **Angus, William** | | 2876168 |
| Crimond, Aberdeenshire | | Private |
| **Angus, William** | | 2876757 |
| Glass, Huntly, Aberdeenshire | | Lance Corporal |
| **Annand, Andrew (Jock)** | No Photo | 2874878 |
| Woodside, Aberdeen | | Private |
| **Armour, George** | | 2879048 |
| Dunfermline, Fife | | Private |
| **Arnold, George** | | 2876982 |
| Stafford | | Private |
| **Ashton, Reginald** | | 532828 |
| Bedford | | Band Master (WO1) |
| **Atkinson, Norman** | | 2876783 |
| Aberdeen | | Corporal |
| **Aylward, Patrick** | No Photo | 7598910 |
| Sittingbourne, Kent | | Private |
| **Baillie, George** | | 2876710 |
| Aberdeen | | Private |
| **Bain, Charles** | | 2876169 |
| Udny, Aberdeenshire | | Private |
| **Bain, James** | | 2874345 |
| Greenock | | Private |

| Name | Photo | Number |
|---|---|---|
| **From** | | **Rank** |
| **Bainbridge, George** | | 2875367 |
| Throckley, Newcastle on Tyne | | Sergeant / Bandsman |
| **Baird, William** | | 2876993 |
| unknown | | Private |
| **Barclay, James** | | 2877049 |
| Huntly, Aberdeenshire | | Private |
| **Barr, James** | No Photo | 2879494 |
| Glasgow | | Private |
| **Barrett, John** | No Photo | 2691344 |
| Clackmannan | | Private |
| **Barrie, James** | | 2889909 |
| Brechin, Angus | | Private |
| **Barrie, William** | | 2871865 |
| Edinburgh | | Sergeant (Local RQMS) |
| **Barron, James** | | 5437421 |
| Methlick, Aberdeenshire | | Private |
| **Barr-Sim, Albert Derek** | No Photo | 2889970 |
| London | | Private |
| **Baskett, George** | No Photo | 2876956 |
| Malvern, Worcester | | Private |
| **Baskett, James** | | 2879118 |
| Malvern, Worcester | | Private |
| **Beagley, George** | No Photo | 156794 |
| London | | 2nd Lieutenant |
| **Beange, Alexander** | | 2876170 |
| Glasslaw, Aberdeenshire | | Private |

| Name | Photo | Number |
|---|---|---|
| From | | Rank |
| Beddard, George | No Photo | 3322175 |
| Stoneferry, Hull, Yorkshire | | Private |
| Beedie, Alexander | | 2876277 |
| New Deer, Aberdeenshire | | Private |
| Beer, Henry Charles | No Photo | 2867590 |
| Aberdeen | | Lance Corporal |
| Bell, Andrew | | 2876858 |
| Stonehaven, Kincardineshire | | Private |
| Benge, Henry | No Photo | 4462670 |
| Penge, London | | Private |
| Bennett, James | | 2888226 |
| Bearsden, Dunbartonshire | | Lance Corporal |
| Benning, Alfred | No Photo | 2874866 |
| Woolwich, London | | Private |
| Bent, Percival | | 2865598 |
| Tonbridge Wells, Kent | | Sergeant / Bandsman |
| Bey, Norman | | 2879175 |
| Tarland, Aberdeenshire | | Private |
| Bird, Harry | No Photo | 2876974 |
| Bradford, Yorkshire | | Private |
| Birse, Robert | No Photo | 2880272 |
| Inverurie, Aberdeenshire | | Private |
| Bisset, Alexander | | 2879129 |
| Niagara Falls, Canada | | Private |
| Black, Archbald | | 2879290 |
| Newtonmearns, Renfrewshire | | Private |

| Name | Photo | Number |
|---|---|---|
| From | | Rank |
| Black, Frederick | | 2873923 |
| Aberdeen | | Lance Corporal |
| Black, George | | 836132 |
| Peterhead, Aberdeenshire | | Private |
| Black, William | | 2883081 |
| Aberdeen | | Private |
| Blackwood, Eric | No Photo | 222056 |
| Glasgow | | 2nd Lieutenant |
| Booth, Frank | No Photo | 3322177 |
| Huddersfield, Yorkshire | | Corporal |
| Boswall, Alexander | | 2876994 |
| Edinburgh | | Private |
| Bourne, Henry | No Photo | 3321650 |
| Ealing, London | | Private |
| Bowie, William | | 2875197 |
| Buckie, Banffshire | | Private |
| Bowley, Stanley | No Photo | 2889838 |
| Bledlow Ridge, Buckinghamshire | | Private |
| Boyes, Andrew | | 2876655 |
| Stirling | | Private |
| Braidwood, William | | 2884675 |
| Edinburgh | | Private |
| Brander, George | | 2868950 |
| Aberdeen | | Private |

169

| Name | Photo | Number |
|------|-------|--------|
| **From** | | **Rank** |
| **Bremner, George** | | 2867145 |
| Aberdeen | | Private |
| **Bremner, John Simpson** | | 2876172 |
| Rothienorman, Aberdeenshire | | Private |
| **Bremner, William** | | 2869632 |
| Aberdeen | | Private |
| **Bremner, William John** | | 2890085 |
| Aberdeen | | Private |
| **Brewster, William** | | 2873870 |
| Downpatrick, Co. Down | | CQMS |
| **Briers, Frederick** | No Photo | 3321837 |
| Haslemere, Surrey | | Private |
| **Brind, Frederick** | | 2890780 |
| Brentwood, Essex | | Boy (Pte) |
| **Brind, Patrick** | No Photo | 2890744 |
| Brentwood, Essex | | Private |
| **Brindle, Edwin** | No Photo | 2886157 |
| Walworth, London | | Private |
| **Brooke, Alfred** | No Photo | 2884708 |
| Barnsley, Yorkshire | | Private |
| **Brooks, James** | | 2876534 |
| Keith, Banffshire | | Private |
| **Brown, Cecil** | No Photo | 2878395 |
| Nigg, Aberdeen | | Private |
| **Brown, Henry** | No Photo | 2874894 |
| Glasgow | | Private |
| **Brown, John** | | 2876664 |
| Preston, Lancashire | | Lance Corporal |

| Name | Photo | Number |
|------|-------|--------|
| **From** | | **Rank** |
| **Brown, James** | | 2876379 |
| Montrose, Angus | | Sergeant |
| **Brown, Percy William** | | 2876136 |
| Aberdeen | | Sergeant |
| **Brown, Richard** | | 2876171 |
| Nigg, Aberdeen | | Corporal |
| **Brown, William** | | 2876375 |
| Fyvie, Aberdeenshire | | Private |
| **Brownlie, James** | No Photo | 2876766 |
| Wishaw, Lanarkshire | | Private |
| **Bruce, Charles** | No Photo | 2884655 |
| Holytown, Lanarkshire | | Private |
| **Bruce, Charles** | | 2876269 |
| Bridge of Don, Aberdeen | | Corporal |
| **Bruce, Frank** | | 2876310 |
| Oldmeldrum, Aberdeenshire | | Private |
| **Bruce, James** | No Photo | 2877915 |
| Ellon, Aberdeenshire | | Private |
| **Bruce, James Alexander** | No Photo | 2876430 |
| Dundee, Angus | | Private |
| **Bruce, John** | | 2876328 |
| Aberdeen | | Private |
| **Bruce, Lewis, Peter** | | 2881416 |
| Skene, Aberdeenshire | | Private |
| **Bruce, Robert** | No Photo | 2211039 |
| Elgin, Moray | | CSM (Local RSM) |

170

| Name | Photo | Number |
|---|---|---|
| From | | Rank |
| Buchan, Henry | | 2876281 |
| Forgue, Huntly, Aberdeenshire | | Lance Corporal |
| Buchan, James | | 2876426 |
| Longside, Peterhead | | Private |
| Buchan, John | No Photo | 2927429 |
| Haddington, East Lothian | | Private |
| Buchanan, Charles | No Photo | 3312672 |
| Glasgow | | Private |
| Burgess, Charles | | 2876258 |
| Keith, Banffshire | | Lance Corporal |
| Burness, Robert | | 2876701 |
| Hamilton, Lanarkshire | | Private |
| Burnett, Charles James Edward | | 2876389 |
| Turriff, Aberdeenshire | | Private |
| Burnett, James (Tibby) | No Photo | 2874727 |
| Turriff, Aberdeenshire | | Sergeant |
| Burnett, James | | 2876444 |
| Longside, Peterhead | | Private |
| Burnett, Kenneth Moubray | | 75693 |
| Oldmeldrum, Aberdeenshire | | Captain |
| Burns, William (Billy) | | 2881921 |
| Inverurie, Aberdeenshire | | Private |
| Burr, John, L. M | No Photo | 2885019 |
| Aberdeen | | Private |
| Butterfield, Arthur | | 2876898 |
| Shildon, County Durham | | Private |

| Name | Photo | Number |
|---|---|---|
| From | | Rank |
| Byrne, Clemont | | 2875441 |
| Ballykinlar, Co. Down | | Lance Sergeant / Bandsman |
| Byrne, Horace | No Photo | 2874232 |
| Ballykinlar, Co. Down | | Sergeant |
| Cain, George | No Photo | 2884658 |
| Hamilton, Lanarkshire | | Lance Corporal |
| Calder, William | | 2872624 |
| Lumphanan, Aberdeenshire | | Company Quartermaster Sergeant |
| Callum, Joshua | No Photo | 3322353 |
| Sunderland, Co. Durham | | Lance Corporal |
| Cameron, Andrew | | 2877108 |
| Braemar, Aberdeenshire | | Sergeant |
| Cameron, John | | 2876892 |
| Edinburgh | | Private |
| Campbell, Alexander | | 2876474 |
| Strathdon, Aberdeenshire | | Private |
| Campbell, Daniel | | 2876576 |
| Coatbridge, Lanarkshire | | Private |
| Campbell, Duncan | No Photo | 152309 |
| Stonehaven, Kincardineshire | | 2nd Lieutenant |
| Campbell, Gordon | No Photo | 2876951 |
| Worcester | | Lance Corporal |
| Campbell, Henry | No Photo | 2879498 |
| Port Dundas, Glasgow | | Private |
| Campbell, Hugh | No Photo | 2885865 |
| Kirkintilloch, Dunbartonshire | | Private |

171

| Name | Photo | Number |
|---|---|---|
| From | | Rank |
| Campbell, John (Jock) | | 2884170 |
| Portsoy, Banffshire | | Private |
| Campbell, Robert | No Photo | 2889830 |
| Oxshott, Surrey | | Private |
| Campbell, William | No Photo | 4386554 |
| North England (no details | | Private |
| Campbell, William | No Photo | 2876678 |
| Inverness | | Corporal |
| Campleman, Henry | | 2874252 |
| Glasgow | | Corporal / Bandsman |
| Carle, James | | 2876334 |
| St Fergus, Peterhead | | Private |
| Carr, William | | 830999 |
| Peterhead, Aberdeenshire | | Private |
| Carrick, Thomas | No Photo | 3322354 |
| Darlington, Co. Durham | | Private |
| Carrol, Francis | | 3050201 |
| Edinburgh | | Sergeant A/CQMS (Bandsman) |
| Carrol, James | No Photo | 2878396 |
| Tamnavoulin, Banffshire | | Private |
| Carroll, Edward | No Photo | 2873840 |
| Stone, Staffordshire | | Private |
| Cass, Thomas | | 3184402 |
| unknown | | Private |
| Casserly, John | No Photo | 3322148 |
| Glasgow | | Private |
| Cassie, Angus | | 2878447 |
| New Pitsligo, Aberdeenshire | | Private |

| Name | Photo | Number |
|---|---|---|
| From | | Rank |
| Cassie, Webster | | 2876268 |
| Maud, Aberdeenshire | | Lance Corporal |
| Catto, Norman | | 2875594 |
| Aberdeen | | Sergeant |
| Caulfield, Bryne | | 2876865 |
| Aberdeen | | Private |
| Caulfield, Hugh (Sandy) | | 2873600 |
| Aberdeen | | Private (Bandsman) |
| Chalmers, Harry | | 2876941 |
| Banff, Banffshire | | Private |
| Chalmers, James | No Photo | 2877937 |
| Cruden Bay, Aberdeenshire | | Lance Corporal |
| Chalmers, James Smith | | 2876387 |
| Banff, Banffshire | | Lance Corporal |
| Chalmers, John (Jackie) | | 2876628 |
| Methlick, Aberdeenshire | | Private |
| Chalmers, William | | 1664943 |
| Aberdeen | | Lance Corporal |
| Chapman, James | | 2876525 |
| Unknown | | Private |
| Charles, Edward | | 2876613 |
| Aberdeen | | Private |
| Charles, Thomas | | 2876549 |
| Dalkeith, Midlothian | | Private |

172

| Name | Photo | Number |
|---|---|---|
| From | | Rank |
| Charles, Walter | | 2876840 |
| Edinburgh | | Private |
| Chase, Frank | | 2879111 |
| Portsmouth, Hampshire | | Private |
| Chaytor, Robert | No Photo | 108208 |
| Thirsk, Yorkshire | | Lieutenant |
| Cheyne, James | | 2885047 |
| Fraserburgh, Aberdeenshire | | Private |
| Cheyne, William | | 2876439 |
| Maud, Aberdeenshire | | Private |
| Chisholm, James | | 2877911 |
| Portsoy, Banffshire | | Private |
| Christie, Alexander | | 836547 |
| Fraserburgh, Aberdeenshire | | Private |
| Christie, David | | 2875943 |
| Aboyne, Aberdeenshire | | Private |
| Christie, Donald | | 2876296 |
| Lumphanan, Aberdeenshire | | Sergeant |
| Christie, George | | 2876346 |
| Dyce, Aberdeen | | Private |
| Christie, John | No Photo | 2875173 |
| Oldmeldrum, Aberdeenshire | | Private |
| Christie, William | | 2876314 |
| Aberdeen | | Lance Corporal |

| Name | Photo | Number |
|---|---|---|
| From | | Rank |
| Christie, William | | 2876282 |
| Lumphanan, Aberdeenshire | | Private |
| Clark, Alfred | | 2878440 |
| Fraserburgh, Aberdeenshire | | Private |
| Clark, George | No Photo | 2889843 |
| Lancing, Sussex | | Private |
| Clarke, Edward | No Photo | 2889362 |
| London | | Private |
| Clayton, Joseph | No Photo | 2876767 |
| Wishaw, Lanarkshire | | Private |
| Close, Allan | No Photo | 56434 |
| Stroud, Gloucestershire | | Captain |
| Clyne, David | | 2876454 |
| Stonehaven, Kincardineshire | | Private |
| Clyne, George | | 2878924 |
| Aberdeen | | Private |
| Cobban, Anthony | | 2876073 |
| Rhynie, Aberdeenshire | | Sergeant |
| Cobban, James | No Photo | 834167 |
| Macduff, Banffshire | | Private |
| Cochrane, Horace | No Photo | 776389 |
| Portsmouth, Hampshire | | Private |
| Cockie, Edward | | 2877266 |
| Lumphanan, Aberdeenshire | | Lance Corporal |
| Codd, James | No Photo | 2889844 |
| Bletchingly, Surrey | | Private |

173

| Name | Photo | Number |
|---|---|---|
| From | | Rank |
| Colley, Joseph | | 2879020 |
| Campsall, Doncaster, Yorkshire | | Private |
| Collie, Angus | | 2874524 |
| Kingussie, Inverness-shire | | Company Sergeant-Major |
| Collie, William | | 2869600 |
| Laurencekirk, Kincardineshire | No Photo | Private |
| Collings, George | | 3383637 |
| Burnley, Lancashire | No Photo | Corporal |
| Collins, Francis | | 2876420 |
| Unknown | | Sergeant |
| Collins, Norman | | 2876165 |
| Edinburgh | | Lance Corporal |
| Constable, Charles | | 2885805 |
| Aberdeen | | Private |
| Cooney, Alfred | | 7604982 |
| Ayr, Ayrshire | No Photo | Private |
| Cooper, Alexander | | 2876954 |
| Aberdeen | | Private |
| Cooper, John | | 2877306 |
| Fintray, Aberdeenshire | | Private |
| Cooper, Roy | | 2876517 |
| Dyce, Aberdeen | | Private |
| Copeland, Andrew | | 3318883 |
| Ayr, Ayrshire | No Photo | Private |
| Coutts, Alexander Cran | | 2876175 |
| Unknown | | Sergeant |

| Name | Photo | Number |
|---|---|---|
| From | | Rank |
| Coutts, Wilfred | | 2876687 |
| Nigg, Aberdeen | | Private |
| Coutts, William | No Photo | 2871271 |
| Aberdeen | | Sergeant |
| Cowie, Alexander | No Photo | 2875884 |
| Udny, Aberdeenshire | | Private |
| Cowie, Arthur | | 2876224 |
| Buckhurst Hill, Sussex | | Private (Bandsman) |
| Cowie, John George | | 2879101 |
| Buckie, Banffshire | | Private |
| Craib, Robert | | 2875942 |
| Cruden Bay, Aberdeenshire | | Private |
| Craig, William (Snuffy) | | 2876114 |
| Glasgow | | Private |
| Craigie, William | | 2879160 |
| Dundee | | Corporal |
| Crichton, Gordon | | 2876005 |
| Colchester, Essex | | Private |
| Crookshanks, John Ralph | | 2877424 |
| Aberdeen | | Private (Bandsman) |
| Cruickshank, Sydney | | 2876861 |
| Fetteresso, Kincardine | | Corporal |
| Cruickshank, George | | 2876399 |
| Peterhead, Aberdeenshire | | Private |
| Cullinane, James | No Photo | 2876333 |
| Not Known | | Lance Corporal |

174

| Name | Photo | Number |
|---|---|---|
| From | | Rank |
| Cumming, John | | 2877358 |
| Cornhill, Banffshire | | Private |
| Cumming, Thomas | | 2876795 |
| Inverkeilor, Angus | | Private |
| Cunningham, George | No Photo | 102988 |
| Not Known | | Lieutenant |
| Cuthbert, Hugh | | 2873121 |
| London | | Sergeant (Bandsman) |
| Darby, John | | 2876431 |
| Caversham, Reading | | Private (Bandsman) |
| Daverson, Albert Bristow | No Photo | 2883702 |
| Brighton, Sussex | | Private |
| Davidson, George | No Photo | 2872560 |
| Kilsyth, Stirlingshire | | Sergeant |
| Davidson, George | | 2875319 |
| Aberdeen | | Private |
| Davidson, George (Doddie) | | 2876575 |
| Fraserburgh, Aberdeenshire | | Private |
| Davidson, Peter | | 2876634 |
| Aberdeen | | Private |
| Davidson, Robert | | 2876649 |
| Auchinblae, Kincardineshire | | Private |
| Davidson, Theodore | | 2876455 |
| Aberdeen | | Corporal Bandsman |
| Davidson, William | | 2875673 |
| Insch, Aberdeenshire | | Lance Sergeant |

| Name | Photo | Number |
|---|---|---|
| From | | Rank |
| Davison, Robert | No Photo | 3322427 |
| Amble, Northumberland | | Private |
| Dawson, Alexander | No Photo | 2876408 |
| Cairnie, Aberdeenshire | | Sergeant |
| Dawson, James | | 2875907 |
| Unknown | | Private |
| Dawson, William | No Photo | 2875944 |
| Unknown | | Lance Corporal |
| Day, Edward | No Photo | 2889847 |
| KentishTown, London | | Private |
| Day, Ernest | No Photo | 2889848 |
| Rochester, Kent | | Private |
| de Meir, Guillermo ("Mo") | No Photo | 129023 |
| Insch, Aberdeenshire | | 2nd Lieutenant |
| Denne, Victor | | 20249 |
| Littlehampton, Sussex | | Major |
| Depo, David | | 836369 |
| Rothesay, Bute | | Private |
| Devine, James (Hamish) | No Photo | 2888242 |
| Greenock, Renfrewshire | | Lance Corporal |
| Dick, Alfred | | 2875875 |
| Woodside, Aberdeen | | Lance Corporal |
| Dickie, David | No Photo | 2876359 |
| Edyal, Forfarshire | | Private |
| Dickson, Frederick (Teddy) | | 857642 |
| Edinburgh | | Private |

175

| Name | Photo | Number |
|------|-------|--------|
| **From** | | **Rank** |
| **Dickson, Robert** | | 2876593 |
| Leuchers, Fife | | Private |
| **Dickson, Thomas** | No Photo | 2885780 |
| Glasgow | | Private |
| **Dingwall, Alexander** | | 827117 |
| Edinburgh | | Private |
| **Dobbins, James** | | 2876834 |
| Unknown | | Private |
| **Docherty, James** | | 2885195 |
| Waterloo, Lanarkshire | | Private |
| **Donald, Ian** | | 2876894 |
| Coalburn, Lanarkshire | | Private |
| **Donald, John** | | 2876568 |
| Edinburgh | | Corporal |
| **Donald, William** | | 2875354 |
| Kemnay, Aberdeenshire | | Lance Corporal |
| **Dougan, Michael** | | 2885055 |
| New Mains, Lanarkshire | | Private |
| **Drummond, James** | | 2876654 |
| Stonehaven, Kincardineshire | | Private |
| **Drummond, William** | | 2876728 |
| Whiterashes, Aberdeenshire | | Private |
| **Dryden, David** | No Photo | 2867319 |
| Edinburgh | | Lance Corporal |

| Name | Photo | Number |
|------|-------|--------|
| **From** | | **Rank** |
| **Duffy, John** | | 2879008 |
| Edinburgh | | Private |
| **Duguid, George** | | 2880677 |
| Rothiemay, Aberdeenshire | | Private |
| **Duke, Walter** | | 39441 |
| Lockerbie, Dumfries-shire | | Major |
| **Duncan, Albert** | | 2876856 |
| Bellhaven, Dunbar | | Private |
| **Duncan, Alexander** | No Photo | 2871017 |
| Unknown | | Private |
| **Duncan, James** | | 2876736 |
| Newmachar, Aberdeenshire | | Private |
| **Duncan, James** | | 2878268 |
| Ballater, Aberdeenshire | | Private |
| **Duncan, John** | | 841047 |
| Keith, Banffshire | | Private |
| **Duncan, Thomas** | | 2872737 |
| Aberdeen | | Private |
| **Duncan, William** | | 2876453 |
| Montrose, Angus | | Private |
| **Durno, Alexander (Sandy)** | | 2876738 |
| Kinellar, Aberdeenshire | | Private |
| **Durward, William** | | 2876339 |
| Glenbervie, Kincardineshire | | Private |

176

| Name | Photo | Number |
|------|-------|--------|
| From | | Rank |
| **Duthie, Robert** | | 2876457 |
| Keith, Banffshire | | Sergeant |
| **Edwards, Ernest** | No Photo | 2876670 |
| Blackburn, Lancashire. | | Lance Sergeant |
| **Elder, Allan** | | 2876877 |
| Inverbervie, Kincardineshire | | Private |
| **Elder, Henry** | | 2876671 |
| Inverbervie, Kincardineshire | | Private |
| **Elliot, George** | | 406004 |
| Dalkeith, Midlothian | | Corporal |
| **Elliot, Kenneth** | No Photo | 2875364 |
| Exeter, Devon | | Private |
| **Ellis, Gordon** | | 2876077 |
| Catterline, Kincardineshire | | Corporal |
| **Ellis, Ian Bartlett** | | 2876259 |
| Catterline, Kincardineshire | | Lance Sergeant |
| **Elsey, Herbert** | No Photo | 3320260 |
| Huddersfield, Yorkshire | | Lance Corporal |
| **Elsmie, George** | | 67200 |
| Unknown | | Captain |
| **Emmett, John** | | 2877060 |
| Edinburgh | | Lance Corporal |
| **English, Charles** | | 2876675 |
| Peterhead, Aberdeenshire | | Private |
| **Entwhistle, Richard** | No Photo | 2879489 |
| Edinburgh | | Private |

| Name | Photo | Number |
|------|-------|--------|
| From | | Rank |
| **Esslemont, John** | | 2877448 |
| Aberdeen | | Private |
| **Ewen, James** | | 2870233 |
| Fettercairn, Kincardineshire | | Lance Sergeant |
| **Ewen, William** | | 2876778 |
| Tarland, Aberdeenshire | | Private |
| **Falconer, Lewis** | No Photo | 2875796 |
| Cullen, Banffshire | | Private |
| **Fallon, Patrick** | | 2876590 |
| Glasgow | | Private |
| **Farquhar, Alexander** | | 2879177 |
| Keith, Banffshire | | Private |
| **Farquhar, Charles** | | 2875263 |
| Buckie, Banffshire | | Private |
| **Farquhar, George** | | 2876368 |
| Cullen, Banffshire | | Private |
| **Farquhar, Ludovic Gordon** | No Photo | 49380 |
| London | | Captain |
| **Ferguson, Alexander** | No Photo | 2883876 |
| Hareleeshill, Lanarkshire | | Lance Corporal |
| **Ferguson, William Hogg** | No Photo | 176943 |
| Taunton, Somerset | | 2nd Lieutenant |
| **Fettes, Richard** | | 2876147 |
| Huntly, Aberdeenshire | | Private |

| Name | Photo | Number |
|---|---|---|
| **From** | | **Rank** |
| **Findlay, Alexander** | | 2876295 |
| Turriff, Aberdeenshire | | Private |
| **Findlay, David** | No Photo | 2874531 |
| Swindon, Wiltshire | | Private |
| **Findlay, Donald** | | 2876342 |
| Banchory, Kincardineshire | | Private |
| **Findlay, James** | No Photo | 2877001 |
| Newburgh, Fife | | Lance Corporal |
| **Finnie, Robert** | | 2876182 |
| Aberchirder, Banffshire | | Private |
| **Fletcher, Robert** | No Photo | 176944 |
| Aberdeen | | 2nd Lieutenant |
| **Flett, David** | | 2889999 |
| Findochty, Banffshire | | Private |
| **Forbes, Edward** | | 2876931 |
| Bathgate, Lanarkshire | | Private (Bandsman) |
| **Forbes, James** | No Photo | 2876466 |
| Aberdeen | | Private |
| **Forbes, James** | No Photo | 2884562 |
| Cambuslang, Lanarkshire | | Private |
| **Forbes, Robert** | | 2889044 |
| Forres, Moray | | Private |
| **Forrest, Norman** | | 2876409 |
| Kemnay, Aberdeenshire | | Corporal |
| **Forsyth, Albert** | No Photo | 2876402 |
| Huntly Aberdeenshire | | Corporal |

| Name | Photo | Number |
|---|---|---|
| **From** | | **Rank** |
| **Forsyth, Simon** | | 2876183 |
| Mintlaw, Aberdeenshire | | Private |
| **Foster, William** | | 2732988 |
| Fauldhouse, West Lothian | | Lance Corporal |
| **Fraser, Donald** | No Photo | 2888706 |
| Edinburgh | | Private |
| **Fraser, Gordon** | | 2876635 |
| Huntly Aberdeenshire | | Corporal |
| **Fraser, Henry** | No Photo | 2876343 |
| Wartle, Aberdeenshire | | Sergeant |
| **Fraser, Lawrence** | | 2878251 |
| Aberdeen | | Lance Corporal |
| **Fraser, Samuel** | | 2876545 |
| Aberdeen | | Private (Drummer) |
| **Fraser, Stanley** | | 2876424 |
| Aberdeen | | Private |
| **Fraser, William** | No Photo | 2876506 |
| Methlick, Aberdeenshire | | Private |
| **French, Douglas** | | 2876286 |
| Findochty, Banffshire | | Private |
| **French, Walter** | | 2819143 |
| Findochty, Banffshire | | Private |
| **Friel, Edward** | No Photo | 2883879 |
| Bellshill, Lanarkshire | | Private |
| **Frisken, James** | No Photo | 2884681 |
| Unknown | | Private |

| Name | Photo | Number |
|---|---|---|
| **From** | | **Rank** |
| **Fuller, Malcolm** | No Photo | 102549 |
| Chelmsford, Essex | | Captain |
| **Fyffe, Donald** | | 2876773 |
| Aberdeen | | Private |
| **Gallacher, David** | | 2876625 |
| Linlithgow, West Lothian | | Private |
| **Gallacher, Edward** | | 2876550 |
| Glasgow | | Private |
| **Gallacher, Hugh** | | 2876873 |
| Wishaw, Lanarkshire | | Private |
| **Gammack, Charles** | | 2876414 |
| St Fergus, Aberdeenshire | | Private |
| **Gammack, James** | No Photo | 2875520 |
| Unknown | | Private |
| **Gardner, Lewis** | | 3054708 |
| Edinburgh | | Lance Corporal |
| **Gauld, Magnus** | | 2878266 |
| Portsoy, Banffshire | | Private |
| **Gent, John** | No Photo | 7589642 |
| Chorley, Lanarkshire | | Sergeant (RAOC) |
| **Gerrard, William** | | 2876650 |
| Belhelvie, Aberdeenshire | | Private (Piper) |
| **Gibb, Alexander** | | 2875351 |
| Aberchirder, Aberdeenshire | | Private |
| **Gibb, Charles** | | 2876265 |
| Dyce, Aberdeen | | Private |

| Name | Photo | Number |
|---|---|---|
| **From** | | **Rank** |
| **Gibb, John** | | 2874771 |
| Oyne, Aberdeenshire | | Private |
| **Gibb, Kenneth** | | 2876221 |
| Elgin, Moray | | Sergeant |
| **Gibbs, Robert** | No Photo | 2880946 |
| Croydon, Surry | | Private |
| **Gibson, Adam** | No Photo | 2879291 |
| Edinburgh | | Private |
| **Gibson, Charles** | | 103908 |
| Aberdeen | | Lieutenant |
| **Gibson, Ernest** | No Photo | 2881414 |
| Ellon, Aberdeenshire | | Lance Corporal |
| **Gibson, Peter** | No Photo | 2885059 |
| Coalburn, Lanarkshire | | Corporal |
| **Gibson, William Henry** | No Photo | 2871179 |
| Belvedere, Kent | | Private |
| **Gifford, Harold** | | 2876841 |
| Leeds, Yorkshire | | Private |
| **Gilbert, Arthur** | | 2880737 |
| Skene, Aberdeenshire | | Corporal |
| **Gilbert, Robert** | | 2885227 |
| Kemnay, Aberdeenshire | | Lance Corporal |
| **Glennie, Peter** | | 2876184 |
| Newburgh, Aberdeenshire | | Private |
| **Goodall, Harry** | No Photo | 852599 |
| Huntly, Aberdeenshire | | Private |

179

| Name | Photo | Number |
|---|---|---|
| From | | Rank |
| Goodfellow, Adam | | 2876943 |
| Banff, Banffshire | | Private |
| Goodlad, William | | 2876581 |
| Lerwick, Shetland | | Private |
| Gordon, Alexander | | 2876735 |
| Montrose, Angus | | Private |
| Gordon, Charles | | 2870612 |
| Aberdeen | | Lance Corporal |
| Gordon, George | No Photo | 2876400 |
| Rhynie, Aberdeenshire | | Private |
| Gordon, James | | 2876032 |
| Aberdeen | | Corporal |
| Gordon, Noel | No Photo | 71205 |
| Bearsden, Glasgow | | Captain |
| Gordon, Ronald | No Photo | 2879187 |
| Montrose, Angus | | Lance Corporal |
| Gowling, Albert | | 3055031 |
| Edinburgh | | Private |
| Graham, Alexander | No Photo | 2889054 |
| Grangemouth, Stirlingshire | | Private |
| Graham, William | | 1557 |
| London | | Lieutenant Colonel |
| Grainger, John Herdman | No Photo | 3322328 |
| Chopwell, Co.Durham | | Private |
| Grant, Alexander (Sandy) | | 2876355 |
| Turriff, Aberdeenshire | | Private (Bandsman) |

| Name | Photo | Number |
|---|---|---|
| From | | Rank |
| Grant, Anton Kray | | 2879039 |
| Kininmonth, Aberdeenshire | | Private |
| Grant, Charles | No Photo | 2876245 |
| Keith, Banffshire | | Lance Corporal |
| Grant, G. Gray | | 94145 |
| Glendronach, By Huntly, Aberdeenshire | | Captain |
| Grant, James | | 2876752 |
| Mintlaw, Aberdeenshire | | Corporal |
| Grant, John | | 2877242 |
| Aboyne, Aberdeenshire | | Private |
| Grant, John James | | 2818900 |
| Archiestown, Moray | | Private |
| Grant, Robert | | 2876872 |
| Aberdeen | | Private |
| Grassick, Forbes | | 2876779 |
| Aberdeen | | Private |
| Gray, George John | | 2876367 |
| Bridge of Marnoch, Aberdeenshire | | Corporal |
| Gray, George Simpson | | 2876287 |
| Macduff, Banffshire | | Private |
| Gray, James | | 2876322 |
| Aberdeen | | Private |
| Gray, Robert | | 2876275 |
| Forgue, Huntly, Aberdeenshire | | Corporal |

180

| Name | Photo | Number |
|------|-------|--------|
| From | | Rank |
| Gray, William | | 2875816 |
| Boyndie, Banffshire | | Private |
| Gray, William Scott | | 2876971 |
| Forgue, Huntly, Aberdeenshire | | Corporal |
| Greenlaw, William | | 2876942 |
| Macduff, Banffshire | | Private |
| Greeves, Harold | | 2865694 |
| Birmingham | | Company Quartermaster Sergeant |
| Greig, Alan | | 2881322 |
| Keith, Banffshire | | Private |
| Grieve, James | | 2876720 |
| Aberdeen | | Private |
| Grieve, John | No Photo | 2877176 |
| Unknown | | Private |
| Grieve, Sydney | No Photo | 2876495 |
| Echt, Aberdeenshire | | Private |
| Griffin, Michael | No Photo | 3322234 |
| Glasgow | | Private |
| Grubb, Charles | | 2876989 |
| Kirkcaldy, Fife | | Private |
| Gunn, William | | 2876095 |
| Aberdeen | | Private |
| Hall, George | | 2876508 |
| Keith, Banffshire | | Private |

| Name | Photo | Number |
|------|-------|--------|
| From | | Rank |
| Hall, Norman | | 2876353 |
| Monymusk, Aberdeenshire | | Private |
| Hall, Robert Arthur | | 2876304 |
| Brae, Shetland | | Private |
| Hallowes, Geoffrey | | 132514 |
| London | | 2nd Lieutenant |
| Hamilton, Ian | | 2876876 |
| Weymouth, Dorset | | Corporal |
| Hamilton, Thomas | | 2876694 |
| Motherwell, Lanarkshire | | Corporal |
| Hannan, Thomas | No Photo | 2979040 |
| Airdrie, Lanarkshire | | Private |
| Hardie, James | | 2878862 |
| Banchory, Aberdeenshire | | Private |
| Harper, Thomas | No Photo | 2883893 |
| Airdrie, Lanarkshire | | Private |
| Harrold, James | | 2876332 |
| Lhanbryde, Moray | | Corporal |
| Harter, Michael | | 66174 |
| Cirencester, Gloucestershire | | Captain |
| Harvey, Samuel | | 2875041 |
| Hillsborough, N.Ireland | | Corporal Bandsman |
| Hastie, John | | 2875531 |
| Cruden Bay, Aberdeenshire | | Private |

181

| Name | Photo | Number |
|---|---|---|
| **From** | | **Rank** |
| Hay, James | | 2876237 |
| Dunlugas, Banffshire | | Private |
| Hay, Thomas | No Photo | 3318991 |
| Newcastle Upon Tyne | | Private |
| **Haynes, Stafford** | | 2876827 |
| Blackpool, Lancashire | | Lance Corporal (Bandsman) |
| Henderson, Alexander | No Photo | 2878086 |
| Wartle, Aberdeenshire | | Private |
| Henderson, Douglas | No Photo | 2875951 |
| Fordoun, Kincardineshire | | Private |
| **Henderson, James** | No Photo | 2876961 |
| Glasgow | | Private |
| **Henderson, Jonathan** | | 2876372 |
| Huntly, Aberdeenshire | | Private |
| **Henderson, Robert** | | 64642 |
| Unknown | | Captain |
| **Henderson, Robert** | No Photo | 2877793 |
| Leith, Midlothian | | Private |
| Henry, John | No Photo | 2878625 |
| Auchnagatt, Aberdeenshire | | Sergeant |
| **Hepburn, Alexander** | | 2876384 |
| Auchterless, Aberdeenshire | | Private |
| **Hepburn, Alexander** | | 2876532 |
| Fauldhouse, West Lothian | | Corporal |
| **Hepburn, Archibald** | | 2875872 |
| Pitmedden, Aberdeenshire | | Sergeant |

| Name | Photo | Number |
|---|---|---|
| **From** | | **Rank** |
| **Hepburn, Douglas** | No Photo | 2876059 |
| Unknown | | Sergeant |
| **Hepburn, Jonathan** | No Photo | 2878244 |
| Aberdeen | | Private |
| **Hill, William** | | 2876410 |
| Ythanbank, Schivas | | Private |
| **Hillock, William** | No Photo | 2040682 |
| Motherwell, Lanarkshire | | Lance Corporal |
| **Holden, Robert** | | 2879104 |
| Edinburgh | | Private |
| **Hope, Andrew** | | 3056316 |
| Edinburgh | | Private |
| **Hopkins, James** | No Photo | 2883527 |
| Coalburn, Lanarkshire | | Private |
| Horne, Alexander | | 2077856 |
| Aberdeen | | Private |
| **Horne, David** | No Photo | 2882957 |
| Glasgow | | Private |
| **Houghton, Walter** | | 2876838 |
| Brentwood, Essex | | Private (Bandsman) |
| **Howatt, James** | | 2876158 |
| Fraserburgh, Aberdeenshire | | Corporal |
| **Howie, Charles Bain** | | 2876363 |
| Lonmay, Aberdeenshire | | Private |
| **Hughes, Patrick** | No Photo | 2883941 |
| Eddlewood, Lanarkshire | | Private |

182

| Name | Photo | Number |
|---|---|---|
| **From** | | Rank |
| **Hume, Andrew** | | 2875538 |
| Durham, Co. Durham | | Corporal |
| **Hume, Archibald** | | 3244946 |
| Motherwell, Lanarkshire | | Private |
| **Hunter, Thomas** | | 2876313 |
| Ellon, Aberdeenshire | | Corporal |
| **Hunter, William Brown** | | 2876881 |
| Lanark, Lanarkshire | | Private |
| **Hunter, William Dunlop** | | 3318210 |
| Glasgow | | Private |
| **Hutchieson, James** | No Photo | 156799 |
| Amersham, Bucks. | | 2nd Lieutenant |
| **Hutchison, Ronald** | No Photo | 2889828 |
| Tidworth, Surrey | | Lance Corporal |
| **Ibbertson, William** | No Photo | 2876370 |
| Nethybridge, Inverness-shire | | Private |
| **Iggo, John** | | 2876209 |
| Carmont, Kincardineshire | | Lance Corporal |
| **Imray, Robert** | | 2876622 |
| Selkirk, Selkirkshire | | Lance Corporal |
| **Ingram, James** | | 2876257 |
| Portsoy, Banffshire | | Private |
| **Ingram, Robert** | | 2876185 |
| Maud, Aberdeenshire | | Lance Corporal |

| Name | Photo | Number |
|---|---|---|
| **From** | | Rank |
| **Ingram, Robert** | | 2876500 |
| Belhelvie, Aberdeenshire | | Lance Corporal |
| **Ingram, William** | | 2876210 |
| Dyce, Aberdeenshire | | Private |
| **Innes, James** | | 2876415 |
| Marnoch, Aberdeenshire | | Private |
| **Innes, William Alexander Disney** | | 44937 |
| Haddo House, Aberdeenshire | | Major |
| **Irvine, Robert (Bobby) Hugh** | | 113410 |
| Drumoak, Aberdeenshire | | Lieutenant |
| **Irvine, Robert Laurence** | | 2879052 |
| Whalsay, Shetland | | Private |
| **Jackman, Philip** | No Photo | 7583867 |
| Wybridge, Devon | | Sergeant |
| **Jamieson, Alexander** | | 3244179 |
| Mintlaw, Aberdeenshire | | Private |
| **Jamieson, Andrew John** | | 2876448 |
| North Roe, Shetland | | Private |
| **Jamieson, John (Jack)** | | 2877746 |
| Newmachar, Aberdeenshire | | Corporal |
| **Jamieson, William** | No Photo | 2877261 |
| Not known | | Private |
| **Jappy, William John** | No Photo | 2875587 |
| Wick, Caithness | | Private |

183

| Name | Photo | Number |
|---|---|---|
| **From** | | **Rank** |
| **Jardine, William Stevenson** | | 2875371 |
| Huntly, Aberdeenshire | | Sergeant |
| **Jeffrey, (Jaffrey) Robert** | | 2876509 |
| Auchingoul, Aberdeenshire | | Private |
| **Johnson, Victor** | No Photo | 859165 |
| Stoke on Trent, Staffs | | Lance Corporal |
| **Johnston, Archbald** | | 2885065 |
| Bucksburn, Aberdeen | | Lance Corporal |
| **Johnston, David** | | 2876713 |
| Aberchirder, Aberdeenshire | | Private |
| **Johnston, Henry** | | 2876156 |
| Buckie, Banffshire | | Private |
| **Johnston, James** | | 2876288 |
| Aberchirder, Aberdeenshire | | Private (Piper) |
| **Johnston, James** | | 2879289 |
| Girvan, Aberdeenshire | | Private |
| **Johnston, John** | | 2876619 |
| Edinburgh | | Private |
| **Johnston, Robert (Bert)** | | 2876371 |
| Rathen, Fraserburgh, Aberdeenshire | No Photo | Private |
| **Johnstone (Alias Kirkwood), Alexander** | | 2876558 |
| Fauldhouse, West Lothian | | Private |
| **Johnstone, Thomas** | | 164367 |
| Edinburgh | No Photo | Captain |

| Name | Photo | Number |
|---|---|---|
| **From** | | **Rank** |
| **Jones, Thomas** | No Photo | 2890094 / 204896 |
| Unknown | | Private / 2nd Lieutenant |
| **Joss, Gordon,** | No Photo | 2876262 |
| Gamrie, Banffshire | | Private |
| **Keith, George** | | 2875889 |
| Methlick, Aberdeenshire | | Private |
| **Kellas, Harry** | | 2876714 |
| Aberchirder, Aberdeenshire | | Private |
| **Kellas, William** | | 2876651 |
| Tarland, Aberdeenshire | | Private |
| **Kemp, Alexander** | No Photo | 2873278 |
| Cults, Aberdeen | | Sergeant |
| **Kemp, George** | No Photo | 2874064 |
| Bucksburn, Aberdeen | | Private |
| **Kemp, William** | | 2876320 |
| Aberdeen | | Lance Corporal |
| **Kenn, William** | No Photo | 2880747 |
| Stonehaven, Kincardineshire | | Private |
| **Kennedy, John** | No Photo | 2875549 |
| Aberdeen | | Private |
| **Kennedy, William** | | 2875904 |
| Stonehaven, Kincardineshire | | Private |
| **Kerr, Hector** | | 2876707 |
| Aberchirder, Banffshire | | Corporal |
| **Kimpin, Patrick John** | No Photo | 2867701 |
| Maud, Aberdeenshire | | Private |
| **King, James** | | 2876113 |
| Ayr, Ayrshire | | CQMS |

184

| Name | Photo | Number |
|------|-------|--------|
| **From** | | Rank |
| **King, Victor** | No Photo | 2889874 |
| Barking, Essex | | Private |
| **Kirk, Douglas** | | 2876596 |
| Strathmiglo, Fife | | Lance Sergeant |
| **Knight, Frank** | | 2874564 |
| Huntly, Aberdeenshire | | Sergeant |
| **Knox, Andrew** | | 556299 |
| Alnwick, Northumberland | | Corporal |
| **Knox, Henry** | | 2875846 |
| New Deer, Aberdeenshire | | Private |
| **Laing, Douglas** | No Photo | 2885228 |
| Strachan, Aberdeenshire | | Private |
| **Laing, John** | | 2876421 |
| Perth, Perthshire | | Lance Corporal (Piper) |
| **Laing, Robert** | | 2876627 |
| Edinburgh | | Lance Sergeant |
| **Laird, Frank** | | 2876747 |
| Unknown | | Private |
| **Laird, George Alexander** | | 2876949 |
| Huntly, Aberdeenshire | | Private |
| **Laird, William** | | 2876398 |
| Cairnie, Aberdeenshire | | Private |
| **Lapsley, Robert** | No Photo | 2883245 |
| Carstairs, Lanarkshire | | Lance Corporal |

| Name | Photo | Number |
|------|-------|--------|
| **From** | | Rank |
| **Lavery, James** | | 2876001 |
| Dumbarton | | Private |
| **Lawrence, James** | No Photo | 153398 |
| Glenfarg, Perthshire | | 2nd Lieutenant |
| **Lawson, Albert** | | 3597764 |
| Carlisle, Cumberland | | Private |
| **Lawson, Robert** | | 2878821 |
| Buckie, Banffshire | | Private |
| **Leckie, John** | No Photo | 211470 |
| Weybridge, Surrey | | 2nd Lieutenant |
| **Leckie, Peter** | No Photo | 156801 |
| Weybridge, Surrey | | 2nd Lieutenant |
| **Lee, David** | No Photo | 2877496 |
| Marykirk, Kincardineshire | | Private |
| **Leech, Ernest** | No Photo | 2876616 |
| Leeds, Yorkshire | | Private |
| **Lees, Richard Gilbert** | | 10909 |
| Aberdeen | | Major |
| **Leiper, George** | No Photo | 3322245 |
| Aberdeen | | Private |
| **Leiper, William** | | 2876784 |
| Aberdeen | | Private (Bandsman) |
| **Leslie, James** | | 2876246 |
| Unknown | | Private |
| **Lindsay, James** | | 2885144 |
| Kintore, Aberdeenshire | | Private |

185

| Name | Photo | Number |
|---|---|---|
| **From** | | **Rank** |
| **Littlejohn, Duncan** | No Photo | 2873660 |
| Laurencekirk, Kincardineshire | | Lance Corporal |
| **Lobban, David** | | 2876250 |
| Udny Station, Aberdeenshire | | Private |
| **Logan, Herbert** | No Photo | 2875425 |
| Wife interned in Singapore | | Corporal |
| **Logan, John** | No Photo | 2885202 |
| Perth | | Private |
| **Lorimer, William** | | 2876425 |
| Aberdeen | | Private |
| **Lovie, Hector** | | 2876624 |
| Banchory, Kincardineshire | | Private (Bandsman) |
| **Low, William** | | 2870244 |
| Banchory, Kincardineshire | | CSM |
| **Lyle, Alexander** | No Photo | 2885295 |
| Lanark | | Corporal |
| **Lyon, Ivan** | | 66175 |
| Farnham, Surrey | | Captain |
| **Macallan, Alexander** | No Photo | 2885103 |
| Aberdeen | | Lance Corporal |
| **Macartney, William** | No Photo | 2870137 |
| Harrogate, Yorkshire | | Private |
| **Macbeth, Hugh** | No Photo | 2885088 |
| Fort William, Inverness-shire | | Private |
| **MacDonald, Alexander** | | 2874280 |
| Oyne, Aberdeenshire | | Private |

| Name | Photo | Number |
|---|---|---|
| **From** | | **Rank** |
| **Macdonald, Alexander** | No Photo | 2879006 |
| Portree, Skye | | Private |
| **Macdonald, Donald** | No Photo | 407734 |
| Portree, Skye | | Private |
| **Macdonald, James** | No Photo | 2874175 |
| Edinburgh | | Private |
| **Mackenzie, Ian** | | 2879288 |
| Stirling | | Private |
| **Mackenzie, Ronald** | No Photo | 2876891 |
| London | | Private |
| **Mackie, Albert** | No Photo | 2876463 |
| Aberdeen | | Private |
| **Mackie, Andrew** | No Photo | 2885147 |
| Coatbridge, Lanarkshire | | Private |
| **Mackie, Edward** | | 2876852 |
| Ballater, Aberdeenshire | | Private |
| **Mackie, George** | | 2876381 |
| Fyvie, Aberdeenshire | | Private |
| **Mackie, William** | No Photo | 2879250 |
| Fyvie, Aberdeenshire | | Private |
| **Mackie, William Alexander** | | 2882556 |
| Banff, Banffshire | | Private |
| **MacKinnon, Hugh** | No Photo | 187146 |
| Buenos Aires, Argentina | | 2nd Lieutenant |
| **MacKinnon, Robert** | | 2873837 |
| Plymouth, Devon | | Sergeant (Bandsman) |

186

| Name | Photo | Number |
|------|-------|--------|
| **From** | | **Rank** |
| **MacLean, Simon** | No Photo | 2873074 |
| Culloden, Inverness-shire | | Lance Corporal |
| **MacLeod, Murdo** | No Photo | 33807 |
| Tarbert, Isle of Harris | | Chaplain |
| **Macrae, John** | No Photo | 2879292 |
| Edinburgh | | Private |
| **Macrae, John Harrison** | No Photo | 2876679 |
| Kilsyth, Stirlingshire | | Private |
| **Main, George** | | 2885767 |
| Aberdeen | | Private |
| **Main, James** | | 2878297 |
| Kemnay, Aberdeenshire | | Private |
| **Main, William** | | 2867469 then 73220 |
| Aberdeen | | Lieutenant (Quarter Master) |
| **Mair, George Reid** | | 2876564 |
| Stonehaven, Kincardineshire | | Private |
| **Malcolm, James** | | 2878815 |
| Stonehaven, Kincardineshire | | Private |
| **Marnoch, James** | | 2879043 |
| Crathes, Aberdeenshire | | Lance Corporal |
| **Marr, Douglas** | No Photo | 130890 |
| Unknown | | 2nd Lieutenant |
| **Marritt, George** | No Photo | 2884749 |
| York, Yorkshire | | Corporal |
| **Marsh, Reginald** | No Photo | 3321759 |
| London | | Private |

| Name | Photo | Number |
|------|-------|--------|
| **From** | | **Rank** |
| **Martin, Robert** | | 2876669 |
| Inverkeithing, Fife | | Private |
| **Martin, William** | | 2876659 |
| Gartly, Aberdeenshire | | Private |
| **Marwick, James Craigie** | | 2874198 |
| Aberdeen | | Corporal |
| **Massie, James (Busty)** | | 2869598 |
| Huntly, Aberdeenshire | | Private |
| **Masson, James** | | 2876725 |
| Montrose, Angus | | Private |
| **Mathers, James** | | 2876526 |
| Montblairie, Banffshire | | Private |
| **Mathers, William** | | 2873793 |
| Aberdeen | | Private |
| **Matthew, Albert** | | 2876839 |
| Boddam, Aberdeenshire | | Private |
| **Matthew, George** | | 2876443 |
| Unknown | | Private |
| **McAllan, Charles** | | 2885231 |
| Aberdeen | | Private |
| **McAllan, James** | | 2876734 |
| Aberdeen | | Private |

| Name | Photo | Number |
|---|---|---|
| **From** | | **Rank** |
| **McAlley, Robert** | No Photo | 2879286 |
| Dundee | | Private |
| **McArthur, John** | | 2875485 |
| Peterhead, Aberdeenshire | | Private |
| **McArthur, Robert** | No Photo | 7575045 |
| Glasgow | | Private |
| **McBride, Peter** | | 2876308 |
| Glasgow | | Corporal |
| **McCall, Richard Donald** | No Photo | 4614088 |
| Skipton, Yorkshire | | Private |
| **McDonald, Alexander James** | | 2871657 |
| Dinnet, Aberdeenshire | | Corporal |
| **McDonald, David** | No Photo | 2879285 |
| Strathtay, Perthshire | | Private |
| **McDonald, G** | No Photo | 2884554 |
| Unknown | | Private |
| **McDonald, John** | | 2880690 |
| Bucksburn, Aberdeen | | Private |
| **McDonald, Robert** | | 2876380 |
| Aberchirder, Aberdeenshire | | Lance Corporal |
| **McDougall, William** | No Photo | 2746656 |
| Glasgow | | Private |
| **McGowan, Henry** | No Photo | 2885100 |
| Uddingston, Lanarkshire | | Private |
| **McGregor, Alexander** | | 2879072 |
| Keith, Banffshire | | Private |

| Name | Photo | Number |
|---|---|---|
| **From** | | **Rank** |
| **McGregor, Arthur** | | 2878316 |
| Keith, Banffshire | | Private |
| **McGregor, George** | No Photo | 2877753 |
| Keith, Banffshire | | Lance Corporal |
| **McGregor, James** | | 2876791 |
| Huntly, Aberdeenshire | | Private |
| **McGregor, John** | | 2877536 |
| Keith, Banffshire | | Private |
| **McGregor, John Stewart** | | 2882097 |
| Dinnet, Aberdeenshire | | Lance Corporal |
| **McGregor, Ronald** | | 2875459 |
| Aberdeen | | Sergeant |
| **McGregor, Scott** | | 2876365 |
| Strathdon, Aberdeenshire | | Private |
| **McGurk, Hugh** | | 3054253 |
| Linlithgow, West Lothian | | Private |
| **McHardy, Charles** | | 2876254 |
| Corgarff, Aberdeenshire | | Private |
| **McHardy, James** | No Photo | 2876572 |
| Aberdeen | | Private |
| **McInnes, Roderick** | | 2876187 |
| Aberdeen | | Corporal |

188

| Name | Photo | Number |
|---|---|---|
| **From** | | **Rank** |
| **McIntosh, Andrew** | | 2888556 |
| Drumnadrochit, Inverness-shire | | Private |
| **McIntosh, James** | | 2876496 |
| Dunecht, Aberdeenshire | | Private |
| **McKay, Alexander Sim** | | 829054 |
| Aberdeen | | Corporal |
| **McKay, Alexander** | | 2876255 |
| Balmedie, Aberdeenshire | | Lance Sergeant |
| **McKay, John, (Ian)** | | 2874992 |
| Dufftown, Banffshire | | Lance Sergeant |
| **McKay, Stephen** | No Photo | 2875660 |
| Unknown | | Private |
| **McKay, William** | | 2878442 |
| Aberdeen | | Private |
| **McKean, Frederick** | No Photo | 2879190 |
| Cove Bay, Aberdeen | | Private |
| **McKenzie, George** | | 2879025 |
| Banff, Banffshire | | Private |
| **McKenzie, James** | | 2876541 |
| Rathven, Buckie, Banffshire | | Private |
| **McKenzie, John** | | 2876595 |
| Edinburgh | | Lance Sergeant |

| Name | Photo | Number |
|---|---|---|
| **From** | | **Rank** |
| **McKerlie, Victor** | | 2876702 |
| Burnbank, Lanarkshire | | Lance Corporal (Bandsman) |
| **McKessick, John** | | 2876345 |
| Fyvie, Aberdeenshire | | Lance Corporal |
| **McKimmie, Frank** | | 2876477 |
| Portsoy, Banffshire | | Private |
| **McKinley, Matthew** | | 2876899 |
| Cumnock, Ayrshire | | Private |
| **McKinnon, James** | | 2928928 |
| Longside, Peterhead, Aberdeenshire | | Private |
| **McLean, Duncan** | | 2874899 |
| Aberdeen | | Corporal |
| **McLean, Peter** | | 2883070 |
| Peterhead, Aberdeenshire | | Lance Corporal |
| **McLeish, Frank** | | 2879002 |
| Carnoustie, Angus | | Private |
| **Mcleod, Alexander** | | 1661787 |
| Aberdeen | | Corporal |
| **McLeod, Andrew** | No Photo | 870299 |
| Edinburgh | | Lance Corporal |
| **McLeod, Harry** | | 2875021 |
| Huntly, Aberdeenshire | | Private |

189

| Name | Photo | Number |
|------|-------|--------|
| **From** | | **Rank** |
| **McLeod, Hector** | | 2876758 |
| Drumblade, Aberdeenshire | | Private |
| **McLuckie, John** | No Photo | 2879934 |
| Littleborough, Lancashire | | Private |
| **McMaster, David** | | 2876507 |
| Ellon, Aberdeenshire | | Corporal |
| **McNab George** | | 2885735 |
| Peterculter, Aberdeenshire | | Private |
| **McNabb, Robert** | No Photo | 2885454 |
| Liverpool | | Private |
| **McNally, John** | | 7681724 |
| Ladywood, Birmingham | | Private |
| **McRobbie, Andrew** | | 2879033 |
| Turriff, Aberdeenshire | | Private |
| **McRobbie, George** | | 2875976 |
| Banchory, Kincardineshire | | Corporal |
| **McShane, William** | | 2875960 |
| Aberdeen | | Private |
| **Mearns, Robert** | | 2876505 |
| Oldmeldrum, Aberdeenshire | | Private |
| **Meldrum, George** | | 2876211 |
| Ballindalloch, Banffshire | | Corporal |

| Name | Photo | Number |
|------|-------|--------|
| **From** | | **Rank** |
| **Meldrum, William** | | 2877421 |
| Huntly, Aberdeenshire | | Private |
| **Melville, John Murray** | | 2888645 |
| Maidenhead, Berks | | Private |
| **Mennie, James** | | 2875778 |
| Knock, Banffshire | | Private |
| **Mennie, William** | | 2876853 |
| Knock, Banffshire | | Private |
| **Menzies, Archibald** | | 2876810 |
| Dundee, Angus | | Private |
| **Merchant, William** | | 2879026 |
| Aberdeen | | Private |
| **Michie, Charles** | | 2876189 |
| Tough, Aberdeenshire | | CQMS |
| **Michie, George** | | 2875971 |
| Tough, Aberdeenshire | | Sergeant |
| **Middleton, Albert** | | 2869710 |
| Auchterless, Aberdeenshire | | Private |
| **Middleton, Ritchie** | | 2879173 |
| Maryculter, Aberdeenshire | | Private |
| **Middleton, William** | No Photo | 2875856 |
| Drumlithie, Kincardineshire | | Sergeant |

190

| Name | Photo | Number |
|---|---|---|
| **From** | | **Rank** |
| **Millar, Thomas** | | 2876698 |
| Glasgow | | Private |
| **Milne, Alexander** | | 2869674 |
| Monymusk, Aberdeenshire | | Regimental Sergeant-Major |
| **Milne, Charles** | | 2866704 |
| Aberdeen | | Sergeant |
| **Milne, Charles** | | 2876396 |
| Rhynie, Aberdeenshire | | Private |
| **Milne, Colin** | | 2876518 |
| Rhynie, Aberdeenshire | | Lance Corporal |
| **Milne, Frederick** | | 2874259 |
| Rhynie, Aberdeenshire | | Sergeant |
| **Milne, Harold** | No Photo | 2878400 |
| Lumphanan, Aberdeenshire | | Private |
| **Milne, John McGregor** | | 2876351 |
| Oyne, Aberdeenshire | | Private |
| **Milne, John William** | | 2876223 |
| Aberdeen | | Private Bandsman |
| **Milne, Leslie** | No Photo | 2877033 |
| Bankhead, Aberdeen | | Corporal |
| **Milne, Robert** | No Photo | 2874717 |
| Turriff, Aberdeenshire | | Lance Corporal |

| Name | Photo | Number |
|---|---|---|
| **From** | | **Rank** |
| **Milne, Robert** | | 2876212 |
| Premnay, Aberdeenshire | | Sergeant |
| **Milton, Alexander** | | 2869802 |
| Keith, Banffshire | | Company Sergeant-Major |
| **Milton, James** | | 2875801 |
| Aberlour, Banffshire | | Sergeant |
| **Milton, Peter** | | 2875799 |
| Aberlour, Banffshire | | Lance Sergeant |
| **Minty, James** | | 2876548 |
| Auchnagatt, Aberdeenshire | | Private |
| **Mitchell, Alexander** | | 2876061 |
| Huntly, Aberdeenshire | | Private |
| **Mitchell, George** | No Photo | 2876385 |
| Rothienorman, Aberdeenshire | | Private |
| **Mitchell, James** | | 2876391 |
| Turriff, Aberdeenshire | | Private |
| **Mitchell, John** | No Photo | 2869636 |
| New Deer, Aberdeenshire | | Sergeant |
| **Mitchell, Peter** | | 2879054 |
| Lumsden, Aberdeenshire | | Lance Corporal |
| **Moffat, Charles** | No Photo | 2885299 |
| Lanark, Lanarkshire | | Private |
| **Moffat, George** | No Photo | 2879284 |
| Dundee, Angus | | Private |

191

| Name | Photo | Number |
|---|---|---|
| **From** | | **Rank** |
| **Moggach, Gordon** | | 2876488 |
| Rothiemay, Banffshire | | Private |
| **Moir, Alexander** | | 2876190 |
| Ellon, Aberdeenshire | | Private |
| **Moir, Andrew** | | 2876464 |
| Peterhead, Aberdeenshire | | Private (Piper) |
| **Moir, James** | | 2869425 |
| Ellon, Aberdeenshire | | Private |
| **Moir, James** | | 2877146 |
| Kintore, Aberdeenshire | | Private |
| **Moir, John** | | 2876305 |
| Aberdeen | | Private |
| **Moir, William** | | 2876217 |
| Auchleuchries, Ellon, Aberdeenshire | | Private |
| **Moir, William Alexander** | | 2876297 |
| Udny Station, Aberdeenshire | | Private |
| **Moir-Byres, George Francis** | | 69179 |
| London | | Captain |
| **Mollinson, William** | | 2876264 |
| Cruden Bay, Aberdeenshire | | Corporal |
| **Monro, John Gartside** | No Photo | 77690 |
| London | | Captain |

| Name | Photo | Number |
|---|---|---|
| **From** | | **Rank** |
| **Montgomery, Carr** | | 2876761 |
| Edinburgh | | Lance Corporal |
| **Morgan, Arthur** | | 2876361 |
| Peterhead, Aberdeenshire | | Private |
| **Morgan, Benjamin** | | 2875814 |
| Insch, Aberdeenshire | | Corporal |
| **Morgan, Robert** | | 2875457 |
| Longside, Peterhead, Aberdeenshire | | Private |
| **Morison, Gilbert** | | 2876907 |
| Aberdeen | | Private |
| **Morrice, Alexander** | | 2883080 |
| Aberdeen | | Private |
| **Morrice, Alexander George** | | 2876362 |
| Peterhead, Aberdeenshire | | Lance Corporal |
| **Morrice, James Reid** | | 2876611 |
| Aberdeen | | Sergeant |
| **Morrison, Charles** | | 2879155 |
| Auchterless, Aberdeenshire | | Private |
| **Morrison, John** | | 2876154 |
| Buckie, Banffshire | | Private |
| **Morrison, John Patterson** | | 2876510 |
| Montrose, Angus | | Private |

192

| Name | Photo | Number |
|------|-------|--------|
| From | | Rank |
| Morrison, William | | 3321222 |
| Glasgow | | Private |
| Morton, Charles | | 3308703 |
| Glasgow | | Corporal |
| Moses, Herbert | No Photo | 2889878 |
| Portslade, Sussex | | Private |
| Mowatt, James (Jimmy) | | 2883082 |
| Laurencekirk, Kincardineshire | | Private |
| Mullen, Alexander | No Photo | 846164 |
| Dundee, Angus | | Lance Corporal |
| Munro, Alfred | | 2886263 |
| Aberdeen | | Private |
| Murch, Francis (Jim) | | 2876243 |
| Guist, Norfolk | | Corporal Bandsman |
| Murdoch, James | | 2872442 |
| Nairn, Nairnshire | | Sergeant (Pipe Major) |
| Murphy, James | No Photo | 2877304 |
| Glasgow | | Private |
| Murphy, William | No Photo | 3130372 |
| Irvine, Ayrshire | | Private |
| Murray, David | | 2876441 |
| Cruden Bay, Aberdeenshire | | Sergeant |
| Murray, Edward S. | | 2870500 |
| Fyvie, Aberdeenshire | | Company Sergeant-Major |

| Name | Photo | Number |
|------|-------|--------|
| From | | Rank |
| Murray, John | | 2876056 |
| Turriff, Aberdeenshire | | Lance Corporal |
| Murray, Robert | No Photo | 2885010 |
| Glasgow | | Private |
| Mutch, Alexander | | 2876218 |
| New Deer, Aberdeenshire | | Private |
| Mutch, John | | 2871659 |
| Ellon, Aberdeenshire | | Private |
| Mutch, John | | 2876629 |
| Auchleuchries, Aberdeenshire | | Private |
| Mutch, Oliver | | 2879068 |
| Aberdeen | | Private |
| Napier, James Burr | | 2876793 |
| New Deer, Aberdeenshire | | Private |
| Neave, Alexander | No Photo | 2876324 |
| Aberdeen | | Lance Sergeant |
| Neill, Robert | | 2879106 |
| Lisburn, Co. Antrim | | Corporal |
| Neilson, Walter | | 2876626 |
| Boullieston, Lanarkshire | | Private |
| Ness, Donald | | 2876503 |
| Dunecht, Aberdeenshire | | Private |

| Name | Photo | Number |
|---|---|---|
| **From** | | **Rank** |
| **Nimmo, Thomas** | No Photo | 3240091 |
| Edinburgh | | Private |
| **Nish, James** | | 2876338 |
| Elgin, Moray | | Private |
| **Niven, Harry** | | 2876642 |
| Buckie, Banffshire | | Private (Piper) |
| Niven, William | | 2880078 |
| Huntly, Aberdeenshire | | Private |
| **Noble, William** | No Photo | 2888222 |
| Linlithgow, West Lothian | | Lance Corporal |
| **Nunneley, David** | No Photo | 77691 |
| Fremington, Devon | | 2nd Lieutenant |
| **O'Brien, Denis** | No Photo | 2879415 |
| Glasgow | | Private |
| **O'Brien, John** | No Photo | 4270431 |
| London | | Private |
| **O'Donnell, Pierce (Percy)** | | 2876690 |
| Edinburgh | | Private (Bandsman) |
| **Ogg, William** | | 2879029 |
| Keith, Banffshire | | Private |
| **Ogilvie, Alexander** | | 2873275 |
| Glass, Aberdeenshire | | WO2 QSM |
| **Ogston, John** | | 2876740 |
| Fraserburgh, Aberdeenshire | | Lance Corporal |

| Name | Photo | Number |
|---|---|---|
| **From** | | **Rank** |
| **O'Neill, Joseph** | | 2876469 |
| Lerwick, Shetland | | Lance Corporal |
| **Ormiston, James** | | 2876612 |
| Edinburgh | | Corporal |
| **Ormiston, Thomas** | No Photo | 2872468 |
| Dundee, Angus | | Sergeant |
| **Orr, James** | No Photo | 2885106 |
| Newmains, Lanarkshire | | Private |
| Osborne, William | No Photo | 2876483 |
| Kirriemuir, Angus | | Private |
| **Oxford, Henry Isa** | No Photo | 2876777 |
| Unknown | | Private |
| **Pallant, Archibald** | | 2867720 |
| Middlesbrough | | Sergeant (ORS) |
| **Palmer, Angus** | | 2876863 |
| Portsoy, Banffshire | | Private |
| **Palmer, Richard** | | 2876570 |
| Aberdeen | | Private |
| **Pantridge, James Francis (Frank)** | | 128673 |
| Hillsborough, Co. Down | | Captain |
| **Paris, Alexander (Alistair)** | | 2876571 |
| Inverness, Inverness-shire | | Private |

| Name | Photo | Number |
|---|---|---|
| **From** | | Rank |
| **Parley, Alexander** | | 2874254 |
| Edinburgh | | Private |
| **Paton, Harry** | | 409768 |
| Dundee, Angus | | Private |
| **Payne, Jack** | | 2876228 |
| Woking, Surrey | | Lance Corporal |
| **Peart, Robert** | | 2879172 |
| Gateshead, Co. Durham | | Lance Corporal |
| **Pemberton, Leslie** | No Photo | 6665722 |
| Langley, Herts. | | Private |
| **Penman, Thomas** | | 2876968 |
| Leven, Fife | | Private |
| **Petch, George Arthur** | No Photo | 3319043 |
| Newcastle on Tyne | | Private |
| **Peterkin, James** | No Photo | 2871383 |
| Aberdeen | | QMS (ORS) |
| **Petrie, Hugh Simpson** | | 2872962 |
| Aberdeen | | Corporal (Bandsman) |
| **Petrie, Kenneth** | | 2884113 |
| Kinnethmont, Aberdeenshire | | Private |
| **Petrie, William** | | 2878085 |
| Kemnay, Aberdeenshire | | Private |

| Name | Photo | Number |
|---|---|---|
| **From** | | Rank |
| **Phillips, Thomas** | | 2876340 |
| Aberdeen | | Lance Corporal |
| **Phimister, James** | No Photo | 2878092 |
| Aberdeen | | Private |
| **Pirie, John** | | 2876252 |
| Newmachar, Aberdeenshire | | Private |
| **Pirie, William** | | 2876251 |
| Newmachar, Aberdeenshire | | Private |
| **Porter, Alexander** | | 2876780 |
| Skene, Aberdeenshire | | Private |
| **Priestley, John** | No Photo | 3319117 |
| Bradford, Yorkshire | | Private |
| **Prise, Robert (Bob)** | | 2874449 |
| King Edward, Banffshire | | Corporal |
| **Quinn, Frank** | | 3310489 |
| Glasgow | | Corporal |
| **Quirie, William** | | 2875986 |
| Strichen, Aberdeenshire | | Lance Corporal |
| **Raeper, Robert** | | 2876648 |
| Fyvie, Aberdeenshire | | Private |
| **Rankin, George** | No Photo | 2879991 |
| Mauchline, Ayrshire | | Lance Corporal |

195

| Name | Photo | Number |
|------|-------|--------|
| **From** | | **Rank** |
| **Rattray, Alexander** | | 2875543 |
| Ballater, Aberdeenshire | | Private |
| **Rattray, Lancelot** | | 2877031 |
| Dyce, Aberdeenshire | | Corporal |
| **Reeves, Frank** | No Photo | 6911716 |
| Unknown | | Private |
| **Reid, Albert** | | 2877569 |
| Banchory, Kincardineshire | | Private |
| **Reid, George** | No Photo | 2876868 |
| St Fergus, Aberdeenshire | | Private |
| **Reid, William** | | 2820620 |
| Unknown | | Private |
| **Reynolds, Andrew John** | | 2876985 |
| Edinburgh | | Private |
| **Richards, David Beattie** | No Photo | 2884759 |
| Pontefract, Yorkshire | | Lance Corporal |
| **Riddell, George** | | 2876511 |
| Insch, Aberdeenshire | | Private |
| **Riddoch, Alexander** | | 2876274 |
| Huntly, Aberdeenshire | | Private |
| **Riddock, Robert** | No Photo | 2876668 |
| Partick, Lanarkshire | | Private |

| Name | Photo | Number |
|------|-------|--------|
| **From** | | **Rank** |
| **Riley, Frank** | | 96006 |
| Stonehaven, Kincardineshire | | Captain |
| **Ritchie, Alfred** | | 2885695 |
| Aberdeen | | Private |
| **Ritchie, George** | | 2879015 |
| Peterhead, Aberdeenshire | | Private |
| **Ritchie, James** | | 2876263 |
| Kintore, Aberdeenshire | | Corporal |
| **Ritchie, John** | | 2879195 |
| Aberdeen | | Private |
| **Ritchie, William** | | 2875924 |
| Udny Green, Aberdeenshire | | Private |
| **Roake, G** | | 2873505 |
| Unknown | | Private (Bandsman) |
| **Robb, Hugh** | | 2876349 |
| Inverbervie, Kincardineshire | | Private |
| **Roberts, George** | No Photo | 186375 |
| Edinburgh | | 2nd Lieutenant |
| **Roberts, Percy** | | 2873087 |
| Glasgow | | Private (Bandsman) |
| **Robertson, Alexander** | No Photo | 2875838 |
| Inverurie, Aberdeenshire | | Lance Corporal |

| Name | Photo | Number |
|---|---|---|
| From | | Rank |
| Robertson, Alexander | | 2879148 |
| Kintore, Aberdeenshire | | Private |
| Robertson, Charles | | 2879166 |
| Keith, Banffshire | | Private |
| Robertson, Christopher | | 2876680 |
| Lerwick, Shetland | | Sergeant |
| Robertson, Farquhar | | 2876418 |
| Aberdeen | | Private |
| Robertson, James | No Photo | 2884060 |
| Glasgow | | Private |
| Robertson, John (Jack) | | 2875848 |
| New Deer, Aberdeenshire | | Private |
| Robertson, John | | 2876253 |
| Kintore, Aberdeenshire | | Private |
| Robertson, Robert (Bobby) | | 2879183 |
| Dundee, Angus | | Private |
| Robertson, Samuel | | 2876427 |
| Ellon, Aberdeenshire | | Private (Piper) |
| Robertson, Thomas | No Photo | 2884617 |
| Motherwell, Lanarkshire | | Private |
| Robinson, John Thomas ("Nuggy") | No Photo | 6745728 |
| Limerick, Ireland | | Private |
| Roper-Caldbeck, Reggie | | 204894 |
| Scaynes Hill, Sussex | | Captain |

| Name | Photo | Number |
|---|---|---|
| From | | Rank |
| Rose, Frank | | 2879062 |
| Dundee, Angus | | Private |
| Rose, John | | 834928 |
| Peterhead, Aberdeenshire | | Private |
| Rose, William | | 2876376 |
| Aberdeen | | Private |
| Ross, Alexander | | 2876875 |
| Fordoun, Kincardineshire | | Private |
| Ross, Hugh | | 132517 |
| Graffham, Sussex | | 2nd Lieutenant |
| Ross, John | | 2875462 |
| Aberdeen | | Private |
| Ross, John | | 2876732 |
| Glassel, Kincardineshire | | Sergeant |
| Ross, Peter | | 2876279 |
| Midmar, Aberdeenshire | | Lance Sergeant |
| Ross, Robert | | 2889885 |
| Dagenham, Essex | | Private |
| Ross, William | | 2876681 |
| Clydebank, Glasgow | | Lance Corporal |

197

| Name | Photo | Number |
|---|---|---|
| **From** | | **Rank** |
| **Rothney, Arthur Morgan,** | | 2876195 |
| Mintlaw, Aberdeenshire | | Private |
| **Russell, John** | | 130751 |
| Swanage, Dorset | | 2nd Lieutenant |
| **Russell, John** | No Photo | 174509 |
| Midhurst, Sussex | | 2nd Lieutenant |
| **Sandison, James** | | 68263 |
| Hatton, Aberdeenshire | | 2nd Lieutenant |
| **Sang, William** | | 2876493 |
| Dufftown, Banffshire | | Private |
| **Sangster, George** | | 2876957 |
| Ellon, Aberdeenshire | | Private |
| **Sangster, John (enlisted as Grant, John)** | | 2877014 |
| New Deer, Aberdeenshire | | Private |
| **Sangster, Robert** | | 2876248 |
| Fraserburgh, Aberdeenshire | | Private |
| **Sarjanston, Ronald** | No Photo | 2889886 |
| London | | Private |
| **Scorgie, John** | | 2888446 |
| Clochan, Banffshire | | Private |
| **Scott, Bertram** | | 2875158 |
| Aberdeen | | Sergeant |
| **Scott, George** | No Photo | 2889831 |
| Unknown | | Private |

| Name | Photo | Number |
|---|---|---|
| **From** | | **Rank** |
| **Scott, James** | | 2880277 |
| Braemar, Aberdeenshire | | Private |
| **Scott, Randall** | | 2868908 |
| Farnborough, Hampshire | | Company Sergeant-Major |
| **Scott, Roy** | No Photo | 2879196 |
| Queensland, Australia | | Private |
| **Scroggie, George** | | 2875608 |
| Alford, Aberdeenshire | | Private |
| **Sey, John** | | 2876336 |
| Alford, Aberdeenshire | | Sergeant |
| **Shaw, Percy** | No Photo | 6978297 |
| Springhead, Lancashire | | Lance Corporal |
| **Shea, Frank** | | 2876196 |
| Unknown | | Private |
| **Shearer, Duncan** | | 2876273 |
| Insch, Aberdeenshire | | Private |
| **Sherwood, Ian** | No Photo | 2890066 |
| Potters Bar, Middlesex | | Private |
| **Shirran, Jamieson** | | 2876219 |
| Aberdeen | | Sergeant |
| **Shulman, Sydney** | No Photo | 2889889 |
| Windsor, Berks. | | Private |
| **Sim, George** | | 2876331 |
| Cruden Bay, Aberdeenshire | | Sergeant |

198

| Name | Photo | Number |
|------|-------|--------|
| **From** | | Rank |
| **Sim, Walter** | | 2876490 |
| Kintore, Aberdeenshire | | Private |
| **Simmons, Anthony** | No Photo | 2889827 |
| Godalming, Surrey | | Private |
| **Simmons, George** | | 2876837 |
| Walsall, Staffordshire | | Private |
| **Simpson, Alexander** | | 2885796 |
| Aberdeen | | Corporal |
| **Simpson, Alexander** | | 2884260 |
| Aberdeen | | Private |
| **Simpson, Henry** | | 2879035 |
| Methlick, Aberdeenshire | | Private |
| **Simpson, James** | | 2877045 |
| Portsoy, Banffshire | | Corporal |
| **Simpson, Joshua** | | 2879144 |
| Mintlaw, Aberdeenshire | | Private |
| **Simpson, Leslie** | No Photo | 3322372 |
| Stockton on Tees, Co. Durham | | Private |
| **Simpson, Norman** | | 2876405 |
| Insch, Aberdeenshire | | Private |
| **Simpson, William** | | 2875477 |
| Insch, Aberdeenshire | | CQMS |

| Name | Photo | Number |
|------|-------|--------|
| **From** | | Rank |
| **Simpson, William** | | 2876347 |
| Alford, Aberdeenshire | | Private |
| **Sivewright, Alexander** | No Photo | 2874740 |
| Aberdeen | | Private |
| **Sivewright, Charles** | | 873924 |
| Macduff, Banffshire | | Private |
| **Sivewright, Henry (Harry)** | | 2876870 |
| Macduff, Banffshire | | Private |
| **Skene, William** | | 2876478 |
| Aberdeen | | Private |
| **Skene, Thomas** | | 2876335 |
| Skene, Aberdeenshire | | Sergeant |
| **Skene, Thomas** | | 2876447 |
| Unknown | | Private |
| **Slattery, John** | No Photo | 3321712 |
| South Shields, Co. Durham | | Private |
| **Slessor, William** | | 2875079 |
| Longside, Peterhead | | Private |
| **Smart, Alexander** | | 2877319 |
| Inverurie, Aberdeenshire | | Lance Sergeant |
| **Smith, Alexander** | | 2875530 |
| Turriff, Aberdeenshire | | Private |

199

| Name | Photo | Number |
|------|-------|--------|
| **From** | | **Rank** |
| **Smith, Alexander** | | 2879133 |
| Dundee, Angus | | Private |
| **Smith, Alistair** | | 2876724 |
| Aberdeen | | Private |
| **Smith, Anthony** | | 2876481 |
| Edinburgh | | Private |
| **Smith, Charles** | | 2820899 |
| Keighley, Yorkshire | | Private |
| **Smith, Edward** | | 2877794 |
| Laurencekirk, Kincardineshire | | Private |
| **Smith, Gordon** | No Photo | 2888677 |
| London | | Lance Corporal |
| **Smith, George** | No Photo | 2875895 |
| St Cyrus, Montrose | | Private |
| **Smith, George** | | 2876562 |
| Inverbervie, Aberdeenshire | | Lance Corporal |
| **Smith, Hector** | | 2876242 |
| Aberdeen | | Sergeant |
| **Smith, Hector** | | 2881511 |
| Skene, Aberdeenshire | | Private |
| **Smith, Henry (Harry)** | | 235499 |
| Dumfries | | Chaplain |

| Name | Photo | Number |
|------|-------|--------|
| **From** | | **Rank** |
| **Smith, James** | | 2876199 |
| Forgue, Aberdeenshire | | Private |
| **Smith, James** | No Photo | 2881379 |
| Huntly, Aberdeenshire | | Private |
| **Smith, James** | No Photo | 2889893 |
| London | | Private |
| **Smith, James Peter** | | 2877219 |
| Aberdeen | | Private |
| **Smith, John** | | 2875926 |
| Montrose, Angus | | Private |
| **Smith, John Alexander** | | 2876272 |
| Old Deer, Aberdeenshire | | Corporal |
| **Smith, John Thom** | | 2875230 |
| Turriff, Aberdeenshire | | Private |
| **Smith, Kenneth** | No Photo | 2876938 |
| Keith, Banffshire | | Private |
| **Smith, Thomas** | | 2876606 |
| Aberdeen | | Private |
| **Smith, Victor** | | 2874582 |
| Alford, Aberdeenshire | | Private |
| **Smith, William** | | 2876867 |
| Forgan, Fife | | Private |
| **Souter, Cameron** | | 2876599 |
| Stirling, Stirlingshire | | Private |

| Name | Photo | Number |
|---|---|---|
| **From** | | **Rank** |
| **Spence, Robert** | No Photo | 2871799 |
| Linlithgow, West Lothian | | RQMS |
| **Spence, William** | | 2876155 |
| Buckie, Banffshire | | Corporal |
| **Spittel, Ernest** | No Photo | 2889908 |
| London | | Private |
| **Stark, William** | | 2876554 |
| Edinburgh | | Sergeant |
| **Steel, James** | | 2878973 |
| Aberdeen | | Private |
| **Stephen, Alexander** | | 2876236 |
| Aberdeen | | Private |
| **Stephen, David** | | 2876373 |
| Ellon, Aberdeenshire | | Private |
| **Stephen, Robert** | No Photo | 2876730 |
| Huntly, Aberdeenshire | | Sergeant |
| **Stevenson, Henry West** | | 844254 |
| Macduff, Banffshire | | Private |
| **Stevenson, Robert** | | 775459 |
| Glasgow | | Private |
| **Stewart, Alexander R.** | | 2885705 |
| Aberdeen | | Private |

| Name | Photo | Number |
|---|---|---|
| **From** | | **Rank** |
| **Stewart, Alexander** | | 2883860 |
| Shotts, Lanarkshire | | Private |
| **Stewart, George** | | 2869547 |
| Kincardine O'Neil, Aberdeenshire | | Private |
| **Stewart, Gordon** | No Photo | 2874959 |
| Insch, Aberdeenshire | | P/L/C |
| **Stewart, James** | | 2876459 |
| Unknown | | Private |
| **Stewart, John** | | 854828 |
| Fraserburgh, Aberdeenshire | | Private |
| **Stewart, John (Ginger)** | No Photo | 2880733 |
| Lhanbryde, Moray | | Private |
| **Stewart, John** | | 2819471 |
| Keith, Banffshire | | Private |
| **Stewart, Matthew** | No Photo | 2874188 |
| London | | Lance Corporal |
| **Stewart, Samuel** | No Photo | 2885799 |
| Hamilton, Lanarkshire | | Private |
| **Stewart, Vincent Irvine Derek** | | 189551 |
| Bogawantalawa, Ceylon (Sri Lanka) | | 2nd Lieutenant |
| **Stewart, William** | No Photo | 2976402 |
| Lochore, Fife | | Private |
| **Still, William** | | 2874044 |
| Edinburgh | | Private |

201

| Name | Photo | Number |
|---|---|---|
| **From** | | **Rank** |
| **Stilson, Robert** | | 2876756 |
| Aberchirder, Aberdeenshire | | Private |
| **Stitt, John (Jack)** | | 10895 |
| Aberdeen | | Lieutenant Colonel |
| **Stolworthy, John** | | 2879041 |
| Bradwell, Suffolk | | Lance Corporal |
| **Stopper, George** | | 2885707 |
| Aberdeen | | Private |
| **Strachan, Edward** | | 2876326 |
| Maud, Aberdeenshire | | Private |
| **Strachan, Hunter** | No Photo | 2879495 |
| Glasgow | | Private |
| **Strachan, James** | | 2876200 |
| Peterhead, Aberdeenshire | | Private |
| **Strachan, John** | No Photo | 2885773 |
| Drumlithie, Kincardineshire | | Private |
| **Strachan, Norman** | | 2871200 |
| Liss, Hampshire | | Company Sergeant-Major |
| **Strachan, William** | | 2878635 |
| Fetterangus, Aberdeenshire | | Private |
| **Struthers, John** | | 2885710 |
| Aberdeen | | Private |
| **Stuart, Alexander** | No Photo | 2882540 |
| Macduff, Banffshire | | Private |

| Name | Photo | Number |
|---|---|---|
| **From** | | **Rank** |
| **Stuart, Charles Forbes** | | 2876261 |
| Lumsden, Aberdeenshire | | Private |
| **Stuart, Douglas Haig** | | 2876598 |
| Aberdeen | | Private |
| **Stuart, John** | | 2872330 |
| Fraserburgh, Aberdeenshire | | Private |
| **Summers, George** | No Photo | 2879466 |
| Fraserburgh, Aberdeenshire | | Private |
| **Summers, James** | No Photo | 2875032 |
| Tarves, Aberdeenshire | | Private |
| **Sutherland, Alexander** | | 2868831 |
| Bucksburn, Aberdeen | | Private |
| **Sutherland, David** | No Photo | 2888468 |
| Edinburgh | | Corporal |
| **Sutherland, George Hendry** | | 2876298 |
| Aberdeen | | Sergeant |
| **Sutherland, George** | No Photo | 2883817 |
| Rhynie, Aberdeenshire | | Private |
| **Symington, Percy George** | No Photo | 137031 |
| Troon, Ayrshire | | 2nd Lieutenant |
| **Tavendale, Henry** | No Photo | 2881341 |
| Stonehaven, Kincardineshire | | Sergeant |
| **Taylor, Alexander** | | 2876748 |
| Rathven, Buckie | | Private (Piper) |
| **Taylor, Alexander Jesse** | No Photo | 6665914 |
| Not known | | A/CQMS) |

| Name | Photo | Number |
|---|---|---|
| From | | Rank |
| Taylor, Charles | | 2881760 |
| Crathie, Aberdeenshire | | Lance Corporal |
| Taylor, Douglas | | 825497 |
| Fraserburgh, Aberdeenshire | | Sergeant |
| Taylor, Edward | | 406008 |
| Aberdeen | | Corporal |
| Taylor, Ernest | No Photo | 4129416 |
| Manchester | | Private |
| Taylor, James (Dherzi) | | 2875631 |
| Fraserburgh, Aberdeenshire | | Private |
| Taylor, James | No Photo | 2883818 |
| Bieldside, Aberdeen | | Private |
| Taylor, John Davidson | No Photo | 2874983 |
| Old Deer, Aberdeenshire | | Private |
| Taylor, John James | No Photo | 193438 |
| London | | 2nd Lieutenant |
| Taylor, Peter | No Photo | 2882550 |
| Longmanhill, Banffshire | | Private |
| Taylor, Peter | | 2876857 |
| Aboyne, Aberdeenshire | | Private |
| Taylor, Robert | | 2876657 |
| Turriff, Aberdeenshire | | Private |
| Taylor, William | | 2876374 |
| Kincardine O'Neill, Aberdeenshire | | Lance Corporal |
| Telford, John | No Photo | 2883944 |
| Larkhall, Lanarkshire | | Private |

| Name | Photo | Number |
|---|---|---|
| From | | Rank |
| Tennant, Charles | No Photo | 2876366 |
| Dufftown, Banffshire | | Private |
| Thain, John | | 2876358 |
| New Byth, Aberdeenshire | | Private |
| Thom, David Imray | | 2568691 |
| Aberdeen | | Private |
| Thompson, Robert | No Photo | 2875056 |
| Blaydon, Co.Durham | | WO2 (PSM) |
| Thomson, Charles | No Photo | 2885933 |
| London | | Private |
| Thomson, David | No Photo | 841003 |
| Aberdeen | | Private |
| Thomson, George | | 2876632 |
| Ellon, Aberdeenshire | | Private |
| Thomson, James | | 2876636 |
| Not known | | Private |
| Thomson, James Alexander | | 2878841 |
| Botriphnie, Banffshire | | Private |
| Thomson, James Christie | No Photo | 2883800 |
| Rothiemay, Banffshire | | Corporal |
| Thomson, James | | 2876437 |
| Oldmeldrum, Aberdeenshire | | Private |
| Thomson, John | | 2876395 |
| Marnoch, Banffshire | | Private |

203

| Name | Photo | Number |
|---|---|---|
| **From** | | **Rank** |
| **Thomson, John** | | 3322299 |
| Arbroath, Angus | | Private |
| **Thomson, Matthew** | | 2876729 |
| Ellon, Aberdeenshire | | Private |
| **Thomson, William** | | 2320214 |
| Clochan, Banffshire | | Private |
| **Thomson, William** | | 2877251 |
| Crathie, Kincardineshire | | Private |
| **Thorburn, John** | No Photo | 2888390 |
| Kirkintilloch, Dunbartonshire | | Private |
| **Timlin, Thomas** | | 3185246 |
| Glasgow | | Private |
| **Todd, Joseph** | No Photo | 3322376 |
| Seghill, Northumberland | | Private |
| **Toogood, William** | | 2879483 |
| Haddington, East Lothian | | Private |
| **Topp, Edward** | | 2873868 |
| not known | | CQMS |
| **Tough, Alexander** | | 2876828 |
| Huntly, Aberdeenshire | | Private |
| **Tough, Ernest** | | 2885244 |
| Culter, Aberdeen | | Private |

| Name | Photo | Number |
|---|---|---|
| **From** | | **Rank** |
| **Troup, James** | | 2876163 |
| Alford, Aberdeenshire | | Private |
| **Trussell, Leslie** | No Photo | 2876318 |
| Barking, Essex | | Private |
| **Turnbull, James** | No Photo | 2879081 |
| Newcastle on Tyne | | Private |
| **Tweedie, John** | No Photo | 2885218 |
| Airdrie, Lanarkshire | | Private |
| **Urquhart, Alastair** | | 2883851 |
| Aberdeen | | Private |
| **Valetta, John** | No Photo | 3242287 |
| not known | | Private |
| **Varley, Joseph Henry** | No Photo | 4271739 |
| Newcastle on Tyne | | Private |
| **Waistell, Harry** | No Photo | 3322408 |
| not known | | Lance Corporal |
| **Walker, Charles** | | 2873378 |
| London | | Private (Bandsman) |
| **Walker, George** | | 2876241 |
| Bucksburn, Aberdeen | | Private |
| **Walker, Hugh** | | 2879470 |
| Renfrew, Renfrewshire | | Private |
| **Walker, James** | | 2884225 |
| Fraserburgh, Aberdeenshire | | Private |

| Name | Photo | Number |
|------|-------|--------|
| **From** | | Rank |
| **Walker, John** | No Photo | 3322303 |
| Finchley, Middlesex | | Private |
| **Walker, John Murray** | No Photo | 2926943 |
| Richmond, Yorkshire | | Private |
| **Walker, Joseph** | No Photo | 2885713 |
| Aberdeen | | Private |
| **Walker, Peter** | | 2882392 |
| Kinnoir, Aberdeenshire | | Private |
| **Walker, Robert** | | 2885831 |
| Insch, Aberdeenshire | | Private |
| **Walker, Thomas** | No Photo | 2885400 |
| not known | | Private |
| **Walker, Thomas** | No Photo | 2885889 |
| Glasgow | | Private |
| **Walker, Thomas (Ginger)** | | 2876798 |
| Aberdeen | | Private (Bandsman) |
| **Walker, William** | No Photo | 2873220 |
| Govan, Glasgow | | Private |
| **Wallace, John** | | 2876792 |
| Huntly, Aberdeenshire | | Private |
| **Wallace, John Murray** | | 2876354 |
| Fetterangus, Aberdeenshire | | Private |
| **Wallace, John (Nellie)** | No Photo | 2888398 |
| Glasgow | | Lance Corporal |
| **Ward, Thomas** | No Photo | 3322259 |
| Bradford, Yorkshire | | Lance Corporal |

| Name | Photo | Number |
|------|-------|--------|
| **From** | | Rank |
| **Watson, D** | No Photo | 2749170 |
| Not Known | | Sergeant |
| **Watson, John** | No Photo | 2879485 |
| Greenford, Essex | | Private |
| **Watson, Thomas** | | 2883948 |
| Newmains, Lanarkshire | | Private |
| **Watt, Alexander** | | 2876645 |
| Finzean, Aberdeenshire | | Private |
| **Watt, George** | No Photo | 2875353 |
| Aberdeen | | Sergeant |
| **Watt, George David** | No Photo | 2875970 |
| Forfar, Angus | | Corporal |
| **Watt, Gordon Innes** | | 2876884 |
| Ellon, Aberdeenshire | | Private (Bandsman) |
| **Watt, James Cruden** | No Photo | 820156 |
| Tain, Ross-shire | | Lance Sergeant |
| **Watt, James Cruden** | | 2876589 |
| Fraserburgh, Aberdeenshire | | Lance Corporal |
| **Watt, John** | | 2876393 |
| New Pitsligo, Aberdeenshire | | Private |
| **Watt, Robert** | No Photo | 2885862 |
| Haddington, Midlothian | | Private |
| **Watt, William** | | 2870033 |
| Collieston, Aberdeenshire | | Private |

205

| Name | Photo | Number |
|---|---|---|
| **From** | | **Rank** |
| **Watters, Peter** | | 2876976 |
| Unknown | | Private |
| **Waugh, Henry** | No Photo | 2888398 |
| Dalmellington, Ayrshire | | Lance Corporal |
| **Webster, James** | | 2865818 |
| Aberdeen | | Sergeant |
| **Welsh, George** | | 2875715 |
| Insch, Aberdeenshire | | Private |
| **Welsh, John** | | 2876739 |
| Keith, Banffshire | | Private |
| **West, Frank** | | 2876204 |
| not known | | Private |
| **Wharmby, Stanley** | No Photo | 2886915 |
| Famworth, Lincolnshire | | Lance Corporal |
| **Wheatley, Arnold** | No Photo | 2884776 |
| Thorbury, Yorkshire | | Private |
| **White, Andrew** | | 2879060 |
| Lerwick, Shetland | | Private |
| **Whitelaw, David** | | 2876103 |
| Glasgow | | Corporal |
| **Whitelaw, John Falconer** | No Photo | 157632 |
| Edinburgh | | Captain |
| **Whyte, Henry** | No Photo | 2876205 |
| not known | | Private |

| Name | Photo | Number |
|---|---|---|
| **From** | | **Rank** |
| **Whyte, Peter** | | 2883830 |
| Insch, Aberdeenshire | | Private |
| **Wilkes, Ronald** | | 2876959 |
| Birmingham | | Private |
| **Wilkie, Charles** | No Photo | 2883919 |
| Coatbridge, Lanarkshire | | Private |
| **Wilks, Harold Taylor** | No Photo | 3322417 |
| Saltburn, Yorkshire | | Private |
| **Will, Gavin** | | 7362611 |
| New Deer, Aberdeenshire | | Private |
| **Will, Robert** | No Photo | 2883814 |
| Drumoak, Aberdeenshire | | Private |
| **Williamson, Andrew** | | 2879056 |
| Fraserburgh, Aberdeenshire | | Private |
| **Williamson, J A** | No Photo | Not Known |
| | | Chaplain |
| **Williamson, John** | No Photo | 3188859 |
| Bellshill, Lanarkshire | | Private |
| **Willox, John** | | 2876280 |
| Fetterangus, Aberdeenshire | | Corporal |
| **Willox, Robert** | | 2883815 |
| Peterhead, Aberdeenshire | | Private |
| **Wilson, Alexander** | | 2876502 |
| Portsoy, Banffshire | | Private |

| Name | Photo | Number |
|---|---|---|
| **From** | | **Rank** |
| **Wilson, Duncan** | | 2882048 |
| not known | | Lance Corporal |
| **Wilson, George** | No Photo | 2876289 |
| not known | | Private |
| **Wilson, George Angus** | No Photo | 7887495 |
| not known | | Private |
| **Wilson, James** | | 2876392 |
| Turriff, Aberdeenshire | | Private |
| **Wilson, John** | | 2876602 |
| not known | | Lance Corporal |
| **Wilson, John** | No Photo | 2889825 |
| St Helens, Lancashire | | Private |
| **Wilson, John** | No Photo | 3322309 |
| not known | | Private |
| **Wilson, John William** | No Photo | 3322419 |
| Chilton, Co. Durham | | Private |
| **Wilson, Peter** | | 2875699 |
| Buckie, Banffshire | | Private |
| **Wilson, Richard** | | 2876781 |
| Aberdeen | | Private |
| **Wilson, Thomas** | | 2876609 |
| Blantyre, Lanarkshire | | Private |
| **Wilson, William** | No Photo | 2886796 |
| Bootle, Liverpool | | Private |
| **Winchester, Gordon** | | 841251 |
| Macduff, Aberdeenshire | | Private |

| Name | Photo | Number |
|---|---|---|
| **From** | | **Rank** |
| **Winton, Andrew** | | 2872532 |
| Aberdeen | | Company Sergeant-Major |
| **Winton, Norman** | | 2883825 |
| Cairnie, Aberdeenshire | | Private |
| **Wiseman, Robert** | | 2876580 |
| Lerwick, Shetland | | Private |
| **Witty, Frederick** | | 2876737 |
| Fraserburgh, Aberdeenshire | | Lance Corporal |
| **Wolstenholm, Robert** | No Photo | 2884782 |
| Dewsbury, Yorkshire | | Corporal |
| **Wood, Alexander** | No Photo | 2879027 |
| Macduff, Banffshire | | Private |
| **Wood, Alexander Wilson** | | 875116 |
| Macduff, Banffshire | | Corporal |
| **Wood, Archibald** | | 2883812 |
| Rothienorman, Aberdeenshire | | Private |
| **Wood, James** | | 2879011 |
| Fraserburgh, Aberdeenshire | | Private (Piper) |
| **Wood, John** | No Photo | 2876700 |
| Musbiggin, Northumberland | | Private |
| **Wood, John** | No Photo | 3322258 |
| Middlesbrough, Teesside | | Private |
| **Wood, Peter** | No Photo | 2883945 |
| Shotts, Lanarkshire | | Private |

207

| Name | Photo | Number |
|---|---|---|
| **From** | | **Rank** |
| **Wood, Thomas** | No Photo | 3322264 |
| Hull, Yorkshire | | Lance Corporal |
| **Wood, William** | | 2876883 |
| Brechin, Angus | | Private |
| **Woodall, Joe** | No Photo | 3322265 |
| Halifax, Yorkshire | | Lance Corporal |
| **Woolfson, Cecil** | | 2875509 |
| St. Mary's, Norfolk | | Private |
| **Wray, Alexander** | | 2876618 |
| Stockton on Tees, Co. Durham | | Private |
| **Wright, William** | | 3055080 |
| Edinburgh | | Private |

| Name | Photo | Number |
|---|---|---|
| **From** | | **Rank** |
| **Wynn, George** | | 2879128 |
| Edinburgh | | Private |
| **Yeates, Albert** | | 2876247 |
| Newton Abbot, Devon | | Lance Corporal |
| **Young, Alexander** | No Photo | 2874092 |
| Gourdon, Montrose | | Private |
| **Young, George** | | 2876294 |
| Portlethen, Kincardineshire | | Private |
| **Young, John** | | 2883928 |
| Airdrie, Lanarkshire | | Private |
| **Young, William** | | 2876638 |
| King Edward, Aberdeenshire | | Corporal |

# Bibliography

The Collection of the Gordon Highlanders' Museum, Aberdeen

William Ross Young & John Duff, *A Gordon Highlander if Ever I Saw One*, 2007

John Murray Melville, *Tomorrow -The New Day*, 1990 (unpublished)

A Black, *Threads – A Personal Account of Military Service in the Far east 1939 to 1945*, 1988 (unpublished)

Brian Coutts, *George S McNab – Gordon Highlander & Far East Prisoner of War*, (unpublished)

Paul Gibbs Pancheri, *Volunteer*, Paul Gibbs Pancheri, Bucks. 1998

Aberdeen Journals, *The Press & Journal; Peoples Journal; Evening Express*, 1942 - 1945

Files WO 344–361/1 to 344–410/1; WO 373/47, National Archives

# Index